M000313836

Special Economic Zones in Africa

Special Economic Zones in Africa

Comparing Performance and
Learning from Global Experiences

Thomas Farole

  THE WORLD BANK

in cooperation with the Investment Climate Department of the World Bank

© 2011 The International Bank for Reconstruction and Development / The World Bank
1818 H Street NW
Washington DC 20433
Telephone: 202-473-1000
Internet: www.worldbank.org

All rights reserved

1 2 3 4 14 13 12 11

This volume is a product of the staff of the International Bank for Reconstruction and Development / The World Bank. The findings, interpretations, and conclusions expressed in this volume do not necessarily reflect the views of the Executive Directors of The World Bank or the governments they represent.

The World Bank does not guarantee the accuracy of the data included in this work. The boundaries, colors, denominations, and other information shown on any map in this work do not imply any judgement on the part of The World Bank concerning the legal status of any territory or the endorsement or acceptance of such boundaries.

Rights and Permissions
The material in this publication is copyrighted. Copying and/or transmitting portions or all of this work without permission may be a violation of applicable law. The International Bank for Reconstruction and Development / The World Bank encourages dissemination of its work and will normally grant permission to reproduce portions of the work promptly.

For permission to photocopy or reprint any part of this work, please send a request with complete information to the Copyright Clearance Center Inc., 222 Rosewood Drive, Danvers, MA 01923, USA; telephone: 978-750-8400; fax: 978-750-4470; Internet: www.copyright.com.

All other queries on rights and licenses, including subsidiary rights, should be addressed to the Office of the Publisher, The World Bank, 1818 H Street NW, Washington, DC 20433, USA; fax: 202-522-2422; e-mail: pubrights@worldbank.org.

ISBN: 978-0-8213-8638-5
eISBN: 978-0-8213-8639-2
DOI: 10.1596/978-0-8213-8638-5

Cover photo: A to Z Textiles, Kisongo EPZ, Tanzania

Library of Congress Cataloging-in-Publication Data
Farole, Thomas.
  Special economic zones in Africa : comparing performance and learning from global experiences / Thomas Farole.
     p. cm.
  Includes bibliographical references.
  ISBN 978-0-8213-8638-5 — ISBN 978-0-8213-8639-2 (electronic)
  1. Economic zoning—Africa, Sub-Saharan. 2. Enterprise zones—Africa, Sub-Saharan. 3. Export processing zones—Africa, Sub-Saharan. 4. Africa, Sub-Saharan—Economic policy. I. Title.
  HC800.F373 2011
  338.8'7—dc22

2010048276

Contents

Boxes

Tables

Foreword

Low-income countries looking for development models have often turned to the experience of Asian countries, most recently China, whose growth in the past 30 years has been unparalleled in history. The story of China's economic growth is inextricably linked to the use of "special economic zones" (SEZs). The transformation of Shenzhen, a small fishing village in the 1970s, into today's city of almost 9 million is an illustration of the effectiveness of the SEZ model in the Chinese context.

Many African countries continue to struggle to compete in industrial sectors and to integrate into the global value chains that generate the goods and services that are demanded by consumers around the globe. SEZs offer a potentially valuable tool to overcome some of the existing constraints to attracting investment and growing exports. But as this book explains clearly, governments that take a "build it and they will come" approach to SEZs do so at their peril. Indeed, the African experience with SEZs has not been anywhere near as successful as policy makers hoped it would be. What explains this? And to what degree might SEZs help contribute to improved competitiveness in African and other low-income economies?

This book provides the first comprehensive assessment of Africa's recent experience with developing SEZs, drawing lessons from in-depth survey and case study research. It provides compelling evidence on the factors that determine success in SEZ programs, and charts the performance of a representative sample of African SEZs against regional and global standards.

Although for the most part the performance of SEZs has been relatively disappointing, the book's analysis also reveals much heterogeneity in the effectiveness of SEZs, both in Africa and around the world. This diversity—in terms of objectives, institutional approaches, and operational models—suggests opportunities. The Export Processing Zone models that were at the heart of the success of traditional zone programs in East Asia and Latin America during the 1970s through the 1990s are no longer relevant in the postcrisis world; they are likely to fail in Africa. But by focusing on comparative advantage and on integration—with national industrial policies, among government institutions and the private sector, and between zones and domestic markets—SEZs have the potential to contribute to improving Africa's competitiveness and its integration with the global economy, thereby helping to create jobs and raising incomes.

This book provides a wealth of information for researchers, policy makers, and the development community at large. As the World Bank Group continues its efforts to support investment, job creation, and industrial development in Africa and in low-income countries around the world, it is critical that we build on such evidence-based analysis to assist with the consideration, design, and implementation of potentially valuable but complex policy instruments like SEZs. This book makes a valuable contribution to that effort.

Bernard Hoekman
Director, International Trade Department
World Bank

Acknowledgments

This study was prepared by Thomas Farole (senior economist World Bank, International Trade Department) and developed in cooperation with the Bank's Investment Climate Department.

Many individuals and organizations provided substantial support. I would like to extend thanks to the following:

- The private firms, special economic zone (SEZ) authorities, governments, and other stakeholders—in Bangladesh, the Dominican Republic, Ghana, Honduras, Kenya, Lesotho, Nigeria, Senegal, Tanzania, and Vietnam—who took the time to reply to surveys and to meet with us to share their insights and experiences.
- Guillermo Arenas, who led the analysis of the survey data and provided input throughout.
- Claude Baissac, who led the work in chapter 2 and wrote the research agenda section of chapter 8.
- The consultants who carried out the surveys and conducted case studies across these countries, including Org-Quest and Mustafizul Hye Shakir (Bangladesh), Grupo Delphi (Dominican Republic), Francis Aidoo (Ghana), FIDE (Honduras), Kenya School of Professional Studies (Kenya), Activquest Pty (Lesotho), Etude Economique Conseil

(Nigeria), Sidiki Guindo (Senegal), Anthony Mveyange (Tanzania), and Mekong Economics (Vietnam); and Lim Pao Li and Jean Marie Burgaud, who led the case study research across most of the countries and provided invaluable input based on their combined 70-plus years of experience with SEZs.

- Staff in World Bank and IFC offices around the world who helped us make contact with consultants and stakeholders, and provided important input in the early stages of the study. Among others, special thanks to Ganesh Rasagam, Martin Norman, Josaphat Kweka, Giuseppe Iarossi, Papa Demba Thiam, Gilberto de Barros, Alain d'Hoore, Ismail Radwan, Markus Scheurmaier, Quong Doan, Musabi Muteshi, and Dante Mossi.

- Michael Engman, who played a critical role during the project's early stages, helped develop the survey, and led much of the initial research in West Africa, the Dominican Republic, and Honduras.

- Peter Walkenhorst, who conceived the project, secured the funding, and got it off the ground.

- Gokhan Akinci, Etienne Kechichian, Sumit Manchanda, and Igor Kecman of the Investment Climate Department.

- Stacey Chow for her support in coordinating the production process, and for her advice throughout.

- Aimee Yuson, Mary Ann van Oordt, and Charumathi Rao, who provided excellent support in all financial and administrative matters throughout the project

Many thanks also to Greg Elms, Michael Engman, Bernard Hoekman, Jose Lopez-Calix, Sumit Manchanda, Martin Norman, José Guilherme Reis, and Markus Scheurmaier, who provided comments on the report and earlier versions of some chapters; to Richard Auty, Deborah Brautigam, Naoko Koyama, Denisse Pierola, Deborah Porte, Cornelia Staritz, Xiaoyang Tang, Swarnim Wagle, Douglas Zeng, and Min Zhao, who provided input on aspects of this work; and to participants at seminars in Hyderabad (World Free Zone Convention), Nairobi (World Bank–African Economic Research Consortium–Japan International Cooperation Agency), and Cairo (IFC "Deep Dive"), where initial findings from parts of this report were presented. And thanks to the many other people who helped us and are not mentioned here.

The study was carried out under the overall supervision of Mona Haddad (sector manager, International Trade Department). Peer reviewers were Vincent Palmade and Dorsati Madani (Finance and Private Sector Development, Africa Region) and Leora Klapper (Development Economics, Finance and Private Sector Development).

Finally, thanks to the Bank-Netherlands Partnership Program (BNPP), which provided the generous financial support for the project.

Abbreviations

AGOA	African Growth and Opportunity Act
ALAFA	Apparel Lesotho Alliance to Fight AIDS
APIX	Agence national de Promotion et de Investments du Senegal
ARTEP	Asian Regional Team for Employment Promotion
ASEAN	Association of Southeast Asian Nations
ASEZ	Aqaba Special Economic Zone
ATC	Agreement on Textiles and Clothing
BEPZA	Bangladesh Export Processing Zones Authority
BICF	Bangladesh Investment Climate Fund
BPO	business process outsourcing
BWM	Benjamin William Mkapa (SEZ)
CADF	China-Africa Development Fund
CAFTA	Central America Free Trade Agreement
CBI	Caribbean Basin Initiative
CEPII	Centre d'Etudes Prospectives et d'Informations Internationales
CIC	Investment Climate Department of the World Bank
CMT	cut, make, and trim
CNMC	China Nonferrous Metal Mining (Group) Company

CNZFE	Consejo Nacional de Zonas Francas de Exportación
COMESA	Common Market for Eastern and Southern Africa
COMTRADE	Common Format for Transient Data Exchange
DIFZ	Dakar Industrial Free Zone
DISEZ	Dakar Integrated Special Economic Zone
EAC	East African Community
ECOWAS	Economic Community of West African States
EDF	European Development Fund
EFE	Entreprise Franche d'Exportation
EPZ	export processing zone
EPZA	Export Processing Zones Authority
EU	European Union
FDI	foreign direct investment
FIAS	Foreign Investment Advisory Service
FTZ	free trade zone
FZ	free zone
GDP	gross domestic product
GFZB	Ghana Free Zones Board
GIPC	Ghana Investment Promotion Centre
GPN	global production network
GSP	Generalized System of Preferences
HIV/AIDS	human immunodeficiency virus/acquired immune deficiency syndrome
ICFTU	International Confederation of Free Trade Unions
IDA	International Development Association
IFC	International Finance Corporation
IFTZ	Integrated Free Trade Zone
IIA	Investment Incentive Act
ILO	International Labour Organization
IMP	Industrial Master Plan
IPA	investment promotion authority or agency
IPC	Instituto Politécnico Centroamericano
IT	information technology
JAFZA	Jebel Ali Free Zone Authority
JV	joint venture
LDC	least-developed country
LNDC	Lesotho National Development Corporation
LTEA	Lesotho Textile Exports Association
M&E	monitoring and evaluation
MA-TTRI	Market Access Tariff Trade Restrictiveness Index

MB	megabyte
MBP	Millennium Business Park
MERCOSUR	Mercado Común del Cono Sur
MFA	Multi Fibre Arrangement
MIC	middle-income country
MNC	multinational corporation
MOU	memorandum of understanding
MPIP	Multipurpose Industrial Park
MTICM	Ministry of Trade and Industry Cooperatives and Marketing
NAFTA	North American Free Trade Agreement
NEPZA	Nigerian Export Processing Zones Authority
NGO	nongovernmental organization
NPV	net present value
OECD	Organisation for Economic Co-operation and Development
OGFZA	Oil and Gas Free Zones Authority
PDC	Penang Development Corporation
PIA	Promotion of Investment Act
PIO	Pioneer Industries Ordinance
PPP	public-private partnership
PRONAF	Programa Nacional Fronterizo
PSDC	Penang Skills Development Centre
PSI	Presidential Special Initiative
R&D	research and development
SACU	Southern African Customs Union
SADC	Southern African Development Community
SCM	Agreement on Subsidies and Countervailing Measures
SDT	Special and Differential Treatment
SEZ	special economic zone
SIP	Suzhou Industrial Park
SME	small or medium enterprise
SOE	state-owned enterprise
TA	technical assistance
UN	United Nations
UNCTAD	United Nations Conference on Trade and Development
UNCTC	United Nations Centre on Transnational Corporations

UNIDO	United Nations Industrial Development Organization
USAID	United States Agency for International Development
VAT	value added tax
WEPZA	World Economic Processing Zones Association
WITS	World Integrated Trade Solution
WTI	World Trade Indicators
WTO	World Trade Organization

Overview

Background

Economic zones have grown rapidly in the past 20 years.[1] In 1986, the International Labour Organisation's (ILO's) database reported 176 zones in 47 countries; by 2006, it reported 3,500 zones in 130 countries. This huge growth occurred despite many zones having failed to meet their objectives; however, many others are contributing significantly to growth in foreign direct investment (FDI), exports, and employment, as well as playing a catalytic role in integration into global trade and structural transformation, including industrialization and upgrading.

With some exceptions, Sub-Saharan African countries adopted economic zones only recently, with most programs initiated in the 1990s. The consensus from previous research is that African zones have generally underperformed, with the significant exception of those in Mauritius and the partial exception of those in Kenya and possibly Madagascar and Lesotho.[2]

There has been a long-running debate over the value of economic zones as a policy instrument. Many economists view zones as a second-best policy, preferring economy-wide liberalization of trade and investment. But some researchers and policymakers point to the potential of

1

economic zones to overcome market and coordination failures, and to act as catalysts of both market forces and political-economic reforms.

Despite three decades of research on economic zones, many important questions remain unanswered. There is a lack of systematic analysis on the performance of economic zones around the world; policymakers are forced to rely on the same small handful of case studies (some now 10–20 years old). For African policy makers, virtually no research exists on the performance of zone programs in the region.

This study aims to address some of these questions and deliver an analysis that is both data-driven and policy-focused. The objective of the study is to explore the experience of zone programs—with a particular focus on Sub-Saharan Africa—to understand the factors that contribute to static and dynamic outcomes. It aims to provide input to the question of whether and how zones can make a significant contribution to job creation, diversification, and sustainable growth in African and other low-income countries.

The study draws on research conducted across 10 countries, focusing on 6 countries in Africa (Ghana, Kenya, Lesotho, Nigeria, Senegal, and Tanzania); and four established zone programs in other regions (Bangladesh, the Dominican Republic, Honduras, and Vietnam). The research included two components in each country: (1) a case study, based on secondary research and interviews with investors, zone developers and operators, regulatory authorities, government, and other stakeholders; and (2) surveys of investors operating in the zones. Details of the research methodology can be found in the appendixes. All field research was conducted between May 2009 and January 2010.

The study is confined largely to formal manufacturing-oriented zones. It excludes any detailed discussion of information and communication technology (ICT) parks or science parks, industrial clusters, or other less formal agglomerations. Both ICT and science parks and clusters have close links with SEZs; their relationship is an important topic for future research.

Outcomes to Date in African SEZs

Defining and measuring the success of SEZ programs is far from straightforward. Zones may be established to achieve various objectives.

In assessing performance, we define three types of outcomes: (1) *static economic outcomes*, derived in the short term through the use of economic zones as instruments of trade and investment policy (including primarily investment, employment, and exports); (2) *dynamic economic outcomes*, including technology transfer, integration with the domestic economy, and, ultimately, structural change (including diversification, upgrading, and increased openness); and (3) *socioeconomic outcomes*, including the quality of employment created and gender-differentiated impacts.

Against "static" measures of success, most African programs are not fulfilling their potential and are underperforming compared with the Asian and Latin American programs included in the study. With the possible exception of Ghana, African zones show low levels of investment and exports, and their job creation impacts have been limited; African zones are surprisingly capital-intensive. However, most of the programs are still in the early stages of development, and some show promise. Despite poor nominal performance, the relative contributions of African SEZs to national FDI and exports is in line with global experience; this points to a bigger competitiveness challenge in the region and suggests that the SEZs may not be doing enough to catalyze wider structural change.

Little evidence exists that African programs have made progress toward "dynamic" measures of success. None of the programs studied show signs of zones having played any significant role in facilitating upgrading[3] or catalyzing wider reforms; and integration between the zones and their domestic economies is limited.

Success in meeting socioeconomic objectives has also been elusive. While zones have created job opportunities for poor, mainly rural women (although, outside of possibly Lesotho and Madagascar, this has not been on a scale anywhere near that in Asia and Latin America), most are still failing to deliver quality employment and a living wage. And given the high concentration of female workers in many zones, gender-specific concerns are not yet being effectively addressed. Moreover, in many countries, land acquisition, compensation, and resettlement practices are inadequate.

Worryingly, in the environment since the end of the Multi Fibre Arrangement (MFA) and the global economic crisis, there is a risk that many African zones will shift permanently and prematurely to a low-growth path. While the typical path of a successful zone program is slow-to-moderate growth in the first 5–10 years, followed by a period of exponential growth before eventually reaching maturity, the African zones under study appear to be already experiencing stagnating growth.

The analysis of performance raises questions about the competitiveness of African zone programs and the potential of African zones to compete for labor-intensive manufacturing activities, which have formed the foundation of traditional export processing zone (EPZ) programs and have been the basis of growth in the successful models of East Asia, Central America, and Mauritius.

Determinants of SEZ Success and African Zone Performance against Them

Results from the surveys underscore the importance of the national investment climate, providing quantitative evidence for what has been observed anecdotally—that the success of SEZs is closely linked to the competitiveness of the national economy. We observe strong correlations between SEZ outcomes and measures of national competitiveness and the national investment environment. There are likely to be deep determinants for some of these correlations, but issues of state capacity and governance are of critical importance.

Location and market size matter. Zones with proximate access to large consumer markets, suppliers, and labor tend to be more successful.

In addition, the survey results show clearly that the investment climate inside the zone—specifically, infrastructure and trade facilitation—is linked to program outcomes. The data show a strong correlation between infrastructure quality and the levels of investment, exports, and employment in zones. Trade facilitation shows a similarly strong positive relationship with outcomes. On the other hand, factors related to business licensing and regulations in the zones (e.g., one-stop services) appear to be less critical.

The traditional sources of competitiveness for zones—low wages, trade preferences, and fiscal incentives—are not found to be correlated with SEZ outcomes. This may be, in part, because these factors are often employed as alternatives to making the hard policy choices that lead to improvements in productivity and in the investment environment. The results suggest that these are insufficient substitutes.

On the SEZ-specific factors that matter most to investors and program outcomes—infrastructure and trade facilitation[4]—African SEZs are delivering a much-improved investment climate compared with what is available to firms operating outside the zones. For example, data from the surveys show that, on average across the African SEZs, firms inside the zones report 50 percent less downtime resulting from electricity failures than exporters based outside the zones. Customs clearance times are reported to be 30 percent faster in the zones.

However, this improvement in the investment climate may not be sufficient to attract global investors, because even the improved investment climate inside the zones falls below international standards. And the non-African SEZs in the study show much more substantial improvements inside their zones. For example, despite the 50 percent reduction in electricity-related downtime in the African zones, reported average downtime (44 hours per month) only reaches the average levels outside SEZs in the non-African countries. Non-African SEZs showed an average 92 percent reduction in average downtime, bringing it to only 4 hours per month. A similar pattern is observed in customs clearance.

Policy Conclusions: When Are SEZs an Appropriate Policy Choice?
The cases in which zones have been successful in both static and dynamic outcomes suggest that no orthodox role or model exists for zone development. In small markets, successful zone programs have tended in the first stage to take advantage of location, trade preferences, and labor arbitrage to create large-scale employment and to support a transition away from reliance on natural resource sectors toward the development of a light manufacturing sector. Many of the large-country successes used zones to leverage an existing comparative advantage in factor-cost-based manufacturing to facilitate a transition away from inward-looking development policies to export-led growth. Such zones have offered foreign investors the potential to operate in a protected environment while giving governments the time and context to test reforms. The zones have also helped attract the foreign technology needed to support the transformation of domestic industrial capacity and facilitate scale economies in emerging sectors.

The most complex environment for zones probably exists at opposite ends of the investment climate spectrum—where the national investment climate is so poor that implementing a successful zone is extremely difficult and where the investment climate has so few constraints that the cost to government of maintaining a special trade and investment regime for the program may outweigh any incremental benefits. In the former situation, an SEZ would need to find a way to almost fully circumvent the weak or predatory state[5]; in the latter, an SEZ might still play a role in sectors at the edge of the technology frontier, where coordination challenges and uncertainty constrain investment.

SEZs tend to benefit FDI and larger domestic investors most in the short term; they are not a direct solution for the development of local small and medium enterprise (SME) development. Most SEZs are designed to attract larger businesses, with world-class infrastructure, incentives geared toward exporters, and high lease costs relative to what is available in the local market. Thus, attracting local SMEs into SEZs on a large scale may not be a realistic objective. Instead, the emphasis should be on developing effective links between local SMEs and the globally competitive firms anchored in the zones. This might be achieved through cluster-based policies.

Policy Conclusions: Which SEZ Model is Most Likely to be Effective in Africa?

The global trade and investment context from which assembly-based EPZs emerged has changed significantly in recent years. The rapid growth of SEZs and their success in contributing to export-led growth is due in part to an unprecedented era of globalization of trade and investment that took place during the 1980s and 1990s, with the rise of global production networks (GPNs). But African countries, most of which launched programs only in the late 1990s and 2000s, face a much more difficult competitive environment, resulting from factors such as the emergence and entrenchment of "factory Asia"; the expiration of the Multi Fibre Arrangement; the consolidation of GPNs; and recently slowing demand in traditional export markets. On the other hand, new opportunities may emerge through regional markets, South-South trade and investment, and the growth of services offshoring.

In this changing context, there is reason to question whether the traditional EPZ model, which has been adopted by most African programs,

(1) supports the comparative advantages of most African countries, and (2) provides the potential for the African zone programs to grow to a significant scale and generate spillovers to the wider economy. Much evidence suggests that Africa has a fundamental competitiveness challenge with respect to manufacturing owing to issues of geography, scale, and transaction costs, particularly since China and India have integrated into global markets. If most African zones are unlikely to be competitive as manufacturing export platforms in the near term, they will need to rethink their strategies and move away from the traditional EPZ model.

One implication is that African zones will need to reorient themselves toward activities that better exploit sources of comparative advantage. In many countries, this will be in natural-resource-based sectors (agriculture, minerals, oil and gas, tourism), at least in the near term. This does not mean that there will not also be some manufacturing and services opportunities (including trading and logistics) worth pursuing. Indeed, one of the main opportunities could be to use economic zones to develop improved competitiveness in first- and later-stage processing of resources. But the traditional assembly of imported components is unlikely to be the main driver.

Such an approach should allow African countries to better exploit the dynamic potential of economic zones and to achieve higher employment multipliers, but it will require significant attention to improving the competitiveness of local value chains. As natural-resource-based activities will necessarily involve greater requirements for local supply, this model offers scope for delivering greater job creation through multipliers. It may also offer more potential for spillovers of knowledge and technology from zone-based FDI to the domestic economy through integration with local industry clusters. But the flip side of this approach is that the competitiveness of the zones will depend on the existence of competitive local value chains. In many African countries, serious barriers to competitiveness up and down value chains (especially in the extended value chains typical of the agricultural sector) will need to be addressed.

The shift toward SEZ models offers potential for zones to play a catalytic role as part of integrated regional growth initiatives; for example, as "growth poles." Wide-scale SEZs can be integrated around key trade infrastructure (ports, roads, power projects), with domestic industry clusters and local labor markets. This integration could begin to unlock the potential of zones as catalysts rather than enclaves.

Overcoming land constraints will be critical for African SEZs. Despite substantial amounts of undeveloped land in many African countries, problems related to titles, registration, and connective infrastructure make access to industrial land one of the biggest constraints to investors on the continent. SEZs can play an important role in removing this constraint, but it also means the land acquisition process in zones programs is likely to be challenging in many African countries.

For African zones, regional trade opportunities may be significant, but a bigger opportunity may be to use zones as a tool of spatial industrial policy to support a scaling up of regional production. Economic zones in Africa may be attractive to investors as locations from which specialized regional inputs can be tapped and production scaled up. This implies a strategic focus on SEZs as a component of spatial industrial policy rather than simply as trade and investment policy. It also suggests greater emphasis on the role of SEZs in the regional integration agenda; indeed, while SEZs can support integration, they are often perceived as a risk from a trade policy perspective, as they open up the potential for tariff jumping and leakage of goods across borders.

The development of Chinese-invested SEZs in several African countries presents significant opportunities but also raises some risks. The Chinese Economic and Trade Cooperation Zones under development in four countries in the region have the potential to support industrialization, demonstrate effective SEZ models, and transfer knowledge of SEZ program design and implementation to African governments and the private sector. But the success of these projects is by no means guaranteed. Meeting the objectives of both China and the African countries will require an active partnership and a framework for collaboration that includes engagement from host governments, processes for phasing in local control, communication and enforcement of standards, and support for integration with local economies.

African governments should be more proactive in using their SEZs as reform pilots. Given the competitive weaknesses in the region and the political economy factors that slow reform, Africa's economic zones offer a useful vehicle through which to test reforms. To date, none of the African zone programs appear to have taken this approach. But the programs that are held up as success stories internationally—primarily China but also Mauritius—used their economic zones *expressly* as a vehicle for broader economic reform.

Policy Conclusions: Planning and Implementing Effective SEZ Programs

SEZs are difficult to get right—a number of conditions are required for zones to be successful. Unless a country has a significant comparative advantage in labor costs or a large internal market, a number of factors must come together for a zone to be successful in attracting and retaining investment. These factors include location, policy, planning, legal framework, infrastructure, and management. In addition, an element of serendipity is found in many successful programs; that is, they offered the right solution at the right time (e.g., a formerly closed region opened up to trade or a new trade agreement came into effect).

Despite the perception of zones as enclaves, in practice their success is almost fully intertwined with the national economy, the national investment environment, and the capacity of the government. Zones can tip the competitiveness balance at the margin, but they will not generally shift the paradigm. Critically, most of the factors that determine the success of SEZ programs cannot be confined to the zone program alone but require action at the national level.

One of the main differences between zone programs that have been successful and sustainable and those that have either failed to take off or have become stagnant enclaves is the extent to which they have been integrated in the broader economic policy framework of the country. Successful programs do not simply view zones as a static instrument of trade and investment policy. Zones have not had a catalytic impact in most countries, in part because they have been disconnected from wider economic strategies. Often, zone programs are put in place and then left to operate on their own, with little effort to support domestic investment into the zone or to promote links, training, and upgrading. Unlocking the potential of a zone requires clear strategic integration of the program, and government must play a leading role in potentiating the impact of the zone.

Most zone programs have been designed as instruments for trade and investment; they continue to be built around low labor costs, trade preferences, and fiscal incentives. Each of these factors can help jump-start a zone program, but they are generally not sustainable. In countries with large pools of unskilled labor, low wages may be a source of comparative advantage into the medium term and may outweigh the need for preferences and incentives; but this is not the case in Africa, where labor costs are relatively high and scale is lacking. But when wages, preferences, and incentives are the main levers on which competitiveness is based, they create pressure for distortions and race-to-the-bottom policies, including extending and increasing incentives (rather than addressing more difficult aspects of the investment environment) and granting exemptions on minimum wage and labor rights (rather than addressing productivity or labor market rigidities).

High-level, active, and consistent government commitment to zone programs over a long period is a significant contributor to success—most zones take 5–10 years to begin bearing fruit. Many African countries have shown only a halfhearted commitment to their zones; for example, passing zone laws but failing to implement regulations or provide adequate resources for program management, infrastructure, and promotion. Many programs have suffered from poor trade policy coordination and a failure to establish a policy environment that offers investors confidence in transparency and predictability. In successful zones, policymakers often work closely with the private sector to develop zone policy according to changing needs. Indeed, many successful zones did not get their zone policies right at the start, but succeeded only on their second or third try. A critical factor for success is securing a senior political champion for the zone program and ensuring broad commitment through, for example, an interministerial committee.

More private sector participation in SEZ programs should be encouraged, but ideological prescriptions should be avoided in favor of what is practical in the context. What seems to matter is not so much who runs the program but how they run it: the objectives, incentives, and capacity. Government-run zone programs in Africa have suffered from problems of both governance and capacity. However, there is no guarantee that the private sector will offer a better alternative, as the experience of several African countries attests. But given the large investments required to support zones and their uncertain return, private sector investment is important to reduce government risk in zone programs. Regardless of the role the private sector plays in zone development and management, greater private sector participation in strategic planning and policy decisions affecting zone programs should be encouraged, and the development of public-private institutions promoted.

An effective legal and regulatory framework is a necessary first step for zone program development. A clear and transparent legal and regulatory framework codifies the program strategy and establishes the rules of the game for all stakeholders involved in the process. This framework helps in addressing difficult land issues, facilitating the provision of infrastructure, and ensuring compliance with labor and environmental standards. While its presence is no guarantee of success, the absence of a solid legal and regulatory framework will probably condemn an SEZ program to failure.

De facto implementation is equally important. African zone programs need to improve the capacity, budget, and accountability of regulatory authorities, as well as interagency coordination. Good laws are often applied poorly. In many of the African SEZs, the agency responsible for developing, promoting, and regulating the program lacks resources and capacity to carry out the mandate. Of equal importance, it often lacks the institutional agency to do so. In many successful zone programs, the regulatory agency is often autonomous but anchored to a central ministry (e.g., the president, prime minister, or ministry of finance) and supported by a sustainable budget. Institutional reforms and capacity building are needed in many zone programs.

The location of a zone is too often determined by political rather than commercial or economic considerations. Despite long-standing evidence to the contrary, governments try (and usually fail) to use zones as regional development tools. Almost all the countries under study located at least one zone in a lagging or remote region, but few have done enough to address the infrastructure connectivity, labor skills, and supply access these regions lack. Not surprisingly, FDI shuns these locations in favor of agglomerations where they can access quality infrastructure, deep labor markets, and knowledge spillovers.

Infrastructure quality is a critical gap in many African zones. Delivering more effectively on hard and soft infrastructure inside the zones and integrating zones with the domestic market must be priorities for African zone programs. Most of the African zones offer an infrastructure inside the zone that, while not world class, is of higher quality than that typically available elsewhere in the country. However, in some cases, infrastructure inside the zones mirrors that in the rest of the country, including water shortages; electricity failures; and health, safety, and environmental shortfalls. If the basic internal infrastructure needs cannot be met, a zone has little chance of success.

Co-location of SEZs with trade gateway infrastructure or other major industrial projects may be an efficient solution to the challenge of integration. A problem common to many zones in low-income countries is that quality infrastructure stops at the zone gates. If zones are to be successful, it is critical to address the wider trade-related infrastructure—poor road connectivity and serious port-related delays undermine the competitiveness of many zones. One of the most effective and cost-efficient ways to ensure integration between zones and trade gateways is to co-locate them. Thus, the development of new zones should focus, wherever possible, on locations that are within or adjacent to major ports, airports, or other key trade infrastructure. The combination of core infrastructure and an SEZ environment (which can be used to pilot reforms or address difficult policy issues that cannot be addressed quickly at the national level) offers the potential to unblock some of the most binding constraints to competitiveness in the region.

Policies to promote links between SEZs and the domestic economy are key to realizing the dynamic potential of zones. Countries that have been successful in deriving long-term economic benefits from their SEZ programs have established the conditions for ongoing exchange between the domestic economy and activities based in the zone. These conditions include investment in the zone by domestic firms, forward and backward links, business support, and the seamless movement of skilled labor and entrepreneurs between the zone and the domestic economy. From a policy perspective, this suggests shifting from the EPZ model to an SEZ model that eliminates legal restrictions on forward and backward links and domestic participation. But it also requires the implementation of much broader policies beyond the scope of the SEZ program, including (1) promoting skills development, training, and knowledge sharing; (2) promoting industry clusters and targeting links with zone-based firms at the cluster level; (3) supporting the integration of regional value chains; (4) supporting public-private institutions, both industry-specific and transversal; and (5) ensuring that labor markets are free to facilitate the movement of skilled labor across firms.

Another critical factor for realizing the dynamic potential of SEZs is supporting domestic investment in the zones. Evidence from successful SEZ programs shows a strong role for local investors in the medium term. The inversion from FDI to local firm dominance in SEZs has been seen in Malaysia, Korea, Mauritius, and, recently, in China. The process also appears to be under way in Bangladesh and Vietnam. But in Africa, although the share of locally owned firms is not exceptionally low, overall investment levels (including FDI) are weak. Promoting local investment in zones may involve eliminating policy restrictions and high-investment-level requirements in some zones. Again, such issues go beyond the confines of the zone program itself; they also affect policies dealing with such issues as access to finance and the culture of entrepreneurship.

Addressing social infrastructure needs is critical to ensuring sustainability and realizing the potential for upgrading. By attracting large numbers of workers (usually unskilled) from rural areas, many zones place huge burdens on the social infrastructure of the communities in which they are based. Experience in East Asia shows that providing quality social infrastructure (especially education and health care) is critical to attract the skilled workers needed to support upgrading. This is another example of the policy needs of SEZs extending well beyond what is traditionally considered in most programs.

Most African economic zones need to improve their approach to social and environmental compliance issues. At the national policy level, economic zones should be seen as an opportunity to experiment with policy innovations. Zones have made progress in meeting international norms for labor standards. In almost all the countries studied, wages for unskilled labor were higher inside the zones than outside, and (anecdotally, at least) working conditions were more favorable inside the zones. SEZs are an important source of human capital development and basic work skills acquisition in many low-income countries. However, a gap remains between the de jure and de facto environments in many zones—monitoring compliance with labor standards can be improved in most zones. And despite the large proportion of female workers in most zone programs, little effort has been made to address gender-specific issues in many zones under study. Enforcement of environmental standards in many zones is also weak. Despite this, zones offer an ideal environment for policy experimenting with innovations in both social and environmental policy.

Effective monitoring and evaluation (M&E) is a critical component to address some of the gaps in zone program performance and to more effectively link policy, strategy, and operations. In the absence of effective monitoring of the activities and results of companies operating under zone regimes, African zone authorities are (1) unable to enforce regulations effectively, resulting in abuses of the system and negative externalities (e.g., environmental); (2) unable to determine whether programs have been successful; and (3) unable to make informed decisions about future investment, to participate effectively in policy dialogue, or to respond appropriately to changing needs of investors and the government.

What is the Outlook for Future Support for SEZs?
SEZs are expensive and risky projects, and the margin for error is small. Yet, in some cases, zones have played a critical role in catalyzing diversification, upgrading, and economic growth. Implemented in a comprehensive way, they have the potential to be a useful instrument.

Despite their weak performance to date, SEZs can still play a valuable role in many African countries. These countries are in need of diversification and either are in the early stages of industrialization or have experienced deindustrialization in recent decades. To diversify, they need to attract private investment, particularly FDI. By overcoming infrastructure and land constraints and facilitating economies of scale, SEZs offer the potential to leverage trade preferences to attract investment and support diversification if they designed and implemented effectively.

Sufficient reasons exist for continued support of the SEZ as a policy instrument, but its use should be context-dependent. The environments in which zone programs are developed are complex and heterogeneous, so it is important to avoid overly deterministic approaches. However, it may be useful to establish a clear framework for situations in which SEZs are appropriate, and the likely preconditions for their success. The following are suggested elements of such a framework:

a) Ensure that SEZ programs are focused where they can best complement and support comparative advantage, as validated through a detailed strategic planning, feasibility, and master planning process.
b) Integrate SEZs as part of a broader package of industrial, trade, and economic development policies.
c) Integrate SEZs with support to existing industry clusters rather than as an alternative or greenfield approach to cluster development.

d) Ensure high-level political support and broad commitment—including the establishment of an interministerial committee to oversee program development—before launching any program.

e) Promote exchange between the zone and the domestic environment through both policy and administrative reforms.

f) Support the provision of high-quality hard and soft infrastructure encompassing zones, key urban centers, and trade gateways. (One possible model is the Ghana Gateway project and its multipurpose industrial park.) The focus should be on leveraging SEZs to support existing and planned infrastructure to facilitate the potential for growth catalysts/poles.

g) Put SEZs on the regional integration agenda, with an emphasis on their role in facilitating regional production scale and integrating regional value chains.

h) Ensure the development of sound legal and regulatory frameworks, and cement them by also addressing the challenges of institutional design and coordination.

i) Promote private sector participation and public-private partnerships (PPPs), along with technical assistance for structuring and negotiating PPP deals.

j) Take into greater consideration the capacity of governments to deliver on SEZ programs, particularly given their integrated and long-term nature. This will require a focus on institutional development and political economy factors that influence zone policy and implementation.

k) Establish clear standards with regard to environmental, labor, and social compliance, and identify clear regulatory responsibilities for monitoring and enforcement.

l) Develop and implement a comprehensive monitoring and evaluation (M&E) program from the outset, with safeguards in place to ensure that SEZ program developments remain aligned with strategic and master plans.

m) Recognize the long-term nature of SEZ program development. This means planning beyond short-term project cycles and monitoring progress on an ongoing basis.

Coordination is important. In most cases, no single donor or government will be in a position to support all the financial and technical needs of a country's economic zone program. Coordination of all actors, including those in the private sector, will help ensure effective delivery, particularly given the limited absorption capacity in many zone authorities.

One of the most important areas for coordinated support from donors, governments, and other actors is in the provision of high-quality data, research, and analysis on SEZs, as well as practical advice for SEZ practitioners.[6] Chapter 8 offers some suggestions for a research agenda.

Notes

1. Definitional note: We refer to *zones, economic zones,* and *SEZs* interchangeably as generic terms to encompass a wide range of modern free zone types (FIAS 2008), such as export processing zones (EPZs), free trade zones (FTZs), special economic zones (SEZs), and other spatially defined areas that combine infrastructure and policy instruments with the aim of promoting investment and exports. The countries covered in this research were mainly operating EPZ or FTZ programs, although several were shifting their regimes to become focused on so-called "wide-area" SEZs and other more integrated industrial park models (e.g., Ghana's multipurpose industrial park).

2. Lesotho does not have a zone program per se, but it combines policy instruments to support export manufacturers, including a special fiscal and administrative regime and public provision of industrial infrastructure.

3. "Upgrading" here refers to a shift toward more technology- or knowledge-intensive activities, involving either a shift to new sectors or moving up the value chain in an existing sector.

4. Trade facilitation involves the processes and controls that govern the movement of goods throughout a supply chain, including logistics, transport, trade-related infrastructure, and regulatory and commercial procedures.

5. This may be the situation, for example, in postconflict environments. Additional research is needed to assess the performance of zones in this context.

6. The forthcoming International Finance Corporation (IFC) publication *SEZ Practitioners Guide* is an example of the kind of knowledge products that can play a valuable role in supporting more effective planning and implementation of SEZ programs.

CHAPTER 1

Introduction

Background and Objectives

Special economic zones (SEZs) are spatially delimited areas within an economy that function with administrative, regulatory, and often fiscal regimes that are different (typically more liberal) than those of the domestic economy. Operating through a variety of different forms—such as export processing zones, economic processing zones, free zones, and foreign trade zones—SEZs aim to overcome barriers that hinder investment in the wider economy, including restrictive policies, poor governance, inadequate infrastructure, and problematic access to land.

SEZs have been an important policy instrument for many governments seeking to attract foreign investment, promote export-oriented growth, and generate employment. Their popularity as a policy tool has grown enormously in the past 20 years: in 1986, the International Labour Organisation's (ILO's) database reported 176 zones in 47 countries; by 2006, it reported 3,500 zones in 130 countries. This huge growth of SEZs comes despite many zones having failed to meet their objectives. However, there are a number of examples of zones contributing significantly to growth in FDI, exports, and employment, and playing a catalytic role in (1) integration with global trade and (2) structural transformation, including industrialization and upgrading. These zones are primarily in East Asia (e.g., China, Malaysia, Korea) but also in Latin America (e.g., the Dominican Republic, Costa Rica), the Middle East/North Africa (e.g., United Arab Emirates, Morocco), and Sub-Saharan Africa (e.g., Mauritius). The consensus from previous policy research is that African zones have generally underperformed, with the significant exception of Mauritius and the partial exception of Kenya, and possibly Madagascar and Lesotho. For example, Watson (2001) found that many African zones have suffered from lack of attention to labor and displacement issues, and weak economic management skills have made it impossible for governments to address the multiple challenges of providing high-quality infrastructure, government services, and human capital.

There has been much debate over the years as to the value of SEZs as a policy instrument. Most traditional economic analysis, including major analytical pieces from the World Bank (Warr 1989; Madani 1999), view zones as a second-best policy, preferring economy-wide liberalization. However, other researchers have noted the dynamic, long-run economic impacts of successful zone programs.

SEZ policy and zone management practices have evolved over time, as has the external environment. One notable trend in worldwide SEZ development over the past 15 years has been the growing importance of zones that are privately owned, developed, or operated (FIAS 2008). Moreover, many successful zones have managed to shift their basis of competitiveness, focusing on the quality of services they offer rather than relying on generous packages of fiscal incentives. In addition, while fierce competition for foreign direct investment has emerged from East Asia, multilateral liberalization and the proliferation of preferential trade agreements have opened up new export opportunities that can be exploited effectively within zones. These countervailing forces appear to have further accentuated the differences between SEZs that perform well and those that do not.

However, despite three decades of research on economic zones, many important questions remain unanswered. There is a lack of systematic, data-driven analysis on the performance of economic zones around the world and limited up-to-date analysis of the policies and practices that determine that performance. As a result, policymakers are often forced to rely on the same small handful of case studies (covering a limited range of countries and some now 10–20 years old). For African policymakers, virtually no research exists on the performance of zone programs in the region, outside of Mauritius.

This study addresses some of these gaps and delivers an analysis that is both data-driven and policy-focused. The objective of this study is to explore the experience of zone programs, with a particular focus on Africa, to understand the factors that contribute to outcomes in both a static and dynamic context. It addresses the questions of whether and how zones can make a significant contribution to job creation, diversification, and growth in African countries.

Methodology

This report is a synthesis of findings from two main streams of research conducted for the study: firm-level surveys of investors in SEZs and country case studies of SEZ programs.

SEZ Investor Surveys

Original surveys were designed and conducted with foreign and domestic investors based in SEZs across the 10 countries included in the study. The surveys captured information about investment location decisions and the experience of establishing and operating a business inside the SEZ. A number of questions mirror those asked in the World Bank's Enterprise Surveys, to allow for a comparison of responses from firms based inside and outside the SEZs. The surveys were conducted by local consultants in each country through face-to-face interviews with firm managers and owners. More than 600 surveys were completed across the 10 countries. In each country, surveys were conducted at three of the largest zones in the country (although the African countries all had fewer than three zones). Individual country "survey notes" were developed as an output of this activity. (For a description of the survey methodology and a summary of sampling statistics, see Appendix C.)

Case Studies

Case studies were developed on the SEZ programs in each of the 10 countries. These were based primarily on semistructured interviews conducted in each country with investors, zone developers and operators, regulatory authorities, government representatives, and other stakeholders. Interviews were supplemented by secondary research on the history and development of the SEZ program, along with analysis of SEZ laws, regulations, and other relevant policy and legal documents. Individual country case studies were developed as an output of this activity; details on the stakeholders interviewed and secondary sources reviewed are available in these country case studies. The study covers the following 10 countries:

- Africa: Ghana, Kenya, Lesotho, Nigeria, Senegal, and Tanzania
- Asia: Bangladesh and Vietnam
- Latin America: the Dominican Republic and Honduras

In addition, the study draws on examples from a number of other successful SEZ programs, largely through secondary research on programs in Mauritius, China, Costa Rica, and Malaysia.

A detailed set of criteria was applied to select the sample of countries to be included in the study (for additional information, see Appendix A). These criteria relate mainly to comparability, generalizability, and opportunities for learning. However, they also take into account donor and Bank priorities, as well as practical issues with respect to data collection. The following were the most important factors in country selection:

- The majority of countries are in Sub-Saharan Africa, given the focus of the study on this region; within Africa, we aimed for broad geographical coverage.
- Countries outside Africa were included to identify practices (good and bad) that are relevant for SEZs in African countries.
- Programs had to have been active for at least three years in order to have some history to study.
- The study aimed to include as many low-income (International Development Association) countries as possible.[1]

Structure of the Report

Following this brief introductory chapter, the remainder of the study is structured as follows:

Chapter 2 provides an introduction to SEZs and discusses the main policy debates in the field. It clarifies the definition of zones, taking into account their key structural features and core policy goals. It then explores historic moments in the formation of the modern zone. Finally, it covers the main debates on the contribution to growth and development of the modern zone, with a view to summarizing progress in economic and policy analysis, and outlining the outstanding policy questions.

Chapter 3 looks at the relative performance of SEZs in Africa. It provides a broad, quantitative assessment of outcomes of SEZ programs in terms of exports, investment, and employment. It also looks at longer term economic and social outcomes of these zone programs, including the extent to which SEZs contribute to local economic upgrading through links and spillovers with domestic firms, the quality of the employment they offer, and their gender-differentiated effects.

Chapter 4 helps overcome the research gap on the factors that determine SEZ performance by assessing the quantitative relationship between SEZ program outcomes and several factors, including the investment climate, wages, incentives, location, management, and market access. The chapter draws on a database of SEZs and the results from the SEZ surveys.

Chapter 5 provides a further quantitative investigation based on the results of the SEZ surveys. It focuses on assessing the performance of SEZs in meeting the investment climate requirements of their investors, with a specific focus on Africa.

Chapters 6 and 7 analyze the policies, strategies, and operational practices behind the observed performance in African zones. Drawing on the results of the case study research and examples from other SEZ programs, these chapters document the current or prevailing strategic approaches taken in other zones and the day-to-day implementation of the programs. Emphasis is placed on good practices as well as mistakes to avoid in planning and implementing zone programs. Chapter 6 focuses on policy, planning, and strategy, while Chapter 7 focuses on operations, management, and learning in the SEZs.

Finally, Chapter 8 draws policy conclusions from the findings of the report, designed for policymakers in the African and low-income country context. Specifically, we discuss when the implementation of an economic zone program is most likely to be successful; what type of zone approach is most appropriate for African countries, depending on the context in which they are operating; and how an SEZ program can be most effectively implemented. It outlines a framework of preconditions for successful SEZ programs and suggests an agenda for future research.

Note

1. This criterion helps ensure that findings are transferable across countries; also, it was a specific priority of the trust fund program that supported this study.

References

FIAS (Foreign Investment Advisory Service). 2008. *Special Economic Zones. Performance, Lessons Learned, and Implications for Zone Development.* Washington, DC: World Bank.

Madani, D. 1999. "A Review of the Role and Impact of Export Processing Zones." World Bank Policy Research Working Paper 2238. World Bank, Washington, DC.

Warr, P. 1989. "Export Processing Zones: The Economics of Enclave Manufacturing." *The World Bank Research Observer.* 9 (1): 65–88.

Watson, P. L. 2001. "Export Processing Zones: Has Africa Missed the Boat? Not Yet!" Africa Region Working Paper Series No. 17. World Bank, Washington, DC.

CHAPTER 2

Brief History of SEZs and Overview of Policy Debates

Claude Baissac, lead author

Introduction

The term *economic zones* encompasses a wide variety of related concepts, including free trade zones, free ports, foreign trade zones, export processing zones, special economic zones, free export zones, trade and economic cooperation zones, economic processing zones, and free zones. Despite the many variations in name and form, they can all be broadly defined as *demarcated geographic areas contained within a country's national boundaries where the rules of business are different from those that prevail in the national territory. These differential rules principally deal with investment conditions, international trade and customs, taxation, and the regulatory environment; whereby the zone is given a business environment that is intended to be more liberal from a policy perspective and more effective from an administrative perspective than that of the national territory.*

Even this parsimonious definition[1] does only partial justice to reality, as some countries make no distinction with regard to taxation in their zones, and others have done away with the geographic spatiality of the zone and have instead made it a purely legal space with applicability across the entirety of the national territory or large portions of it. It is therefore not surprising that little consistency exists in the denomination and classification of zones.

In this chapter, we first attempt to clarify the definition of zones, taking into account their key structural features and core policy goals. We then explore historic moments in the formation of the modern zone. Finally, we cover the main debates on the meaning and the contribution to growth and development of the modern zone, with a view to summarizing progress in economic and policy analysis, and outlining the outstanding policy questions.

Defining Economic Zones

The multiplicity of names and forms of economic zones is the result of several factors, including (1) the need to differentiate among types of zones that display very real differences in form and function; (2) differences in economic terminology among countries; (3) zone promoters' desire to differentiate their product from those of the competition; and (4) the consequences of multiple translations. Definitions vary across countries and institutions, and evolve continuously as new types of zones are developed and older types disappear or are adapted. Any attempt at a comprehensive definition of economic zones must be sufficiently broad to encompass the bewildering array of past, present, and future zones, and yet sufficiently precise to exclude those that do not display the essential structural features that make a zone a zone.

Structural Features

The following are the main structural features of a zone:

1. Zones are, primarily, formally delimited portions of the national territory and, secondarily, legal spaces provided with a set of investment, trade, and operating rules that are more liberal and administratively efficient than those prevailing in the rest of the national territory. Zones are therefore defined by a specific *regulatory regime*. This regime may be contained in one or several dedicated laws or through a set of measures contained in a number of texts.

2. The administration of the regime usually requires a *dedicated governance structure*, centralized or decentralized. The attributes of this structure vary according to the nature of the zone regime, the prevalent administrative culture, the number of existing zones, the role of the private sector in developing and operating zones, and many other factors. The

purpose of this structure is what matters: It is to ensure efficient management of the regime and ensure that investors benefit from its provisions.

3. Zones are usually provided with a physical infrastructure supporting the activities of the firms and economic agents operating within them. This infrastructure usually includes real estate, roads, electricity, water, and telecommunications. The infrastructure is usually composed of *industrial or mixed-use activity parks* and key transport infrastructure connecting the zone to its sources, markets, and economic hinterland. Even in countries where zones are legal spaces, industrial or mixed-use activity parks usually exist to host firms.

These features are necessary attributes of zones to varying extents. As we will demonstrate in the following section, not all types of zones display all these attributes at once, although prototypical zones (e.g., export processing zones) tend to include all of them. The determinant structural feature of a zone is that *it benefits from a different regulatory regime from that in the rest of the economy.* The governance, spatial, and infrastructural features are important, but less so.

Policy Intent
Another important attribute of zones is the policy intent that informs their creation. Zones exist because of their policy raison d'être: the social values or return they are expected to generate. Zones are created to generate or participate in the economic transformation of their host countries in a way that is faster or more effective than would be the case without them. They are developed to act as catalysts for growth. What this means, however, varies significantly from country to country and has evolved considerably over the past 30 years. According the 2008 FIAS report, zones are created with four specific (although by no means exclusive) policy goals:

1. *To attract foreign direct investment*: Most new SEZ programs, particularly in some regions, such as the Middle East, are designed to attract foreign investment (FIAS 2008, p. 12).
2. *To serve as "pressure valves" to alleviate large-scale unemployment*: The EPZ programs of Tunisia and the Dominican Republic are frequently cited as examples of programs that have remained enclaves; they have not catalyzed dramatic structural economic change but have nevertheless remained robust job-creating programs.
3. *To support a wider economic reform strategy*: In this view, zones are a simple tool permitting a country to develop and diversify exports.

Zones are a way of reducing anti-export bias while keeping protective barriers intact. The zones of Taiwan-China, Mauritius, and the Republic of Korea follow this pattern.

4. *As experimental laboratories for the application of new policies and approaches*: China's wide-area SEZs are classic examples—financial, legal, labor, and even pricing policies were introduced and tested first within the SEZs before being extended to the rest of the economy.

Using a different perspective, zones can be seen to confer two main types of benefits, which can be realized in the short and long term, respectively:

1. *Static economic benefits* are derived in the relatively short term through the use of economic zones as instruments of trade and investment policy. They are the result of capturing the gains from specialization and exchange, and include employment creation, the attraction of the generation of foreign exchange through exports, and the creation of economic value added.
2. *Dynamic economic benefits* are the longer term structural and developmental benefits that may derive from zones. These encompass the promotion of nontraditional economic activities, hard and soft technology transfers, encouragement of domestic entrepreneurialism, and the promotion of economic openness. At the national level, economic zones are formed with the goal of effecting positive changes in the competitiveness of the country or a region.

Over the past 30 years, the focus has progressively shifted toward the dynamic contribution of zones to economic restructuring and their use as instruments to enhance competitiveness. This is discussed later in the chapter.

In terms of meta-denomination, the emerging consensus is that the term *special economic zone* is both the broadest and the most precise to describe the zones defined here. It is also particularly useful from a definitional and policy development perspective, as the component terms are themselves both sufficiently broad and precise:

1. *Special* refers to the differential regulatory regime that distinguishes the zone from the prevalent domestic economy.
2. *Economic* refers to the broadest type of activities now allowed in zones, without prejudice regarding their nature and focus.

3. *Zone* refers to the physically or legally bounded "economic space" contained in the domestic territory.

A Nomenclature of SEZs

Insofar as the precise nomenclature is concerned, it should reflect the types of SEZs that currently exist or have existed, while accommodating the changes occurring in the dynamic environment. It should be understood as an ideal-typical representation, but a not entirely satisfactory approximation. Here again, the FIAS 2008 nomenclature is valuable, with some adaptations and caveats. The 2008 report says that special economic zones are *"demarcated geographic areas contained within a country's national boundaries where the rules of business are different from those that prevail in the national territory. These differential rules principally deal with investment conditions, international trade and customs, and taxation; whereby the zone is given a business environment more liberal and effective than that of the national territory."*

However, the report includes zones that do not fall or only conditionally fall within this definition, such as enterprise zones created in older industrial and urban centers of advanced economies to support revitalization. While enterprise zones offer investment incentives, they do not provide a specific regulatory regime. Similarly, traditional industrial parks, technology parks, science and research parks, information technology and services parks, and petrochemical zones may not be SEZs under the definition used in this report if they do not have their own regulatory regimes.

Thus, SEZs include the following types:

1. *Commercial free zones, free trade zones,* and *free zones (FZs):* These are the oldest form of SEZ (see Box 2.1) and the most ubiquitous, notably under the *bonded warehouse* format found in the vast majority of seaports and in some airports. Free zones are usually in or near major international transport nodes and are usually under the administration of ports, directly or indirectly. They are also usually physically segregated from both the port's main area and the outside by fences, walls, and gates, because they lie outside the country's custom territory. Their activities are limited to trade-related processes (warehousing, storage, sales, exhibitions) and light processing operations (packaging, labeling, quality control, sorting).

2. *Export processing zones (EPZs):* These made their appearance in the late 1950s/early 1960s as a way to accelerate industrialization and industry-related international trade in developing countries (see Box 2.2).

Box 2.1

Colon Free Zone, Panama

On the Atlantic side of the Panama Canal, the Colon Free Zone occupies an area of 400 hectares. At the nexus of Central, North, and South America and the Caribbean, linking the U.S. eastern and western seaboards, it was opened in 1948 to capitalize on canal traffic and the trade opportunities it presented. The zone offers a liberal trading environment, permitting logistics and trading activities, both wholesale and retail. Its initial focus was trade with South America, but the economic liberalization and greater regional integration of South America has turned Colon into a prominent regional multimodal logistics platform (maritime, rail, air, and road) and trade center. The zone is visited every year by more than 250,000 people, hosts 2,000 enterprises, employs more than 15,000 persons, and imports and exports over $US10 billion of commodities annually. The zone is owned by the state and operated by a semi-autonomous parastatal.

Source: http://www.colonfreezone.com, accessed in May 2010.

The honor of being the first EPZ is usually given to the Shannon Free Zone in Ireland, created in 1958. Shannon provided the basic "grammar" for EPZs, which was replicated across a vast swath of the developing world in the subsequent decades: a fenced-in territory of several hectares offering developed industrial land for rent/lease, situated outside the country's custom territory, benefiting from investment and operational incentives, and supported by simplified administrative procedures. EPZ activities were initially focused exclusively on export markets; investment was restricted to foreign capital; and activities were limited to manufacturing. EPZs have evolved dramatically since the 1990s, and the types of activities permitted have expanded significantly.

3. *Free enterprises (FEs) or single factory/single unit free zones:* This is a variation on the FZ/EPZ in which individual enterprises are provided with FZ/EPZ status and allowed to locate anywhere on the national territory or in a designated part of the territory (see Box 2.3). In some countries, FEs and FZs/EPZs coexist. The U.S. Foreign Trade Zone system provides certain enterprises with a free trade zone (FTZ) status called *subzone.* This status applies to existing enterprises that wish to have the benefits of the FTZ system but whose relocation costs would be too high or to new enterprises that have a compelling reason not to

Box 2.2

Masan Free Zone, Republic of Korea

Created in 1970, the Masan Free Zone became the prototypical export process-ing zone. Initially, it was called the Masan Free Export Zone and was primarily dedicated to attracting FDI in manufacturing export activities. The objective in creating Masan FEZ was to support the development of manufacturing activities that complemented those of the Korean economy but did not compete with them. Thus, investment was constrained by qualification criteria, and the zone was kept relatively small—originally 10 hectares, expanded to 90 hectares. It offered a prime investment and operating environment to qualifying enterprises, including excellent external infrastructure (port, airport, roads) and a high-quality industrial park with solid management and support services. Masan's small size did not detract from its economic impact, which has been significant. It attracted prime foreign enterprises in the electronics industry. In 1971, these enterprises "imported" only 3 percent of their production components from Korea; by 1986, 45 percent of these components were sourced from Korea. The zone achieved one of its crucial objectives: serving as a catalyst for economic diversification through the creation of national competitive clusters in high-value manufactur-ing. Masan was restructured in 2000 to reflect the liberalized global and domes-tic economic environment.

Source: http://www.ftz.go.kr/eng/main.jsp, accessed in May 2010.

locate in an existing FTZ. Some countries have no FZs/EPZs per se, and the FZ/EPZ status is given to individual enterprises. In Mexico, the *maquiladora* status is of this type; for many years, it was geographically restricted to a band along the Mexico-U.S. border.

4. *Freeports*: The term *freeport* in the FIAS (2008) classification can be confusing, as it is used to describe what are generally known as special economic zones. In this classification, the Aqaba Special Economic Zone and the Chinese SEZs would be freeports. These freeports are the largest type of all, as they encompass very large portions of the territory, include urban and rural areas, and incorporate large transport facilities such as ports and airports. Freeports can include entire eco-nomic regions, the populations that live and work in these regions, and all the economic activities that take place there. They can contain or even overlap political and administrative units.

Box 2.3

Mauritius Export Processing Zone

The Mauritius Export Processing Zone (MEPZ) is one of Africa's most famous and successful examples of the free enterprise type of EPZ, in which companies are granted status on an individual basis and are free to locate anywhere on the island, including in industrial parks that are not restricted to MEPZ enterprises. MEPZ enterprises dot the national territory; historically, they have located near labor force pools. Mauritius is only 1,800 km². The small size greatly simplifies access to key infrastructure, as no enterprise is more than 60 km from the international airport and the port. This EPZ strategy allowed the country to avoid having to set up industrial parks to host MEPZs when their numbers reached 600 firms in the late 1980s to mid-1990s.

Mauritius also operates the Mauritius Freeport, which is a small commercial free zone within the island's commercial port in the capital city of Port Louis. Companies must operate within the designated perimeter.

Source: Baissac, C. 2010.

One approach that may be useful in clarifying the definition overlap noted above may be the categorization used by the World Economic Processing Zones Association (WEPZA):

- *Wide-area zones*: These are zones that occupy a surface area greater than 1,000 hectares (100 km²) and with a resident population. Chinese SEZs fall into this category, as does the Aqaba Special Economic Zone.
- *Small-area zones*: These are generally smaller than 1,000 hectares and typically surrounded by a fence. Investors must locate within the zone to receive benefits. They have no resident population, although they may contain worker dormitories. Most EPZs and FTZs are of this type.

In our report, we use the FIAS terminology but replace the term *freeport* with *wide-area SEZ* to describe the Chinese zones.[2] Throughout the report, we use the terms *special economic zone* and *economic zone* in a generic way to refer to all the zones discussed above. When we are making a distinction about a distinct type of economic zone (for example, EPZs) we use the specific term.

The Evolution of Economic Zones—A Brief History

The objective in this section is to trace the evolution of the concept of zones that has led to the modern SEZ. This exercise is subjective and not inclusive—a complete history of SEZs would require much more than these few pages.

Trade-Based Ancestry

Special economic zones are not a new invention. For as long as organized societies have engaged in external trade, there has been a need for secured areas at ports or in strategic locations along trade routes where commodities can be stored or exchanged. These areas became free zones when the commodities circulated free of local prohibitions, taxation, duties, and excises. Many consider the Island of Delos in the Cyclades as the first approximation of a free zone, in the sense that it provided free-trade-like conditions (see Box 2.4).

Between the 13th and 17th centuries, the Hanseatic League (an organization of cities along the Baltic Sea) ran a series of monopoly

---

Box 2.4

Island of Delos

As the birthplace of Apollo and Artemis, Delos was an important religious sanctuary. It attracted worshippers that its productive economy could not support, being only 6 km² and nonagricultural. Thus, it needed to import food, building materials, and objects of worship. The need to import seems to have turned the island into a relatively prosperous and important regional trade platform, concentrating the import of key commodities (e.g., grain, olive oil, wine, cattle, firewood) for the Cyclades archipelago. Beginning about 200 BC, the economy grew substantially, and the island's government spent significant resources expanding the port. Delos also operated as a trading place for slaves, including captives of a very active piracy trade. The island's status as a trading platform improved greatly in 167 BC, when Rome gave it free harbor status for Roman citizens and non-Roman Italians. A year later, in 166 BC, it made Delos a toll-free harbor. This turned the island into a center for Romans operating in Asia Minor and for Greeks, especially after the destruction of Corinth in 146 BC. The Greek historian Polybius, writing around 150 BC, used the term *free port* to describe Delos.

Source: Champion, C.B. 2003; Reger, G. 1994.

trades along sea and land routes. Similarly, across Europe, cities were granted royal privileges and charters giving them monopolies in certain trades or freedom from certain prohibitions, taxes, duties, or excises. The European colonial expansion also rested in large part, at least until the mid-1800s, on the granting of charters and privileges. Most of the early colonial empires were created and administered under that system. Within the territory concessioned, the chartered company exercised a monopoly on free trade. Trading posts were set up—usually at strategic points on coasts and at mouths of navigable rivers—to concentrate trade and resources with the rich hinterlands of the concessioned territories. Hong Kong SAR, China, and Singapore were created in this manner.

Pioneering Manufacturing

The vast majority of early zones were closely associated and generally co-located with ports. By 1900, 11 FTZs existed globally; of these, 7 were in Europe and 4 in Asia. Manufacturing entered the realm of free trade zone activities only in the 20th century. While Shannon was the first explicit export processing zone, the inclusion of production processes in free zones started well before 1958, initially on a very limited and localized basis. The Spanish FTZs were among the first to accommodate industrial production. In the early 1920s, the zone operating at the Port of Cadiz hosted one of the first Ford Motors plants in Europe. In the United States, the Foreign Trade Zone Act of 1934 was a response to protectionist policies introduced in 1930, themselves a reaction to the Great Depression. The act sought to foster international trade by creating an environment that provided better conditions and lower transaction costs. However, manufacturing operations were prohibited in U.S. FTZs until 1950.

These early manufacturing programs in FTZs were of limited scope and required special authorization from the government. The focus of FTZs remained very much on trade. Allowing manufacturing in FTZs was an important step, but FTZs in the strict sense were not the source of the most important innovations. A critical step was the introduction of export-oriented industrialization programs in developing countries and their progressive association with another important development: the *industrial estate*.

Puerto Rico. The 1948 Operation Bootstrap in the Commonwealth of Puerto Rico was a key moment in the development of SEZs. The program's objective was to attract U.S. firms to set up manufacturing operations to serve the mainland U.S. market. This export-oriented strategy sought to provide employment and shift the Puerto Rican economy away from its monocultural plantation structure. The central premise of the project was that mainland firms in sectors facing rising labor costs would need an alternative location with more competitive costs. The program had three primary components. First, its incentives framework rested principally on tax exemptions; for American companies, the island was a de facto free zone, as it was part of the U.S. customs territory and thus faced no import or export duties on commodities traded with the mainland. Second, the Departamento de Fomento focused on investment promotion in the United States, investing US$10 million a year in the process and setting up representation offices. Third, the Industrial Development Company financed the construction of modular industrial buildings for rent by investors.

Shannon Free Zone, Ireland. The next key moment in the evolution of SEZs was the Shannon Free Zone in Ireland. The Shannon approach was original because it combined the attributes of the free trade zone with those of the industrial park into a single, integrated investment, industry, and trade development instrument. Shannon came to represent the quintessential export processing zone, providing the template for many similar developments around the world in the ensuing decades. The package included—

- A differential customs regime
- An investment incentives regime
- Dedicated support functions to facilitate administrative tasks, from investment to labor
- An industrial zone with ready-built infrastructure
- Co-location with a major transport hub

The result was the creation of an industrial enclave that exchanged capital, commodities, and labor flows with the surrounding economy.

Maquiladoras in Mexico. Mexico's *maquiladora* program was another key moment, with its massive regional development orientation. Its overarching goal was to compensate for the 1964 termination of the U.S. Bracero Program,[3] which left Mexico with a severe shortage of employment opportunities—in the main border cities, unemployment was as high as 50 percent. The new program made abundant and cheap labor available to American-owned companies.[4] The scheme required specific legislation to allow and encourage American firms to invest and operate along the border. Until then, Mexico's investment and trade regulations were typically import-substituting. Both countries made changes to facilitate the new program:

- In Mexico, the initial measures allowed the duty-free import of raw materials, components, and capital equipment, provided the finished product was exported and these items remained in bond in Mexico. These operations were permitted only within a 20 km-wide strip in privately owned industrial parks administered by the Programa Nacional Fronterizo (PRONAF). Foreign ownership could not exceed 49 percent.
- In the United States, sections 806.30 and 807 of the Customs Law (1956 and 1963, respectively) ruled that imported products containing U.S.-produced components would be charged duties only on the value of the foreign-produced components and the foreign value added.

Initially, the *maquiladora* program had a limited effect on unemployment, even though more than 200 plants employed 30,000 workers. However, the Mexican government passed a series of legislative acts in the early 1970s,[5] and the number of plants grew to 455 in 1974 and employment to 76,000. Today, these figures have multiplied more than tenfold. The program is credited with leading to the signing of the North American Free Trade Act of 1994 (NAFTA), an inconceivable notion in 1964.

Together, the Puerto Rican, Irish, and Mexican innovations trace a critical evolutionary path of the economic zone concept:

1. Puerto Rico's government pioneered the combination of incentives, promotion, and industrial buildings. However, the island did not develop specific industrial zones, opting instead for a dispersion model.
2. Ireland developed the packaged export processing zone by combining previously unrelated or loosely related components into one strategic geographic location to generate a concentrated economic impact.
3. Mexico adapted this approach for its own requirements by introducing a differential set of rules for the *maquilas* and by restricting investment to qualifying specialized industrial parks in a limited geographic area. Mexico also introduced early forms of private sector participation

in the provision of key services to investors, such as contract manufacturing and the shelter plan.[6]

4. These zones employed a system of reciprocal and complementary trade preferences that applied at the country or firm level, thus creating the efficiency gains that would sustain investment and operation.

The Golden Age of the Export Processing Zone

From the mid-1960s on, the growth imperative across the expanding developing world caused massive commitments to industrialization, primarily through import-substitution and industrial "big push" strategies. But within this overall framework, significant variations developed. Export processing zones were deployed to serve various policy aims, although the general recipe employed the same structural attributes. Taiwan-China and India launched their first EPZs in 1965, with, respectively, Kaoshiung and Kandla. Taiwan-China added the Nantse zone in 1969 and the Taichung zone in 1971. India added the Santacruz zone in 1973. South Korea opened its first zone, Masan, in 1971. Indonesia, Malaysia, the Philippines, Thailand, Singapore, and Sri Lanka all developed zones in this period.

Many of Asia's EPZs experienced rapid and sustained growth. Masan Free Export Zone was created to support the country's industrialization by attracting foreign firms in industries complementary to those of the domestic economy. Thus, unlike many other zones, Masan was not primarily an employment creation instrument. Investment criteria were rigorous, and the zone was initially kept small (10 hectares). Restructured in 2000, Masan is viewed as a runaway success.[7]

Malaysia's first zone opened near Penang Island in 1972. It rapidly became attractive to American firms in particular, which set up manufacturing operations in labor-intensive electronics assembly. Malaysia's EPZs grew by 13.3 percent a year in the 1970s. By 1995, more than 400 firms were operating in the zones. By 2003, the zones employed nearly a million workers, a third of them in increasingly high-tech segments of the electrical and electronics industries. Malaysia's electronics industry, created virtually from nothing within the zones, now produces about 10 percent of the world's semiconductors.

Latin America also took the EPZ route, with Colombia (initially FTZs) and the Dominican Republic as the early adopters. In Colombia, the Barranquilla zone was opened in 1964; in the Dominican Republic, La Romana was inaugurated in 1965. El Salvador, Guatemala, and Honduras followed suit in the early 1970s. After this came Nicaragua in 1976, Jamaica in 1976, and Costa Rica in 1981.

The Middle East and North Africa initially chose to develop FTZs, whose numbers also expanded in the 1960s and 1970s, notably in Egypt, Israel, Jordan, and Syria. Tunisia chose the EPZ route. In the 1990s, manufacturing activities took root, notably through the Qualified Industrial Zone program.

Although most countries in Sub-Saharan Africa did not develop zone programs until the 1990s, several launched earlier initiatives, including Liberia (1970), Mauritius (1971), and Senegal (1974).

By the mid-1980s, EPZs were a fixture of trade and industrial policy in all regions of the world.

Rise of the Chinese Model

No other SEZ program has had as much impact, nationally and internationally, as the Chinese program. Its initiation was a key moment in the development of the modern SEZ. The first zones were established in 1978 as a test of the controlled restructuring of the entire economy through the introduction of capitalism and foreign investment, after more than 30 years of economic and political isolation. Deng Xiaoping described this process as "crossing the river by feeling for stones." He was referring to the introduction of a liberal trade and investment regime in areas of the country that had been opened to trade in previous centuries but closed after 1949. Initially established in the country's coastal areas (three in Guangdong Province and one in Fujian), the number of economic zones increased in the 1980s and 1990s to include a large number of regions and towns, shifting toward the country's heartland.

The strategy proved to be successful. China became the world's largest exporter of manufactures and the leading recipient of FDI among emerging economies. SEZs played a key role: Between 1979 and 1995, the country received 40 percent of international FDI to developing countries. Ninety percent went to the coastal areas; 40 percent to Guangdong Province. The three Guangdong zones absorbed 50 percent of that total. In other words, these three SEZs received a staggering 7.2 percent of the total volume of FDI to emerging markets between 1979 and 1995, and 18 percent of all FDI into China.

Today, China has more than 200 zones of various types, sizes, focuses, and sectoral concentrations: commercial zones, industrial zones, technological zones, and so on. China provides a reference for the use of wide-area SEZs as a tool for economic growth, and it is expanding its model globally with investments in "economic cooperation zones" around the world.

Entry of the Private Sector

As a rule, the SEZs of the 1950s, 1960s, and 1970s were public affairs. Governments planned them, financed them, promulgated the regulations, administered the regime, conducted the investment promotion, interfaced with investors, and managed the real estate side of the operation, including building, renting, and maintaining. The late 1980s and 1990s saw a fundamental change in this model, in response to both push and pull factors. The main push factors were (1) the drive for macroeconomic stability and the resulting need for budgetary and fiscal discipline—it became too expensive for many countries to do it all—and (2) the need to regenerate lackluster free zone programs in some countries. The principal pull factor was the opportunity for private operators to turn zones into profitable real estate ventures and generate income from innovative services to firms.

The development of private sector zones was led primarily by Latin America, first through the *maquiladora* innovation, with its reliance on private industrial parks and value added services such as the shelter plans. The first privately developed and operated export processing zone was probably La Romana Free Zone, developed by the Gulf and Western Corporation in the Dominican Republic in 1969. Soon after, Costa Rica, El Salvador, Honduras, Nicaragua, Guatemala, and Colombia privatized their public zones or created entirely new private zones. Colombia no longer operates public zones. In other countries, public zones have been made to compete with private zones under similar operating conditions to avoid unfair competition. Asia caught on in the 1990s, with Thailand, the Philippines, and Vietnam launching private zones.

Although there has been debate over the efficacy of public versus private approaches in zones (see Box 2.5), anecdotal evidence tends to support the notion that private SEZs are more effective. However, caveats exist. A private zone may be a profitable operation but provide a marginal or negative contribution to the economy. Inversely, a public zone may run at a loss and require subsidization, yet provide positive socioeconomic returns. No comprehensive empirical analysis has been undertaken to answer the question, but the general perspective across the regions is as follows:

- In South America and the Caribbean, the shift to private zones in the 1990s was a major determining factor in the success of many programs.
- East Asia provides ample evidence that public zones have the potential to be well managed and deliver significant economic returns. However,

Box 2.5

The WEPZA Debate on Public versus Private Zones

In 1992, the World Economic Processing Zones Association (WEPZA) held a conference whose proceedings were entitled *Public vs. Private Free Zones*. A key part the conference was a debate between the manager of the public Barcelona Free Zone and the CEO of a Mexican private industrial zone group.

The case for public zones, Juan Torrents, Barcelona Free Zone
• Public zones are instruments of public policy, uniquely capable of providing public goods with broad impact: employment, attracting FDI, improving technology, increasing labor skills, etc.
• They are instruments of industrial policy, focused on the long term. Private zones have no interest in these national strategic issues.
• Public zones have a duty to serve all clients equally, no matter their respective size or origin. Public zones can help small firms in a way that private zones cannot.

The case for private zones, Sergio Bermudez, Grupo Bermudez
• Private zones correspond to the reality of the global economy—by being profit-oriented, they maximize their competitiveness.
• They are divorced from short-term politics and are focused on the long term.
• They must apply strict financial rules, thus maximizing efficiency. This requires innovation and flexibility.
• Investors prefer to deal with a private company rather than with the government. They are shielded from corruption and red tape and have, in case of disputes, a better chance of a positive outcome.

Source: The Services Group. 1999.

the positive experience in East Asia is not restricted to public zones. The Philippines, for example, has had major success (200-plus zones, 3 million employed, 85% of exports from the SEZs) with a completely private program.
• In Africa, continued reliance on public zones may be one factor behind the lackluster performance. But private-sector-led zone programs have also generally failed in the region.

Whatever the performance, privately operated zones are becoming the norm. According to FIAS (2008), while private zones represented only 25 percent of the world's total in the 1980s, by 2006–2007 they accounted for 62 percent of the vastly expanded population of zones.

The Emergence of Public-Private Partnerships

Since the 1990s, innovative PPP mechanisms have blurred the line between the strictly public and the strictly private. PPPs seek to capitalize on the mutual strengths of each sector. Cooperation and division of labor, rather than competition, has become the preferred model:

- The government provides strategy and policy formulation, legislation, regulation, and enforcement—key public goods the private sector cannot or should not provide. A large number of SEZ projects developed on the basis of PPPs require significant public funding. Typically, this includes discounted land prices or free land, external infrastructure, and often internal basic infrastructure, especially for more developmental projects.
- The private sector develops and operates the SEZ project: master planning, investment into core real estate and services infrastructure, construction, management, promotion, and so on.

Six main forms of PPP currently exist, each representing an increase in private participation and thus a progressive shift of risk from the state to the private sector. Among these are service contracts (aspects of management or services are subcontracted to specialist firms for a fee), concessions (which bring private capital to expand on existing infrastructure and turn the zone into a high-value asset), and divesture or privatization (see Box 2.6 for the Colombian experience).

Three key moments stand out in the rise of PPPs in zone programs:

1. In terms of an early division of labor between state and private operators, the *maquiladora* program is critical.
2. The 1992 Subic Bay project in the Philippines was one of the first large SEZ developments based on extensive cooperation and co-investment by public and private parties. It has served as a template for other SEZ projects, including Panama's Pacifico SEZ and Aqaba SEZ in Jordan. These wide-area SEZs combine traditional manufacturing with services, residential living and its necessary amenities, tourism, and environmental protection.
3. Finally, turnkey zones developed by specialist zone development companies such as Jebel Ali Free Zone Authority (JAFZA) or the Chinese

Box 2.6

Privatization of Colombia's Free Zones

Colombia launched its free trade zone program in 1958 as a regional development initiative. It created six public FTZs. Underperformance, financial difficulties, and rampant corruption in the program's administration led to a comprehensive review and the 1991 passage of Law 7. The government decided to turn the zones into EPZs and make them a centerpiece of economic transformation. This would be done in part through the privatization of the existing zones and the creation of additional private zones. In 1992, the public free zone administration was liquidated. In 1993–1994, the zones themselves were liquidated. At the same time, the government adopted Decree 2480, which established a new free zone regime. The Ministry of Foreign Trade, now in charge of the regime, issued terms of reference for the privatization of the liquidated zones. By mid-1995, all but one of the six zones had been privatized under 15-year leases specifying the value of the zones, the required investments, and a detailed development plan. Meanwhile, new private zones were opened across the country. One such zone is the Bogota Free Trade Zone, developed and operated by a private consortium. The country currently operates 10 zones; in 2009, the government announced its intention of substantially expanding the program.

Source: Bolin, R. (ed.) 1993.

Trade and Economic Cooperation Zones represent an evolution of the model. Examples include Djibouti Free Zone and upcoming zones in Senegal (Dakar Integrated Special Economic Zone), Nigeria (Lekki), and Mauritius (JinFei).

Summary of Key Points in the Evolution of SEZs

Table 2.1 summarizes the key developments outlined in this section. From a policy standpoint, the evolution can be summarized as follows:

- In the 1960s and 1970s, export processing zones were developed as addendums to protectionist economic strategies focused on import substitution. The usually lackluster performance of these strategies led countries such as Brazil, India, Kenya, Malaysia, and Mauritius to create enclaves for foreign-oriented activities. EPZs were expected to absorb surplus labor without immobilizing a domestic capital base

Table 2.1   Summary of Key Developments in the Evolution of SEZs

Antiquity and Middle Ages	First free port—Phoenicia	"Public" zones
	Delos—circa 150 BC	
	Hanseatic League and charter cities—13th to 17th centuries	
Colonial Era	Colonial charter companies and trading posts— 17th to mid-19th centuries	Private, then public
	Free port islands—mid-19th to early 20th centuries	
Modern Era	Free trade zones—since early 1900s	Public zones
	Pioneering manufacturing zones—1920s to 1940s	
	Operation Bootstrap—1948	
	Shannon Free Zone—1958	
	Maquiladora—1965	Private zones
	La Romana Free Zone—1969	
	Chinese special economic zones—1978	PPPs
	Subic Bay—1992	
	DISEZ, JinFei, Lekki—2010+	

Source: Authors.

that was oriented toward domestic production. The countries that applied this strategy were initially interested only in the static economic benefits of the tool.

• At the same time, a number of Asian countries chose to focus their economic strategies on exports rather than import substitution. EPZs were primarily developed to act as catalysts in the transition from inward-looking or traditional exports to nontraditional exports. This export-oriented growth model led to the emergence of the newly industrializing countries of East and South East Asia; South Korea and Taiwan-China were the main countries that chose this route.

• China's approach to SEZs has been one of most radical applications of the concept. Once it became clear that the country was failing to effect economic development through the strategies of the Mao era, the government chose to use the first four SEZs, from 1979 onward, as a gigantic experiment in controlled capitalism in a command economy.

• Changes to the international politico-economic order in the 1980s put an end to the inward-looking strategies of the 1950s, 1960s, and 1970s. Economic liberalization saw the protectionist policies of the era dismantled. Many argued that SEZs were losing relevance in this new environment, as trade and investment barriers were disassembled. However, the number of SEZs continued to increase dramatically.

The Scope of SEZs Today—Global Footprint

The lack of consensus on definitions and the absence of comprehensive and reliable data make it hard to measure the true footprint and impact of SEZs. According to the International Labour Organisation (ILO, Boyenge 2007),[8] the number of countries operating SEZs has grown from 25 in 1975 to more than 130. The number of SEZs has exploded, from 79 in 1975 to more than 3,500 (including zones in developed economies), an increase of over 4,000 percent in 30 years. Most of that expansion occurred in the past 20 years. FIAS (2008) gives a figure of 2,500 zones currently operating in emerging and developing economies; this excludes the 700 or so foreign trade zones in the United States and the Western European zones.

SEZs directly employ between 63 million (FIAS) and 68 million (ILO) persons worldwide (see Table 2.2). There is much debate about the employment multiplier effect of SEZs; it is estimated at between 0.25 and 2, depending on the researcher and the region or country of reference. If we use an average multiplier of 1, SEZs would account for an additional 65 million indirect jobs. Thus, in total, SEZs may account for 130 million jobs worldwide, about 1 percent of total global employment. China has the lion's share, with a direct employment figure of 40 million. However, SEZ employment is growing faster in the developing world outside China—from 5 million in 1997 to 26 million in 2006, a fivefold growth in less than 10 years.

Focusing on the approximately 2,500 zones in developing and emerging economies identified by FIAS (2008), Figure 2.1 shows the mix of zones across regions. More than 1,000 zones have been identified in East and South Asia, with a large number in India, China, Vietnam, and the Philippines. Thirty percent of all zones worldwide are in Latin America; most of these in Central America, Mexico, and the Caribbean. Sub-Saharan Africa accounts for only 4 percent of zones; most of these are single factory units, about half of which are in Kenya.[9] Ownership patterns between the public and the private sector also show strong regional patterns: Latin American zones are dominated by the private sector, African and Asian zones are split between public and private sectors, and zones in the Middle East and North Africa as well

Table 2.2   Key Demographic Figures

	1975	1986	1997	2002	2006
Countries with SEZs	25	47	93	116	130
# of SEZs, including advanced economies	79	176	845	3,000	3,500
World direct employment (m)			23	43	66
China direct employment (m)			18	30	40
Rest of world direct employment (m)	1	2	5	13	26

Source: Authors' calculations derived from Boyenge (2007).

Figure 2.1   Regional Breakdown of Zones in Developing and Emerging Economies, 2005

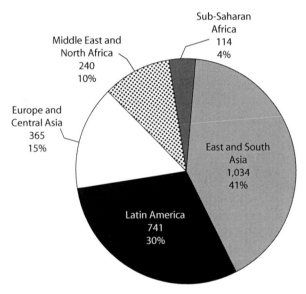

Source: Authors' calculations derived from FIAS (2008).

as Eastern Europe and Central Asia are mainly controlled by the public sector. (For a detailed discussion of ownership patterns in the zones, see Chapter 3.)

Estimations of exports out of SEZs are difficult to come by. According to FIAS, SEZs in emerging and developing countries exported approximately US$850 billion in goods and services annually in the mid-2000s.

This would be approximately 7–8 percent of total global exports and slightly less than 20 percent of exports from emerging and developing economies. If this number is correct, it is extremely significant: It means that SEZs disproportionately contribute to exports in relation to their employment impact. Indeed, the ratio of export contribution of SEZs to direct employment contribution in developing and emerging countries is about 40 to 1. This should not be surprising, as SEZs are primarily focused on export markets, but the magnitude of the ratio has important implications for the economic impact: It suggests that SEZs can play a crucial role in boosting exports from emerging and developing countries, but their relative employment role may be less pronounced.

Investments in SEZs are even more difficult to evaluate. There are two key sets of data, neither of which is very reliable: (1) annual flow of investment into SEZs, and (2) stock of investment. According to FIAS:

> Available data suggest that SEZs are an important destination of FDI in some countries. In the Philippines, for example, the share of FDI flows going to the country's eco-zones increased from 30 percent in 1997 to over 81 percent in 2000 (UNCTAD, 2003). In Bangladesh, $103 million of the $328 million of FDI inflows were registered in EPZs. In Mexico, the share of annual FDI accounted for by *maquiladora* operations increased from 6 percent in 1994 to 23 percent in 2000 (Sadni-Jallab and Blanco de Armas, 2002). And in China, SEZs account for over 80 percent of cumulative FDI. However in many other countries, . . . zones have played a marginal role in FDI attraction and most investment is of domestic origin (FIAS, 2008, p. 35).

Thus, the overall static footprint of SEZs appears to be relatively small but fast-growing. Evidence suggests that they have a disproportionate effect in terms of FDI and exports, and that they are increasing in economic importance.

The SEZ Question—Analytical Perspectives

Few economic development policy tools have been as controversial as SEZs, particularly the EPZ variant. They have been the subject of intense, polarized debates for at least 35 years on almost every aspect of their configuration, raison d'être, and impact. These debates have centered on key economic issues but also on labor, gender, and the environment.

Before proceeding, we should note that few comprehensive sets of aggregate data on SEZs exist, and these sets (such as that of the ILO) are limited in content and breadth. Empirical field research has been limited and often nonsystematic, reducing its aggregate value. Most of the perspectives described here are based on the same limited sets of data and the same limited descriptive literature.

Doing justice to the debates would require significantly more space than is available. The focus here is on the economic meaning and contribution of SEZs. Four broad sets of stakeholders have contributed to the key debates: (1) economists and policy analysts have developed analytic, empirical, theoretical and prescriptive frameworks; (2) policy practitioners have contributed to the development of SEZs and, in doing so, have influenced their make-up and generated experiential narratives; (3) business communities have been affected by SEZs and have supported them or opposed them, depending on their interests; and (4) labor, social, and environmental activists and nongovernment organizations (NGOs) have tended to oppose them or aspects of them, have documented them, and have mobilized resources to improve or discontinue them. Most of the key policy debates have occurred among the first group, although activists have contributed important critiques, and policy practitioners have sought to incorporate prescriptive and critical perspectives to improve on the design and implementation of new zones.

In our brief account, we concentrate on providing a broad view of the key perspectives and frameworks. We introduce the two main types of analysis: (1) formal analysis and (2) descriptive analysis and case studies. We locate them within the three main theoretical approaches to SEZs: (1) trade-based approaches; (2) formal cost-benefit assessments; and (3) endogenous growth perspectives.

Main Types of Analysis

Formal analysis. Most of the initial theoretical work on SEZs has focused on EPZs and has been contributed by *neoclassical economics*, which has long provided the orthodox view. It looks at SEZs for their effect on the efficient allocation of resources within an economy and tries to determine whether they contribute to allocative efficiency or distort it, mostly through prices. In the first case, SEZs would enhance a country's comparative advantage. In the second, they would decrease it. Hamada's pioneering work (1975) is often used as the referent neoclassical analysis of SEZs, and its pessimistic conclusion is usually generalized to all neoclassical analyses of zones. Yet, the growing body of neoclassical analysis is far from cohesive: Rodriguez (1976), Hamilton and Svensson (1982), Miyagiwa (1986), Miyagiwa and Young (1987), Balasubramanyam

(1988), Chaudhuri and Adhikari (1993), Din (1994), Devereux and Chen (1995), and Ge (1993) all differ in their conclusions.

Cost-benefit analysis is an attempt to document the welfare contribution of EPZs in a way that complements the findings of neoclassical analysis. It seeks to quantify the economic flows between zones, their domestic economies, and the rest of the world to determine the net accrued costs and benefits to the domestic economy; specifically, the citizenry. Cost-benefit analysis has been developed within the confines of welfare economics, which concerns itself with two specific problems: "(a) the measurement of real national income, and (b) the efficiency and equity of particular economic outcomes, including the scope for improving them through various instruments of economic policy" (Lal 1983, p. 11). The primary work is by Warr (1989), Spinanger (1984), and Jayanthakumaran (2003). There have also been country studies, such as that of Sawkut et al. (2009).

Starting in the late 1980s and early 1990s, a growing number of analysts took issue with the international trade-based approaches to SEZs and the conclusions they led to. *New growth*, or *endogenous growth theory*, sought to incorporate externalities into the explanation of economic growth; specifically, technology and human capital. This theoretical approach has incorporated microeconomic issues, such as the international distribution of consumption, innovation, and production. While orthodox theories have mostly focused on the static aspects of economic activity (welfare outcomes), new growth has focused on their dynamic aspects (growth and industrial transition outcomes). Most of the new growth work has been descriptive. Formal work is limited; it includes Johansson and Nilssen (1997), Ge (1993), and Tyler and Negrete (2009).

Descriptive Analysis and Case Studies

The descriptive research on zones is vast and rooted in various theoretical foundations. Much of the research has been initiated by international organizations, including the ILO, the OECD, the UN, and the World Bank Group. Some of these institutional studies have represented important milestones in the analysis of zones. This is notably the case with UNIDO (1980), Edgren (1982) for ILO-ARTEP, UNCTAD (1985), UNCTC-ILO (1988), World Bank (1992), and Engman et al. (2007) for OECD. Among the input from activists and NGOs, work by organizations such as the International Confederation of Free Trade Unions (ICFTU) (2003, 2004) has been important and contributed to both debates and policy change.

Individual contributions have significantly increased over the past 20 years. Early work includes Wall (1976), Ping (1979), and Basile and Germidis (1984). Post-1990 work includes Rhee and Belot (1990), Alter (1991), Romer (1993a, 1993b), Kaplinsky (1993), Willmore's (1995) response, Kaplinsky's (1995) reply to Willmore, Johansson (1994), Johansson and Nilsson (1997), Kusago and Tzannatos (1998), Madani (1999), Radelet (1999), Tekere (2000), Cling and Letilly (2001), Schrank (2001), Aggarwal (2005, 2006, 2007, 2010), Milberg (2007), and Tyler and Negrete (2009). These works have spanned the theoretical divide, as will be seen below.

Overview of Key Perspectives

Trade-based perspectives: Formal analysis. As noted above, the initial formal work was primarily rooted in international trade theory. Early findings, especially those of Hamada (1975), were pessimistic about EPZs on the basis of fundamental principles. They were seen as a distortive policy tool set to correct the effects of another distortive policy tool. Indeed, trade, fiscal and quasi-financial incentives under the form of duty drawbacks, tax incentives, and discounted utilities and infrastructure are provided to compensate for high tariffs, import restrictions and quotas, and an overvalued exchange rate. From this perspective, in a free (or freer) trade environment, SEZs would have no raison d'être, as there would be no need for this "countersubsidization" policy instrument. For this reason they are considered to be a second-best policy instrument to the optimal policy of trade liberalization. From a prescriptive standpoint, SEZs should only be deployed in highly distortive environments in which the distortions introduce a disincentive toward exports (anti-export bias). Otherwise, SEZs are welfare-negative. In neoclassical analysis, SEZs are a distortive response to a distortive problem, whether they are welfare-positive or not. The logical conclusion of the analysis is that in an international context of trade liberalization, the need for and relevance of SEZs should decrease as the domestic trade environment becomes neutral (there are no policy biases toward imports, domestic production, or exports) and the country fits its natural comparative advantage.

Later work has produced varied findings. Hamilton and Svensson (1982) concluded that SEZs positively affect allocative efficiency. Miyagiwa (1986), for different reasons, also found SEZs to be welfare-positive, as did Miyagiwa and Young (1987) and Ge (1993). The more recent work has tended to be more optimistic regarding the welfare impact of SEZs and has sought to incorporate certain dynamic impacts, notably in terms of trade liberalization and growth.

Cost-benefit analysis work is empirical insofar as its aim is to evaluate the welfare impact of SEZs on a case basis. Owing to the data constraints that characterize SEZ analysis, few cost-benefit analyses have been conducted. Spinanger (1984) undertook an evaluation of both static and dynamic impacts, and applied it to zones in Malaysia, the Philippines, Singapore, and Taiwan-China. Using market prices, he concluded that in all cases the EPZs had been welfare-positive, but at varying levels.

Warr (1989) conducted a series of analyses in Asia and developed a formal cost-benefit framework based on the "enclave model." The zone is an enclave because it is separated from the domestic economic by investment and trade barriers while being integrated in the international economy through liberal investment and trade conditions. The model selects economic and financial flows that are relevant to the domestic economy and excludes those that are not. Warr posits that the only relevant flows are those between the zone and the domestic economy, while those between the zone and the rest of the world are not relevant. Thus, investments made in the zone by foreign companies are not relevant, nor are profits paid overseas. The importation of equipment, raw materials, and intermediate goods, as well as the technology used to manufacture the finished goods, are excluded. Products manufactured and exported are relevant only up to the proportion of value added that is retained locally: primarily domestic labor, electricity and water, intermediate goods, taxes, and local services.[10] These flows must account for incentives and subsidies, and the social opportunity costs of key domestic entrants.[11]

Warr's analysis showed that most of the benefits generated by zones (Indonesia, Malaysia, and the Philippines) came from foreign exchange earnings and employment. Local purchases of raw materials and tax revenues were marginal. Development and management costs for EPZs and administrative costs of the regime were heavily weighted. This was particularly the case in the Philippines, where the Bataan zone returned a net welfare loss. Warr concluded that zones returned limited benefits and were not engines of development and that their main value was in their capacity to absorb surplus labor in countries in early stages of development. He discounted the dynamic impact of EPZs (1989).

Jayanthakumaran's (2003) cost-benefit analysis using an updated enclave model shows that zones (China, Indonesia, Malaysia, South Korea, and Sri Lanka) had economic internal rates of returns between

10.7 percent and 28 percent, "well above the shadow discount rate of the respective countries" (p. 62). Benefits were significant in relation to employment and taxes, and decreasing in relation to foreign exchange earnings, purchases of domestic raw materials, domestic capital equipment, electricity use, and domestic borrowing. Jayanthakumaran concluded that there was "a strong correlation between the growth of EPZs and the Multi Fibre Arrangement in general" and that the phasing out of the MFA and guaranteed market access "will eventually result in lower rates of return and will be a possible threat to the existing and new EPZs" (p. 64).

Trade-based perspectives: Descriptive and case analyses. Kaplinsky (1993) famously concluded that, on the basis of an analysis of the Dominican Republic's case, EPZs led to "immiserizing employment growth; that is, employment growth which is contingent upon wages falling in international purchasing power" (p. 1861). This conclusion follows an analysis of the country's terms of trade with its principal market (the United States), which declined as the EPZ sector of the economy grew substantially. For Kaplinsky, this phenomenon is a necessary outcome of the "simultaneous commoditization of production and competitive devaluation" (p. 1892) inherent in the EPZ-based growth model.

Madani (1999) summarized the evaluations, experiences, and issues of EPZs in a sample of countries in order to assist in policy formulation and provide guidelines for establishing successful EPZs. Madani argues that EPZs are "not a first policy choice . . . [but] can play a long-term dynamic role in their country's development process if they are appropriately set up, well managed, WTO compatible in [their] incentives, and used as an integrated part of a national reform and liberalization program" (pp. 7–8). However, she argues that countrywide liberalization should be preferred to EPZs and recommends not using EPZs during trade and macroeconomic reform, in part to avoid "discretion" in the policy environment. Finally, Tekere (2000) concludes that EPZs are not a viable strategy for development, primarily because of their costs and negative impact on regional integration. He argues that the emphasis in Africa should be on macroeconomic policy and business climate reform.

Endogenous growth perspectives: Descriptive and case analyses. New growth argues that the trade-based approach has failed to address some key issues, such as (1) the unabated demographic dynamism of SEZs, and the veritable explosion in their number after 1995 and the implementation of the World Trade Organization (WTO) (contradicting the neoclassical explanation; (2) the strong correlation between the use of zones and the development of successful export-led growth; and (3) the economic successes of a few less developed countries (LDCs) following their deployment of zones as a central component of their growth and development strategies. In contrast with trade-based theory, the initial work in this area was essentially descriptive, and formal analysis came at a later stage.

Romer's (1993a, 1993b) analysis of EPZs is indirect and set within a wider theoretical reflection on economic growth and underdevelopment. His work forms part of new growth theory, which is explored further below. Insofar as zones are concerned, the author illustrates their potential role in the crucial task of bridging "idea gaps" in developing countries. In his short case study of Mauritius, Romer argues that the EPZ constituted an environment in which multinational firms (the owners of ideas) could invest and transfer ideas on production and marketing. He explains that there is a strong correlation, however, between macroeconomic stability and the presence of multinationals: "Growth in Mauritius was highly variable over time because the flow of ideas in from the rest of the world is highly sensitive to incentives, and therefore to domestic policy environment" (p. 565).

Pursuing this topic, Johansson (1994) explores the catalytic role EPZs can play. Looking at Mauritius, the author proposes that the success of the zone originated in the fact that it combined foreign technical and marketing expertise with available domestic capital surpluses. Johansson's policy conclusions are as follows: (1) EPZs may have a catalytic effect in the generation of an economy's "export supply response"; (2) this may be particularly important for low-income economies; (3) EPZs can provide important training to labor toward industrial culture; and (4) in the long term they can provide a positive impetus to trade-related reform after having demonstrated the benefits of investment and trade, as happened in the newly industrialized East Asian countries.

Radelet (1999) analyzes the role of EPZs and other export platforms in the development of export-led growth in emerging countries. His work focuses on evaluating the criteria for the success of these platforms in terms of their relationship with the rise of export-led growth. Countries included in the analysis are in Africa, Asia, the Caribbean, and Central and South America. The author concludes that export platforms are an integral component of the development strategies of successful countries, notably in terms of resolving "poor trade policies, weak infrastructure, and inconsistent rule of law" (p. 3). He says they are not silver bullet but "can make an important contribution, both directly and through their demonstration effects, to other exporting firms" (p. 39).

Finally, Collier and Page (2009) focus on the potential of SEZs as a form of spatial industrial policy, particularly for the African region. They argue that, by concentrating infrastructure and an attractive investment climate, SEZs can facilitate agglomerations that may enable African industries to overcome minimum size thresholds and begin to leverage scale economies.

Endogenous growth perspectives: Formal analyses. Johansson and Nilsson (1997) make possibly the first attempt to develop a formal model of the catalytic contribution of EPZs, focusing on the export-supply response of domestic producers. Using a gravity model, the authors assess the impact of EPZs on 14 countries that, combined, represented 94.5 percent of global zone employment in 1986. The control group comprises developing countries without zones. The model is run over the 12-year period from 1980 to 1992.

The first impact measure is that of EPZs over exports. The result differentiates three groups of countries/economies:

- Those in which EPZs have had a strong positive impact on exports: Hong Kong SAR, China, Malaysia, Mauritius, Singapore, and Sri-Lanka. South Korea belongs to this group but shows decreasing significance after 1989.
- Those in which EPZs have had a lesser impact on exports: the Dominican Republic and Mexico.
- Those in which EPZs have had no impact on exports: Egypt, the Philippines, and Tunisia.

The second impact measure is that of EPZ exports over domestic exports in countries that have shown strong results in the first test. This would be the catalytic effect. Owing to data constraints, the authors conduct this test only for Malaysia. There, they find a strong correlation between the two export curves (EPZ and non-EPZ), which suggests a catalytic effect but one that remains constant over time.

Ge (1993) develops a formal model of the dynamic impacts of zones. The framework focuses specifically on the relationship between a low-technology price-taking domestic producer and a monopoly price-making multinational producer. It models how the establishment of an EPZ, under specific conditions of production and market, would affect their relationship, assuming that both firms set up operation in the zone according to a number of scenarios. From this, Ge comes to the following conclusions: (1) In light of the technological externality (the learning factor between the multinational and the domestic firm), EPZs should not be developed through the enclave model but should be opened to extensive domestic participation, both inside and outside the EPZ; (2) conditions for exchanges and learning between domestic firms and foreign firms in EPZs, and between the EPZs and the domestic economy, should be improved so that technology transfers can occur throughout; (3) if this occurs, new firms from previously nonindustrial countries will successfully compete against firms from previously industrial-monopoly countries; and (4) EPZs thus play a catalytic role in creating the conditions for multinational enterprises (MNEs) to invest and, under the appropriate conditions, transfer crucial knowledge, willingly and not. The author concludes by proposing that EPZs are a component of a progressive strategy of economic opening and liberalization.

Other Notable Perspectives on the SEZ Question
In their survey of EPZs, Kusago and Tzannatos (1998) conclude that EPZs have a proven record for absorbing surplus labor in the early stages of industrialization, but that this absorption diminishes as economies transition upward, as in the cases of South Korea and Taiwan, China. Other benefits are found to be less important. Cling and Letilly's (2001) contribution is to answer one question: "Can [free zones] represent a durable focal element of development policy?" (p. 5). They come to three main conclusions: (1) EPZs have worked mostly in a few emerging markets in Asia and South America and, with the exception of a handful of countries, have not succeeded in LDCs; (2) the experience of these emerging markets shows that EPZs are, at best, one of several components of export-oriented industrialization, and one with limited effect on skills and economic value added; and (3) EPZs are undermined by changes in trade rules, notably the WTO's rules on subsidies and countervailing measures,[12] the end of the MFA,[13] and regional trade agreements.

Schrank (2001) asks who is right in the EPZ debate—those who argue "that they offer a gradual 'two-track' alternative to neoliberal 'shock therapy'" (p. 224) or those who believe that they endanger reform by creating liberal enclaves that allow governments to continue protecting inefficient domestic economies. The author provides three narratives to inform an answer: (1) the EPZ life cycle perspective; (2) a historical analysis comparing South Korea, the Dominican Republic, and Mexico; and (3) a quantitative analysis testing variations of national outcomes against measures of state capacity and market size. He concludes that both state capacity and market size are critical in affecting the success of EPZs and they act as effective catalysts for industrial upgrading and economic transformation.

Surveying the latest trends, Milberg (2007) concludes that zones are here to stay but will need to adapt to four main challenges: (1) There is limited room for export-oriented growth in the world (someone must import); (2) the full entry into force of key WTO measures will be deeply felt; (3) the shift to higher technology production will challenge the EPZ model; and (4) there is a need for "social upgrading" to harmonize labor standards between zones and nonzones.

Finally, the labor perspective is perhaps best summarized by two ICFTU publications (2003, 2004), which argue that EPZs are not viable because of the footloose nature of investments attracted by low labor costs, tax incentives, and subsidized infrastructure. The ICFTU considers the overall economic impact of EPZs to be negative because of the low value of the economic activities that are usually attracted to zones and the fact that they do not lead to technology transfer. From a labor rights standpoint, the organization indicts zones on the following counts: (1) lack of respect for freedom of association and the right to strike; (2) nonapplication of domestic labor law and lack of inspections; (3) difficulties with or interdiction of unionization; (4) institutionalization of job insecurity; (5) nonpayment of agreed-upon salaries and overtime pay; (6) abusive working hours; and (7) poor health and safety practices.

Conclusion—The State of the Debate

SEZs' Economic Contribution—Toward Convergence?

The perspectives, theories, and methods summarized here highlight very real differences in perspective on the role and impact of SEZs. These differences are not simply on results but also on the economic policy objectives of SEZs and how they can be measured. The debate is best illustrated by a simple statement of opposition: on the one hand, SEZs as welfare-reducing enclaves that constrict countrywide liberalization; on the other, SEZs as catalytic exclaves that announce and prepare for liberalization. However, this opposition refers mostly to the debate as it was in the 1980s and 1990s. A survey of key perspectives shows that some convergence has occurred in the past 10 years or so on the evaluation of SEZs.

A recent paper on Mauritania by Auty and Pontara (2008) illustrates this convergence. The authors' main focus is economic growth in resource-rich countries, where Dutch disease, rent-seeking, and dependent social capital are typical outcomes of the discovery and exploitation of significant stocks of natural resources. Taking a political economy perspective, and using Mauritania as a case study, they propose that the dual-track strategy promotes a dynamic market economy in "early reform zones" (Track 1), while the rent-distorted economy (Track 2) is gradually reformed as the success of Track 1 drives competitive diversification of the economy while building a proreform political constituency that eventually absorbs Track 2. These early reform zones—with their focus on world-class infrastructure, unsubsidized incentives, and nontraditional activities—are very much in line with the SEZ concept discussed in this report.

From a policy standpoint, the convergence documented here has three main implications:

1. The policy lessons are more complementary than oppositional.
2. There is a greater understanding of the factors and conditions (international, domestic, and internal to the SEZ configuration) that influence the success and failure of SEZs.
3. It is becoming possible to determine whether or not specific countries should develop SEZs and, if they do develop them, to better structure the zone policies and components.

Thus, it should be possible to amend the statement of opposition to the following "convergence": SEZs have the potential to act as catalytic exclaves that announce and prepare for liberalization under certain circumstances and provided certain prerequisites have been addressed. If not, SEZs may, at best, provide limited economic benefits for a limited period and, at worst, may turn into welfare-reducing enclaves that restrict countrywide liberalization.

Outstanding Research Questions

Despite the significant research discussed in this chapter and several decades of vigorous debate over the value and impact of economic zones, many critical questions remain unanswered, and many issues have not yet been analyzed in detail. For example, while many analytical studies and some small-sample comparative studies have looked at the performance of individual zone programs, we still have insufficient comprehensive cross-country analysis of the factors that contribute to zone program success or failure. This is particularly the case for low-income countries and for the Africa region, as most research on zones has been focused where they have been most successful as an instrument for trade and industrialization—in East Asia. In addition, we need a better understanding of the specific investment climate factors that are linked to zone performance.

A second set of issues that the research has not yet resolved is the distinction between static and dynamic outcomes of zone programs. As noted earlier, most of the formal analysis of zone program performance has been concerned with static measures: investment, exports, employment, contributions through taxes, indirect employment, and other short-term mechanisms. On the other hand, much of the descriptive work on the success of economic zones in East Asia depicts processes of structural economic change induced, at least in part, by the economic zones. More rigorous research is needed to assess the dynamic impact of zones across countries and to link the dynamic impact with static impacts, and with specific policies and practices within and related to the zones.

This study addresses those questions. The report draws on the results of case study research and surveys of more than 600 investors in SEZs across the 10 countries and focuses primarily on understanding the performance of economic zones in Africa and other low-income countries, and on the factors that contribute to that performance.

Notes

1. Other definitions exist, some of them for specific legal and technical reasons. For instance, the Revised Kyoto Convention of the World Customs Organization defines free zones as "a part of the territory of a Contracting Party where any goods introduced are generally regarded, insofar as import duties and taxes are concerned, as being outside the customs territory" (cited by Creskoff and Walkenhorst, 2009).

2. Confusingly, some wide area zones contain within them other types of zones, such as FTZs and EPZs. Cities such as Singapore and Hong Kong—sometimes referred to as *freeports* or *free ports*—are not considered special economic zones under this definition. They are economies that offer free-trade-like conditions. However, Singapore does host special economic zones within its territory.

3. The Bracero Program was a 1942 agreement between the United States and Mexico for the supply of temporary workers to support the war effort. After

the war, the program continued under various formats, primarily focused on agricultural labor. The program employed millions of Mexican citizens.

4. The program was formally introduced as the Border Industrialization Program in October 1965. Its focus was job creation and regional development through the attraction of U.S. firms to a narrow strip of land along the border. The program followed a number of earlier initiatives, including the creation of *zonas libres* in the period spanning 1933 to 1939 and PRONAF in the 1950s.

5. Article 321 was added to the Customs Code of the Federation to better integrate with sections 806 and 807 of the U.S. code. A special agency—Comisión Intersecretarial para el Fomento Económico de la Franja Fronteriza Norte y de las Zonas y Perímetros Libres (Intersecretarial Commission for the Economic Development of the Northern Border Zone and of the Free Trade Zones and Ports)—was established to manage the development of the program, and measures were simplified and rationalized. In 1973, the restrictions on foreign ownership were lifted.

6. Shelter plans are production agreements in which the foreign company pays a local shelter company fees to act on its behalf in key activities such as hiring labor, providing factory space, dealing with local authorities, and taxation issues. Production is controlled by the foreign company.

7. In 2007, FDI capital in the zone was US$128 million out of a total investment of US$217 million. Employment stood at 7,500 and exports at US$3.2 billion, with export value per worker nearly US$500,000. The zone contributed 10 percent of the country's trade surplus, and zone enterprises purchased US$1.6 billion from the national economy.

8. ILO counts the SEZs of advanced economies in its statistics, but FIAS does not.

9. Note that the FIAS data do not take into account firms licensed under the Entreprise Franche d'Exportation (EFE) program in Senegal or the Free Zone Enterprises (single factory scheme) in Ghana—see Chapter 3 for more details.

10. Such as accounting and legal services, banking, freight forwarding, and transportation.

11. This is done using shadow prices rather than market prices. Shadow prices are calculated when market prices are distorted and do not reflect their real social opportunity cost.

12. The WTO agreements do not mention SEZs, and zones are not considered to be contrary to the interests of international trade. However, some of the traditional investment incentive measures of certain types of zones are contrary to specific agreements. This is principally the case with the Agreement on Subsidies and Countervailing Measures. This agreement notably prohibits export subsidies and local content subsidies. (For a detailed discussion

of the implications of WTO agreements on SEZ programs, see Chapter 6, Section 5.)

13. The Multi Fibre Arrangement (MFA) originated in 1974 as a mechanism to protect the markets of the main importing countries of Europe and North America. The agreement imposed quota restrictions on the sale of certain categories of apparel.

References

Aggarwal, A. 2005. "Performance of Export Processing Zones: A Comparative Analysis of India, Sri Lanka and Bangladesh." Indian Council for Research on International Economic Relations (ICRIER), New Delhi.

Aggarwal, A. 2006. "Special Economic Zones: Revisiting the Policy Debate. A Discussion of the Pros and Cons of the Controversial SEZ Policy." *Economic and Political Weekly.* Vol. XLI Nos. 43 and 44, November 4–10.

Aggarwal, A. 2007. "Impact of Special Economic Zones on Employment, Poverty and Human Development." Working Paper 194. ICRIER, New Delhi.

Aggarwal, A. 2010. "Economic Impacts of SEZs: Theoretical Approaches and Analysis of Newly Notified SEZs in India." MPRA Paper 20902. http://mpra.ub.uni-muenchen.de/20902.

Alter, R. 1991. "Lessons from the Export Processing Zone in Mauritius. *Finance & Development.* December 1991: 7–9.

Auty, R., and N. Pontara. 2008. "A Dual-track Strategy for Managing Mauritania's Projected Oil Rent." *Development Policy Review* 26 (1): 59–77.

Baissac, C. 2010. Planned Obsolescence: Export Processing Zones and Structural Reform in Mauritius. Mimeo. World Bank. September, 2010.

Balasubramanyam, V. N. 1988. "Export Processing Zones in Developing Countries; Theory and Empirical Evidence." In *Economic Development and International Trade,* ed. David Greenaway, pp. 157–165. Macmillan: London.

Basile, A., and D. Germidis. 1984. *Investing in Free Export Processing Zones.* Paris: OECD.

Bolin, R. (ed). 1993. Public Vs. Private Free Zones. Flagstaff: The Flagstaff Institute

Boyenge, J.P.S. 2007. *ILO Database on Export Processing Zones, Revised.* Geneva: International Labor Organisation.

Champion, C.B. 2003. Roman Imperialism: Readings and Sources. Wiley-Blackwell.

Chaudhuri, T. D., and S. Adhikari. 1993. "Free Trade Zones with Harris-Todaro Unemployment: A Note on Young-Miyagiwa. *Journal of Development Economics* 41: 157–162.

Chen, J. 1993. "Social Cost-Benefit Analysis of China's Shenzhen Special Economic Zone." *Development Policy Review* 11(3): 261–271.

Cling, J. P., and G. Letilly. 2001. "Export Processing Zones: A Threatened Instrument for Global Economy Insertion?" DT/2001/17. Developpement et Insertion Internationale (DIAL), Paris.

Collier, P., and J. Page. 2009. *Industrial Development Report 2009*. Vienna: UN Industrial Development Organization (UNIDO).

Creskoff, S., and P. Walkenhorst. 2009. "Implications of WTO Disciplines for Special Economic Zones in Developing Countries." Policy Research Working Paper 4892. World Bank, Washington, DC.

Devereux, J., and L. L. Chen. 1995. "Export Zones and Welfare: Another Look." *Oxford Economic Papers* 47(4): 704–714.

Din, M. U. 1994. "Export Processing Zones and Backward Linkages." *Journal of Development Economics* 43: 369–385.

Edgren, S. 1982. *Spearheads of Industrialisation or Sweatshops in the Sun? A Critical Appraisal of Labour Conditions in Asian Export Processing Zones*. Bangkok: International Labour Organisation, Asian Team for Regional Employment Promotion.

Engman, M., O. Onodera, and E. Pinali. 2007. *Export Processing Zones: Past and Future Role in Trade and Development*. Paris: OECD.

Foreign Investment Advisory Service (FIAS). 2008. *Special Economic Zones. Performance, Lessons Learned, and Implications for Zone Development*. Washington, DC: World Bank.

Ge, W. 1993. "Export-Processing Zones, Multinational Firms, and the Economic System Transformation." Doctoral dissertation. University of Pennsylvania, Philadelphia.

Hamada, K. 1975. "An Economic Analysis of the Duty-Free Zone." *Journal of International Economics* 4: 225–241.

Hamilton, C., and L.E.O. Svensson. 1982. "On the Welfare Economics of a Duty-free Zone." *Journal of International Economics* 20: 45–64.

ICFTU (International Conference of Free Trade Unions). 2003. "Export Processing Zones—Symbols of Exploitation and a Development Dead End." Brussels, ICFTU.

ICFTU. 2004. "Behind the Brand Names." Brussels, ICFTU.

Jayanthakumaran, K. 2003. "Benefit-Cost Appraisals of Export Processing Zones: A Survey of the Literature." *Development Policy Review* 21(1): 51–65.

Johansson, H. 1994. "The Economics of Export Processing Zones Revisited." *Development Policy Review* 12(4): 387–402.

Johansson, H., and L. Nilsson. 1997. "Export Processing Zones As Catalysts." *World Development* 25(12): 2115–2128.

Kaplinsky, R. 1993. "Export Processing Zones in the Dominican Republic: Transforming Manufactures into Commodities." *World Development* 21(11): 1851–1865.

Kaplinsky, R. 1995. A Reply to Willmore. World Development. 23(3): 537–540.

Kusago, T., and Z. Tzannatos. 1998. "Export Processing Zones: A Review in Need of Update." SP Discussion Paper 9802. World Bank, Washington, DC.

Lal, D. 1983. *The Poverty of Development Economics.* London: Institute of Economic Affairs.

Madani, D. 1999. "A Review of the Role and Impact of Export Processing Zones." World Bank Policy Research Working Paper 2238. World Bank, Washington, DC.

Milberg, W. 2007. *Export Processing Zones, Industrial Upgrading and Economic Development: A Survey.* Geneva: International Labor Organisation.

Miyagiwa, K. F. 1986. "A Reconsideration of the Welfare Economics of a Free Trade Zone." *Journal of International Economics* 21: 337–350.

Miyagiwa, K. F., and L. Young. 1987. "Unemployment and the Formation of Duty-free Zones." *Journal of Development Economics* 26: 397–405.

Ping, H. K. 1979. "Birth of the Second Generation of Free Trade Zones." *Far Eastern Economic Review* (May).

Radelet, S. 1999. "Manufactured Exports, Export Platforms, and Economic Growth." CAER Discussion Papers, Harvard Institute on International Development, Cambridge, MA.

Reger, G. 1994. *Regionalism and Change in the Economy of Independent Delos.* Berkeley: University of California Press.

Rhee, Y. W., and T. Belot. 1990. "Export Catalysts in Low-Income Countries. A Review of Eleven Success Stories." World Bank Discussion Paper No. 72. World Bank, Washington, DC.

Rodriguez, C. A. 1976. "A Note on the Economics of the Duty-Free Zone." *Journal of Development Economics* 6: 385–388.

Romer, P. 1993a. "Idea Gaps and Object Gaps in Economic Development." *Journal of Monetary Economics* 32(3): 543–573.

Romer, P. 1993b. "Two Strategies for Economic Development: Using Ideas and Producing Ideas." Proceedings of the World Bank Annual Conference on Development Economics, pp. 63–91. World Bank, Washington, DC.

Sadni-Jallab, M., and E. Blanco de Armas. 2002. "A Review of the Role and Impact of Export Processing Zones in World Trade: The Case of Mexico." Post-Print halshs-00178444_v1, HAL.

Sawkut, R., S. Vinesh, and F. Sooraj. 2009. "The Net Contribution of the Mauritian Export Processing Zone Using Cost-Benefit Analysis." *Journal of International Development* 21: 379–392.

Schrank, A. 2001. "Export Processing Zones: Free Market Islands or Bridges to Structural Transformation." *Development Policy Review* 19(2): 223–242.

Spinanger, D. 1984. Objectives and Impact of Economic Activity Zones: Some Evidence from Asia. *Weltwirtschaftliches Archiv* 120: 64–89.

Tekere, M. 2000. *Export Development and Export–led Growth Strategies: Export Processing Zones and the Strengthening of Sustainable Human Development.* International Centre for Trade and Sustainable Development. Globalisation Dialogues, Windhoek, Namibia.

The Services Group. 1999. Recommendations for Divestment of Jamaica's Free Zones. A Report for the World Bank. Washington, DC.

Tyler, W. G., and A.C.A. Negrete. 2009. "Economic Growth and Export Processing Zones: An Empirical Analysis of Policies to Cope with Dutch Disease." Latin American Studies Association 2009 Congress, Rio de Janeiro, June 11–14, 2009.

UNCTC-ILO (United Nations Conference on Trade and Development-International Labour Organisation). 1988. *Economic and Social Effects of Multinational Enterprises in Export Processing Zones.* Geneva: UNCTAD-ILO.

UNCTAD. 1985. "Export Processing Zones in Developing Countries: Implications for Free Trade and Industrialization Policies." Report No. TD/B/C.2/211 (1983) and Rev 1. United Nations, Geneva.

UNCTAD. 2003. *World Investment Report 2002: Transnational Corporations and Export Competitiveness.* United Nations, Geneva.

UNIDO (United Nations Industrial Development Organization). 1980. "Export Processing Zones in Developing Countries." UNIDO Working Papers on Structural Changes, No. 10. UNIDO International Centre for Science and High Technology, Vienna.

USAID (United States Agency for International Development). 2007. *Dinamicas recientes de la produccion, el comercio y el empleo en las zonas francas de exportacion de la Republica Dominicana.* USAID Greater Access to Trade Expansion Project. Arlington, VA: Development and Training Services, Inc.

Wall, D. 1976. "Export-Processing Zones." *Journal of World Trade Law* 10: 478–489.

Warr, P. 1989. "Export Processing Zones: The Economics of Enclave Manufacturing." *The World Bank Research Observer* 9(1): 65–88.

Willmore, L. 1995. "Export Processing Zones in the Dominican Republic: A Comment on Kaplinsky." *World Development* 23(3): 529–535.

World Bank. 1992. "Export Processing Zones." Policy and Research Series, No. 20. World Bank, Washington, DC.

CHAPTER 3

Assessing the Outcomes in Africa's SEZs

Introduction

In this chapter, we look at the performance of SEZs in Africa, based on case study research and firm-level surveys of six African zone programs—in Ghana, Kenya, Lesotho, Nigeria, Senegal, and Tanzania—complemented by additional research on two programs each in Asia and Latin America: Bangladesh and Vietnam, and the Dominican Republic and Honduras (for details on the survey methodology, see Appendix C). The chapter includes a broad, quantitative assessment of outcomes of SEZ programs in terms of exports, investment, and employment. It also looks more broadly at longer term economic and social outcomes of these zone programs, including the extent to which SEZs contribute to local economic upgrading through links and spillovers with domestic firms, the quality of the employment they offer, and their gender-differentiated effects.

We find that performance across the African zones is mixed, with Ghana and Lesotho (and in some cases Kenya) performing relatively well on some measures. On the whole, African programs are underperforming relative to the Asian and Latin American programs included in the study. However, most of the programs are still in relatively early stages of development, and some show signs of promise. Specifically, with the possible exception of Ghana (driven largely by cocoa and timber exports through the single factory free zone program), African zones show low levels of investment, exports, and employment. That said, the relative contributions of SEZs in national investment and exports is in line with global experiences, which points to a bigger competitiveness challenge in the region and suggests that the SEZs may not be doing enough to catalyze wider structural change. Indeed, the evidence also indicates that African zones are not yet contributing any significant dynamic benefits to their economies. More worryingly, in the post-MFA, postcrisis environment, there is a risk that the African zones may shift permanently and prematurely to a low-growth path. Finally, the data indicate that, despite the fact that most zone programs are uncompetitive in global terms for labor-intensive activities, many are still failing to deliver quality employment and a living wage to their largely female workforces. Overall, the results raise questions about the current competitiveness of African zone programs and the potential of zones that aim to compete for labor-intensive assembly employment under a traditional export platform (EPZ) model.

Defining and Measuring Success in SEZs

Economic zones are normally established to act as catalysts for trade, investment, and wider economic growth. Most often, they aim to improve competitiveness to facilitate the economic transformation of their host countries faster or more effectively than would be possible without them. In different countries and at different times, however, the specific objectives vary, from attracting FDI to creating employment to experimenting with reforms.

These are all possible objectives by which to measure the success of zone programs. In this chapter, we use a framework that draws on each of these principal objectives to assess zone outcomes (see Figure 3.1). The distinction we make in our framework is between objectives whose outcomes are static in nature and those that are dynamic.

We define *static economic benefits* as those derived in the relatively short term through the use of economic zones as instruments of trade and investment policy. These static benefits are the result of capturing the gains from specialization and exchange. They include employment creation; the attraction of foreign direct investment (FDI); the generation of foreign exchange through exports; and the creation of economic value added. Economic zone programs that are successful in contributing to long-term development leverage these static benefits into *dynamic economic benefits*, which include the promotion of nontraditional economic

Figure 3.1   Framework for Assessing the Outcomes of Economic Zone Programs

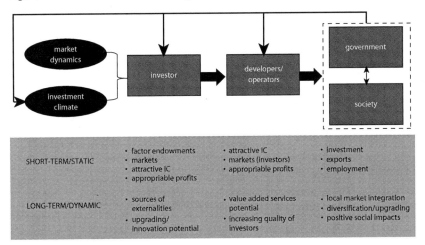

Source: Author.
Note: IC = investment climate.

activities, hard and soft technology transfer, the encouragement of domestic entrepreneurism, and the promotion of economic openness. As part of both the short- and long-term assessment of zones, we look beyond macro-level outcomes to include social impacts as a measure of success— primarily the quality of employment created and the gender-differentiated effects of zones.

As illustrated in Figure 3.1, when we consider the outcomes of zones from a micro perspective, we must consider how the zones meet the objectives of various actors. First are the firms, both foreign and domestic, that decide whether to invest in the zones. This is the starting point: without investors, no benefits, either static or dynamic, will accrue. These firms have specific requirements but, on the whole, are looking for locations that maximize their *appropriable profitability* over some period. We specifically speak of the appropriability of profits for several reasons: It captures the effects of tax holidays and other fiscal incentives that are common in many zone programs; it takes into account issues of exchange control and the ability to repatriate profits, which most zone programs guarantee but which are issues for foreign investors in some markets; and it allows for the impact of broader aspects of the investment climate on the risk calculation of investors. The time period will vary depending on the industry and the firm's strategy. Evidence from sectors such as garments (Rolfe et al. 2003) suggests that this time frame may be very short. But where capital invest-ment, scale economies, and learning curves exist, a longer time horizon is likely. Investors who aim to take advantage of dynamic benefits of eco-nomic zones will also be concerned with accessing sources of externalities (e.g., through industry clustering in zones) and the extent to which the existence of other leading-edge firms and institutions offers the potential for knowledge spillovers and learning.

The second set of stakeholders that must be considered are the zone developers and operators, who may be private or public entities. The objectives of private entities are broadly similar to those of investors: They are looking to maximize profits, which for them come through attracting investors into their zones and, in the longer term, developing new revenue streams that tap into the value added services required by high-quality investors. Public developers and operators may not have the same profit objectives, but the proximate goals of attracting investors and meeting their day-to-day needs should be the same. The third stakeholder is the government and, through it, the local and national society in which the zones are based. These stakeholders rely on investors, developers, and operators for the demand side of the equation. Their short-term goals are generally focused on attracting investment, generating exports (foreign exchange), and creating local employment. The last is normally the most important short-term issue for local communities, along with land appro-priation and environmental impact. In the longer term, these stakehold-ers are concerned with the socioeconomic impact on the local economy and how the zone program contributes to meeting wider economic pol-icy objectives, particularly diversification and upgrading.

Of course, this assumes that government directly reflects the desires of society, which is often not the case. Indeed, especially where government invests in and operates zones, objectives are often focused on narrow eco-nomic grounds that may or may not align well with the needs of local workers and communities, or of the national economy. Political economy factors may play an important role in government decision making and may skew the time horizon and goals away from those of the wider soci-ety (e.g., favoring infrastructure investment instead of community con-cerns about land and environmental impact, or favoring investment that may not deliver quality employment and upgrading opportunities in order to show results and generate income).

Beyond the static, dynamic, and socioeconomic impacts of zones, there is a fourth approach to analyzing zone outcomes: assessing the cost-benefit of zones (e.g., internal rate of return and economic rate of return). Such assessment is closely related to the question of the align-ment between the objectives of zones as economic projects and their objectives as instruments of trade and industrial policy. While we recog-nize that cost-benefit analysis should be a critical part of ex ante and ex post evaluations of zone programs, we do not attempt to use such a framework to assess the programs covered in this study for several rea-sons. First, research such as that of Warr (1989), Jayanthakumaran (2003), and Arce-Alpazar et al. (2005) already provides some evidence that zone programs can, and often are, net positive contributors to eco-nomic welfare. In the absence of a large-sample study showing that the vast majority of zones perform poorly in cost-benefit analysis, political decision makers are unlikely to abandon the instrument of economic zones. In this study we do not have such a large sample, nor do we aim to answer a simple yes-or-no question on the zones as a policy tool. Second, cost-benefit evaluations of individual programs are just that: individual. They are likely to be highly context-dependent, and unless a large sample of studies can be covered, generalizing from such analysis will be of limited value. Finally, the main dynamic benefits of economic zone programs are difficult to measure with any precision. Restricting a cost-benefit analysis to a static accounting exercise is too limited a basis on which to make recommendations on the value of zones as a policy instrument. In this study, we aim to draw lessons that can lead policy-makers to the right decisions about whether to implement an SEZ pro-gram and how to do so in a manner that will result in the best static and dynamic outcomes.

The Global Experience with SEZs

What do we know about the global experience of meeting the objectives of SEZ programs? The evidence is somewhat patchy, as there remains no comprehensive assessment of even a small minority of existing zone pro-grams. Most research has focused on a set of "usual suspects"—mainly East Asian success stories, but also Mauritius and, often more critically, some programs in Latin America. In addition, as noted in Chapter 2, the lack of comprehensive aggregate time series data on SEZs seriously hin-ders the potential to undertake robust assessment of SEZs as a policy tool beyond individual cases.

Macro measures of zone impacts are difficult to come by. On a global basis, the impact of SEZs appears to be relatively small, but it has been growing rapidly over the past two decades. Evidence suggests that for developing and emerging economies, SEZs can play a particularly large role in terms of investment and exports, although their employment impact is moderate.

In terms of the importance of SEZs as locations for global FDI, the limited data available indicate the importance of zones in some countries. Table 3.1 summarizes the findings of Jayanthakumaran (2003) on the impact of SEZs in East Asia. It shows that while SEZs may account for a relatively small share of investment in large economies, in some countries they have been a very substantial contributor; for example, accounting for nearly one quarter of FDI in the Philippines during the 1980s. According to UNCTAD (2003), the share of FDI in SEZs in the Philippines grew to 81 percent by 2000. Similarly, in China, the share of FDI going into SEZs grew dramatically during the 1990s, reaching 80 percent of FDI. In Mexico, *maquiladora* operations accounted for 23 percent of FDI in 2000, up from 6 percent in 1994 (Sadni-Jallab and Blanco de Armas 2002).

The evidence with respect to exports shows a much stronger role of SEZs, although the broad pattern is similar. FIAS (2008) estimates that approximately US$850 billion in goods and services are exported through SEZs in emerging and developing countries annually. This corresponds to nearly 20 percent of exports from these countries. Evidence from East Asian economies shown in Table 3.1 supports the important role of SEZs in developing country exports, particularly in exports from small economies. Data from 2005 (FIAS 2008) show that economic zones dominated the exports of many developing countries in Latin America (Nicaragua, 79%; the Dominican Republic, 77%; Panama, 67%); the Middle East and North Africa (Bahrain, 69%; Morocco, 61%); South and East Asia (Bangladesh, 75%; Philippines, 78%); and even Africa (Madagascar, 80%).

Table 3.1   Relative Importance of SEZs in East Asian Economies (as share of National economy)

	FDI (1980s)	Exports[1] (1980s)	Employment (1995)
Korea	4.0%	1.0%	N/A
Malaysia	13.4%	49.0%	2.1%
Philippines	22.6%	16.0%	0.3%
Indonesia	5.5%	N/A	N/A
China	11.6%	12.0%	12.0%

Source: Jayanthakumaran (2003).

From an employment perspective, while economic zones have made an important contribution to absorbing large-scale unemployment in some countries (e.g., Tunisia, the Dominican Republic, Lesotho), their relative effect has been much less on jobs than on trade and investment. This is not surprising, as the externally traded sector is a minority in almost all economies. Indeed, according to the data from FIAS (2008), the relative contribution of SEZs to exports in developing economies is 40 times greater than its impact on direct employment.

Much of the academic and policy research on economic zones has at its heart the question of whether countries are capturing their dynamic benefits; that is, are they actually managing to use zones to improve long-term competitiveness and effect structural change in their economies? Are SEZs playing a catalytic role in diversification and upgrading? Here there is no large-scale macro evidence, so we must rely on individual and comparative case studies. As discussed in Chapter 2, the findings cover the spectrum: Zones are detrimental to economic upgrading (Kaplinsky 1993); they have limited dynamic potential (Warr 1989); or they are potential catalysts of economic transition (Ge 1999).

Finally (also discussed in Chapter 2), the literature on the labor and social outcomes of SEZ programs is large and wide-ranging, but empirical analysis is limited. One set of studies (c.f. ILO 2003; ICFTU 2003) finds that zones systematically ignore labor standards and rights and have strong negative social impacts. Others (c.f. ILO/UNCTC 1988; Willmore 1995) find that zones can actually promote human development. Detailed empirical analysis by Aggarwal (2005) in South Asia finds that zones generally offer better quality employment than the available alternatives, but, crucially, outcomes are not inherent in the model of zones but rather in their implementation.

SEZs in Africa

Although several African countries launched EPZ or free zone programs in the early 1970s (Liberia in 1970, Mauritius in 1971, and Senegal in 1974), most African countries did not operationalize programs until the 1990s or 2000s.[2] Table 3.2 provides a broad overview of the African zone programs initiated in each decade since the 1970s. It shows that nearly 30 countries in the region (60%) have programs, and over 80 percent of the programs started within the past two decades.

The fact that most African countries are relative latecomers to economic zones. This has several important implications in considering their

Table 3.2   Overview of African Zone Programs by Decade of Launch

1970s	1980s	1990s	2000s
Liberia	Djibouti	Burundi	Gabon
Senegal	Togo	Cameroon	Gambia
Mauritius		Cape Verde	Mali
		Equatorial Guinea	South Africa
		Ghana	Zambia
		Kenya	Eritrea
		Madagascar	Mauritania
		Malawi	Tanzania
		Mozambique	
		Namibia	
		Nigeria	
		Rwanda	
		Seychelles	
		Sudan	
		Uganda	
		Zimbabwe	

Source: FIAS (2008) with author's amendments.

success to date. First, few zones see rapid growth in their early years. Even the most successful zones grew slowly in the first 5–10 years, later shifting to an exponential growth curve before eventually reaching maturity and experiencing slowing growth. Thus, for many African zone programs, it may be too early to pronounce on their success or failure. Second, the macro environment in which these zone programs have been developed differs substantially from that experienced by zones setting up in Asia and Latin America during the 1970s and 1980s. Specifically, most African zones were established during and after the rise of Asia as a manufacturing superpower and the subsequent structural shift in trade and FDI patterns. Thus, the level and nature of competition for traditional manufacturing export platform FDI is a significant factor that may hinder the speed and scale of growth for African zones.

According to FIAS (2008), 114 zones exist in Sub-Saharan Africa—this is somewhere between 3 percent (based on ILO data) and 4.5 percent (based on FIAS data) of the total number of global zones. Africa is obviously a very small player in the SEZ market; however, these figures are broadly in line with the region's share of global trade and investment. The FIAS data indicate that nearly half of these zones are in Kenya, but most of these Kenyan "zones" are, in fact, single factory units licensed as EPZ developers. While they may have the potential under their licenses

·to develop land and facilities for other EPZ users, the vast majority house only their own operations and are not industrial parks. Therefore, the true number of economic zones operating in the region is likely to be much lower than 114.

Insufficient detailed data exist to allow a comprehensive analysis of Africa's performance in SEZs—in terms of investments, exports, and employment—relative to other regions. The data available from the ILO database (Boyenge 2007) does at least give an indication of employment levels in zones—they show that, as of 2006, zones in Africa and the Indian Ocean (Mauritius, Madagascar, and the Seychelles) employed more than a million workers. This is equivalent to 4 percent of worldwide zone employment (excluding China; 1.6% including China). However, half of the total employment in the ILO database is from one country: South Africa.

Anecdotal evidence suggests that success in African zones (even defined narrowly in terms of scope and time) has been limited to a few countries, such as Mauritius, Kenya, Madagascar, and possibly Ghana. In many other countries in the region—including Nigeria, Senegal, Malawi, Namibia, and Mali—zones appear to be struggling for a variety of reasons, including poor location, lack of effective strategic planning and management, and problems of national policy instability and weak governance (Watson 2001). Even where programs have been successful in attracting investment, creating employment, and generating exports, concerns remain over the quality of investment and employment, as well as its sustainability. The recent experience of Madagascar, where employment in the SEZs has collapsed following the prolonged political crisis, illustrates the fragility of the economic zone models implemented in Africa to date.

In the absence of high-quality large-scale cross-country data, we will focus on the six African zone programs covered in our own research, along with the four non-African countries to give perspective on issues that might be generalized for SEZs versus those that appear to be particularly relevant for the African experience. In the next sections, we will compare the performance of African zone programs with the static, dynamic, and socioeconomic objectives discussed earlier.

Results—Static Economic Outcomes in African Zones

This section and the two that follow provide a summary and discussion of outcomes across the 10 zone programs included in the study, with a specific focus on the six African zones. In some cases, comparisons are made with data or experiences of other countries in order to put the discussion into perspective. The data presented come from a variety of sources, including the SEZ investor surveys carried out as part of this study, national zone authorities, and established databases such as UNCTAD's FDI database, UN COMTRADE, and World Development Indicators. (See Appendix C for a discussion of the survey methodology and coverage.)

Note that even for the 10 countries included in our study, data are not comprehensive. In some zone programs (e.g., Nigeria), we were unable to get access to any reliable time series data on the free zone program. In other countries (e.g., Senegal), data were available on the small free zone program but not always on the other parallel programs (the now-defunct "points francs" and the large EFE regime). Moreover, the operation of single factory programs—especially in Ghana and Senegal but also on a smaller scale in Kenya and a much smaller scale in Tanzania—makes direct comparisons and, in some cases, conclusions difficult. Where possible, we have separated data on the zone programs delineated within specific industrial parks or enclaves and dispersed through single factory licensing.

Investment

The first proximate measure of success of an SEZ program is the investment it attracts. Without investment, there will be no employment or exports and no possibility of realizing structural economic benefits. In this section, we review the scale and nature of investment in African SEZ programs to date. We have very limited data on investment patterns in the economic zones of Senegal and Nigeria, so any comparisons that rely on time series data exclude these countries. Table 3.3 summarizes the results on FDI in the SEZs. Note that data on investment in most SEZs do not differentiate FDI from domestic investment, and report only the cumulative value of annual investments rather than providing actual FDI flow data. As a result, we have estimated annual flows by taking the difference in cumulative FDI from one year to the next. We have then compared this to FDI stocks data from UNCTAD and again taken the difference in reported stocks from one year to the next as an estimate for the annual FDI flow.

On measures of FDI stock and FDI per capita, the non-African zones generally outperform the African zones. One exception is Ghana, which experienced large-scale investment in its free zone program during the 2000s. A large majority of FDI in Ghana's program has come through

Table 3.3   SEZ Investment Statistics[3]

	FDI statistics		
	Total SEZ FDI stock (2008) (US$m)	SEZ FDI per capita (2000–2008) (US$)	SEZ FDI as % of total national FDI (2000–2008)
Bangladesh	1,435	6	30
Dominican Republic	2,611	141	18
Vietnam	36,760	325	100
Ghana (Tema)	68	3	48
Ghana (single units)	2,806	120	
Kenya (EPZs)	162	6	20
Kenya (single units)	155		
Nigeria	N/A	<1	<1
Tanzania	210	5	18

Sources: SEZ FDI: author's compilation from individual country SEZ authorities; national FDI data from UNCTAD.

single unit free zones rather than through investment in firms based in the Tema Free Zone. These single unit firms are licensed as free zone companies but entitled to operate anywhere in Ghanaian territory. A similar program operates in Kenya, Senegal, and Tanzania. The last column shows the relative importance of the SEZ program as a source of FDI. It is striking that—with the exception of Nigeria, whose free zone program has failed to attract significant investments by almost any measure—the African zone programs show relatively high contributions to national FDI inflows from the SEZ programs, despite low absolute levels of investment in the SEZs. Thus the relative failure of African SEZ programs to attract investment may be due more to a poor overall investment environment than to the failure of the zone programs themselves.

The data in Table 3.3 also suggest that levels of SEZ contributions to FDI in Kenya and Tanzania are broadly in line with the experiences of East Asia during their early growth period in the 1980s.

So, how does this investment translate into actual firms operating in the SEZs? Figure 3.2 graphs the number of active SEZ-licensed firms in each country under study, distinguishing between those operating in spatially defined zones (or enclaves) and those that operate as single factory units. Again, the gap in scale between the African and non-African zones is evident. The zone program in the Dominican Republic supports more than 550 firms; Honduras has nearly 350 firms; and Bangladesh, nearly 300. Vietnam (data are not presented in the graph for scale reasons)

Figure 3.2   Number of Firms Operating in the Economic Zones, 2009

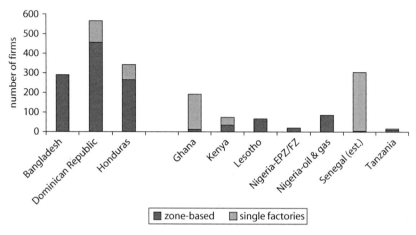

Source: Author's compilation from individual country SEZ authorities.

supports 3,500 firms in its export processing and industrial zones. In contrast, excluding the single factory units, the African zones in the study have, on average, no more than 35 firms operating in them. Such small-scale operations not only have financial implications on program outcomes but are also likely to restrict the potential for their host countries to leverage dynamic benefits through the programs.

Both Senegal and Ghana (with 300 and 180 firms, respectively[4]) have a large number of firms operating through single unit free zone programs. But even taking these into account, the scale of the African programs appears to be limited. Part of the explanation for this (at least relative to Bangladesh and Vietnam, and excepting Nigeria) is size of the population and the economy. A second reason is that the African zones have been established relatively recently.

In exploring the nature of investment in African SEZs, we need to look at the issue of enclave versus single factory zone investments. Many of the African zone programs have opted for single factory models. In Ghana and Senegal, the governments have led the development of a single zone and then opened up the program to allow firms to license their individual factories as SEZs. Kenya and Tanzania have followed a similar model, although they have placed equal emphasis on promoting not just single factory units but private developers investing in SEZ industrial parks. In Honduras and the Dominican Republic, the single factory model is also allowed; however, owing to the strong response of the private sector to zone development opportunities, a wide variety of industrial park options are also available, and most investors have chosen to operate inside an established park.

No strong evidence exists that enclave models are either more or less effective than single factory models on a national basis. Africa's most successful zone program, Mauritius, was based on the single factory model, although the small size of the island means that most EPZ firms are concentrated in a few industrial areas, so too is Malaysia's program. On the other hand, many successful East Asian programs operate under enclave models. Single factory models provide flexibility of location while offering the fiscal and trade-related benefits of zone programs. However, they do not provide the benefits of concentrated infrastructure, administration, and services that are possible in effectively implemented enclave programs. In certain situations, enclave programs tend to be more advantageous than single factory models; for example, when significant challenges exist in the broad economy regarding access to infrastructure or its quality. Enclave programs also work better when resources to deliver on the administrative benefits of zone programs (e.g., licensing, efficient customs administration, value added services) are limited, so that concentrating these resources in one location rather than spreading them over a large geographical area will result in superior service delivery. The evidence in Chapter 5 suggests that single factory free zone firms in Africa fail to reap the investment climate advantages, in both infrastructure and services, available to firms based inside the industrial zones. And enclave programs are more effective where regulatory capacity may not be strong enough to define and enforce the terms on which firms can access single factory licenses, opening up the program to significant risk of rent-seeking by domestic firms that choose to "switch in" to the zone program to access fiscal or other benefits. All these situations hold true in most African countries included in this study; thus, it is somewhat surprising that most of these countries have chosen to emphasize single factory programs.

Figures 3.3 and 3.4 summarize the source of investment in SEZs, including the extent to which companies investing in the zones are foreign or locally controlled, and the source regions of foreign investors. Traditionally, SEZ policy has focused on foreign sources of investment as a priority. However, while SEZs generally need a substantial volume of FDI, at least in the initial stages, to attract the knowledge and technology that can be the basis of structural economic transformation, local investment also plays an important role over time. In fact, most successful zones

Figure 3.3   Ownership Structure of SEZ Investments, 2009[6]

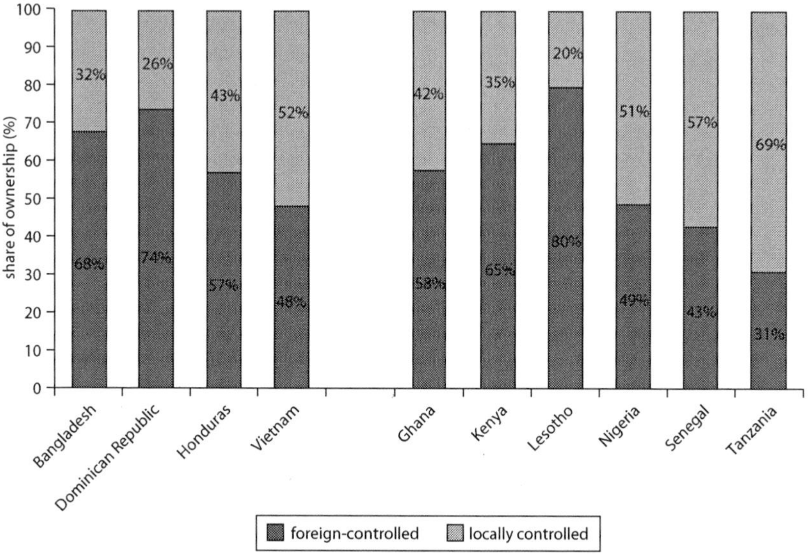

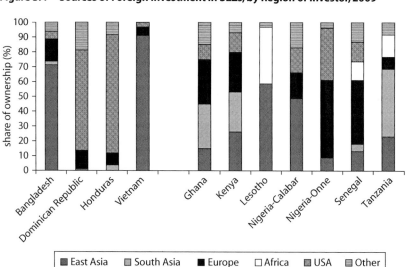

Source: SEZ investor surveys.[7]

Figure 3.4   Sources of Foreign Investment in SEZs, by Region of Investor, 2009[8]

Source: SEZ investor surveys.

that start with substantial FDI are eventually dominated by locally based firms. This was the case, for example, in Mauritius, Malaysia and the Republic of Korea,[5] and a similar pattern is beginning to emerge in China. Looking at our sample countries, we find moderate share of local ownership in most countries, with substantial levels in Vietnam, Senegal, and Tanzania. However, this top-line figure may mask underlying differences in the nature of investment in the African and non-African zones.

Specifically, the non-African zones have shown some evidence of the shift from foreign to local investment. For example, in Vietnam, local share of investment projects rose steadily from around 23 percent in 1995 to over 50 percent by 2008. Local investors have also played critical roles in the zone programs in Honduras and the Dominican Republic (see Box 3.1). In the case of the African zones, however, the same pattern does not appear to hold. For example, new programs, such as that in Tanzania, have had high shares of local investment from the outset. This, in combination with the low levels of FDI attracted into the African zone programs to date, suggests that the relatively high share of local investment may reflect a failure to attract FDI as much as success in attracting local investors. A second explanation—particularly in programs such as Senegal's—is the existence of single unit licenses and the propensity of locally based firms to switch into the SEZ program. On a more positive note, this may reflect the relative perceived advantage of the SEZ operating environment even to local firms and perhaps indicates a pent-up demand for investment opportunities by the domestic private sector. From the available data, we are unable to determine which, if any, of these explanations is true.

Focusing on FDI only, Figure 3.4 illustrates the main sources of investment in each of the zone programs, by region of investment origination. Several points stand out. The first is the general dominance of East Asian investors, particularly in programs focused on the garment and textile sectors (with the exception in the Dominican Republic and Honduras). Second, while the two Asian SEZ programs are mainly used as export platforms by regionally based (Asian) investors and the two Latin American zones (Dominican Republic and Honduras) play a similar role for U.S. investors, the African zones have no such dominant investor source. European investors play a relatively greater role in SEZ investment in the African zones, but they are by no means the dominant source. Indeed, the African zones tend to source investment from a wide variety of locations. For the most part, they have not established themselves as obvious regional export platforms. This is further evidenced by the bar

Box 3.1

Local Entrepreneurs in Latin America's Free Zones: Catalysts and Catalyzed

Honduras

The Honduran government realized early on the need for private sector participation in the establishment of SEZs. Only a few years after the enactment of the free zone law of 1976, the law was extended from the public enclave of Puerto Cortés to a number of other counties to allow private entrepreneurs to establish and operate SEZs. However, while the initial law was neutral with regard to country of origin, in implementation it allowed only foreign exporters to enjoy the benefits for many years. It was not until the enactment of the EPZ law in 1987 that de facto discrimination between domestic and foreign manufacturers ended. Local entrepreneurs, already active in the garment sector, responded quickly to set up not only manufacturing facilities but larger industrial parks. This local participation was seen as an important signal by interested foreign investors, and it played a major role in catalyzing the large FDI that flowed into the *maquila* sector during the 1990s.

Dominican Republic

In the Dominican Republic, the free zone program was also exclusively foreign at the start. Unlike in Honduras, there were no local entrepreneurs with significant investments in the garment sector, but the free zone program helped create a new and sophisticated national entrepreneur class that mastered export strategies and instruments. Local investment grew rapidly during the 1980s and 1990s, rising from 11 percent of free zone firms in 1985 to 35 percent by 2000 (Schrank 2008). A large number of the Dominican companies now operating in the free zones are owned by entrepreneurs who started as employees of foreign-owned companies.

Source: Author.

chart in Figure 3.5, which shows that, outside of Lesotho and possibly Ghana, investment in the zones is spread across a variety of sectors (mainly in "Other manufacturing"), with little evidence of clustering.

Why might African zones be different in this regard? Most investment in SEZ programs is of the export platform variety: It is primarily efficiency- rather than market-seeking. And for most traditional export processing

Figure 3.5   Principal Industry of Operation for SEZ Firms

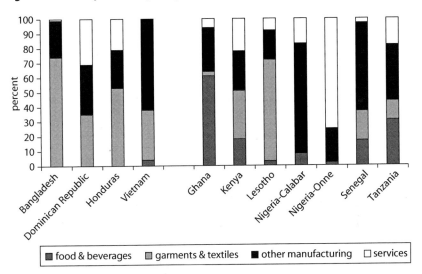

Source: SEZ investor surveys.

activity, the primary determinant of competitiveness is labor cost and productivity. Most African countries have relatively high labor costs, low productivity, and high costs of transport and other inputs. (This is discussed in more detail in Section 8 in this chapter.) Suffice to say that in the absence of comparative advantage in labor-intensive assembly, it is not surprising that African zones have had a poor experience in attracting investment in traditional export processing activities.

Several of these points are worth highlighting in Figure 3.5. First, as noted above, African zones tend to have investment dispersed across a wide set of economic activities; in particular, outside of Lesotho there is little concentration in the garment and textile sector (until recent years, Kenya's program was highly concentrated in garments). Second, while there is virtually no food and beverage activity based in the non-African zones, all the African zone programs show some activity in this sector. It is dominant in Ghana, where most of the investment in cocoa processing takes place in the free zone program. In Kenya, Tanzania, and Senegal, it also plays an important role. This is perhaps not surprising given the importance of the agricultural sector in most African countries. It may also suggest that while they may not be globally competitive as platforms for assembly activity, activities related to the processing of regional natural resources may be a source of comparative advantage for African zones (see Box 3.2).

Box 3.2

Comparative Advantage and Investment in Free Zones

Nigeria

The government of Nigeria put significant investment into its flagship free zone in Calabar during the 1990s. The aim was to develop a base to attract FDI into manufacturing to support the diversification of Nigeria's economy. Despite significant efforts and investment, more than a decade later only a handful of companies are operating in the zone, and only some of them are actually manufacturers. However, a second, smaller initiative to establish a free zone in Port Harcourt to support Nigeria's large oil and gas sector quickly attracted scores of international investors and now employs more than 20,000 workers (compared with little more than 1,000 in Calabar).

Ghana

Similarly, Ghana established a free zone program in the mid-1990s and developed a flagship project at Tema to attract global FDI and position itself as a regional manufacturing and trading hub. Despite programs designed to establish its position in the textile and ICT sectors, Ghana initially struggled to attract investment. However, large-scale foreign and local investors in natural resource sectors—particularly in cocoa processing but also in wood and fish processing—saw the opportunities of the free zone program and have invested heavily, both at Tema and (mainly) through the single factory scheme.

Source: Author.

Exports

The level of exports sustained is probably the most commonly used outcome measure for SEZ programs. Table 3.4 provides a detailed summary of SEZ export levels, growth, and the relative importance of SEZ exports in the national economy. Again, the small scale of the African programs under study stands out on both an absolute and per capita basis (with the exception of Lesotho). We see some evidence of success in Ghana's program. Even in the Tema enclave, which hosts a small number of firms, exports reached US$280 million in 2008; exports from the single factory units were almost four times as high. The success of exports under the Ghana program is partly attributable to cocoa processing activities, which account for a large share of activity under the free zone program and have

Table 3.4 Summary of Key SEZ Export Statistics

| | Exports 2008 (US$m) | Exports per capita 2008 (US$) | SEZ share of national | | Growth in exports | | |
			Non-oil exports	Manufacturing exports	2000–2008 (CAGR)	2000–2004 (avg.)	2004–2008 (avg.)
Bangladesh	2,430	102	15%	16%	13%	11%	16%
Dominican Republic	4,545	462	69%	96%	–1%	0%	–1%
Honduras	4,000 (est.)	550	61%	98%	10%	15%	6%
Vietnam	16,175	188	30%	41%	29%	24%	35%
Ghana (Tema)	281	12	33%	590%	29%	56%	31%
Ghana (single units)	1,019	44					
Kenya (EPZs)	145	4	9%	25%	31%	57%	10%
Kenya (single units)	265	7					
Lesotho	425	211	64%	64%	1%	19%	–7%
Nigeria (Calabar) (est.)	100	1	4%	16%	N/A	N/A	N/A
Senegal (DIFZ)	50	4	16%	42%	26%	144%	–3%
Senegal (single units)	350	29					
Tanzania	59	1	3%	14%	N/A	N/A	N/A

Sources: UN COMTRADE statistics accessed via World Integrated Trade Solution (WITS) and author's calculations based on data from individual country SEZ authorities.

grown robustly since the program was launched in 1995.[9] But the activity goes beyond just cocoa, with firms in Tema involved in prefabricated housing (US$64m in exports) and plastic household products (US$11m in exports). Outside the enclave, the free zone includes several exporters; for example, a tuna processor (US$100m in exports); a processor of fresh fruits and juices (US$33m in exports); and a number of timber companies (together accounting for up to US$200m in exports).

In contrast, Kenya's EPZ program, often held up as an example of African success, looks rather anemic. Even including the single factory units, the program, which has been operating for nearly two decades, accounted for just over US$400 million in exports in 2008—US$11 in exports per capita. The free zone programs in Nigeria and Senegal performed even worse, and Tanzania's program also produced limited exports, although Tanzania's is still in the very early stages of development. As was the case with investment, while nominal exports from the African zone programs were extremely small (on average 10–15 times smaller than the corresponding absolute and per capita exports in the non-African programs), their contribution to national exports was much more in line with international SEZ norms. However, in some countries—particularly Kenya, Nigeria, and Tanzania—the relative contribution of the SEZ program is limited.

Given that many of the African zone programs were established only recently, could the low levels of exports be a function of time? Certainly, this is part of the story. However, as will be shown in Chapter 4, while the age of zone programs is correlated positively with export volumes, this relationship does not hold up as a significant predictor of export outcomes in a large-sample analysis. Data on growth of exports during the period 2000 to 2008 indicate that the African zones, by and large, grew relatively quickly (although in most cases from very small bases) during the decade, at a pace much faster than the non-African zones as a whole. However, within the non-African zones, we have two very different cases: maturing zones in the Dominican Republic and Honduras, where growth is stagnant, and emerging zones in Bangladesh and Vietnam, where growth has been rapid.

A closer look at the growth patterns raises some concerns over many of the African zone programs. As can be seen in Table 3.4, many of the programs experienced rapid growth during the period 2000–2004 but slower growth or even a decline since then. This is partly attributable to the base on which they are growing in each of those periods, but there may also be a structural factor at play: competition from Asia in general, and specifically from the Asian garment sector in the post-MFA environment. In the period 2000–2004, African SEZs (particularly Kenya and Lesotho) benefited enormously from trade preferences to the U.S. market granted under the African Growth and Opportunity Act of 2000 (AGOA). At the same time, they faced limited competition in the U.S. market from Asian producers, who continued to operate under quota restrictions until the MFA expired at the end of 2004. At least in the cases of Kenya and Lesotho, declining competitiveness in the aftermath of the MFA is a well-documented source of export stagnation and employment losses since 2005. (A discussion of the role of the MFA in African SEZ performance and adjustment appears later in this chapter.)

If we look at the typical growth pattern of successful economic zones, it appears that most of the African zones are failing to shift to the exponential growth path that typically occurs somewhere between the 5th and 10th year of operations. Figure 3.6 maps the export growth paths of two successful SEZs—Suzhou in China and Costa Rica—from their first year of operations. Three African programs (Ghana, Kenya, and Lesotho) and three non-African programs (Bangladesh, the Dominican Republic, and Vietnam) are compared.[10] The figure shows that most zone programs start slowly, growing linearly in the initial stages, before hitting a growth inflection point. The two Asian programs then grow exponentially with, as yet, no sign of slowing. The Latin American examples show a slower (although still strong) growth pattern, then hit a point of declining growth or stagnation, although in the case of Costa Rica there is some evidence of a renewed cycle of increasing growth. The differences between the Asian and Latin American growth patterns are probably related to factors such as timing (the Latin American programs launched in the 1970s, while the Asian programs started at the outset of a period of huge growth in production-network-driven global trade in the early 1990s); the concurrence of wider reforms (in Vietnam and China, the zone programs were one small element of major economic reform initiatives that opened their economies for the first time in half a century); and the huge differences in scale between the Latin American and Asian economies under comparison.

Of the three African programs, only Ghana appears to be showing evidence of shifting to the higher growth path, although it is unclear how sustainable this growth will be, as it depends to a large extent on processed commodities (cocoa and timber) that are limited in their availability and face significant cyclical price fluctuations. Figure 3.7 removes China and Vietnam to give a clearer picture of the growth paths of the

Figure 3.6   SEZ Export Growth Trajectories by Year of Operation

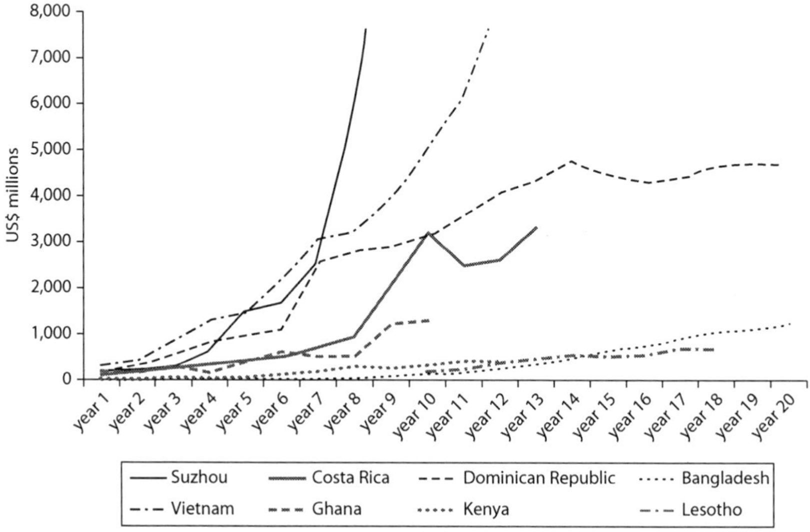

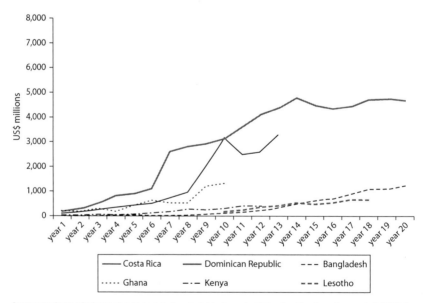

Figure 3.7   SEZ Export Growth Trajectories by Year of Operation, excluding China and Vietnam

Sources: Author's calculations based on data from individual country SEZ authorities; Arce-Alpazar et al. (2005) for Costa Rica; Zhao and Farole (2010) for Suzhou.

African zones against some relevant comparators.[11] It is clear that exports from both Kenya and Lesotho are growing but are failing to take off. In contrast, the formerly slow-growing SEZ program in Bangladesh appears, after 10–12 years, to have moved to a much faster growth path, driven by the country's increasing competitiveness in the global garment market since 2005.

It is also important to explore the markets in which SEZ companies are selling. Here, the first question concerns *export intensity*. Like most economic zone programs around the world, the African zones studied are strongly oriented toward export markets. This is, of course, partly because the zones have been designed and legally regulated to encourage firms to serve export rather than domestic markets. Table 3.5 summarizes the export orientation and specific regulations in place to restrict local sales across the 10 countries in the study. With the exception of Nigeria and Lesotho, all the zone programs under study place significant restrictions on sales to the local market from SEZ-based companies, although changes may be under way in some African programs. For example, in light of East African Community (EAC) integration, member states are considering substantially reducing local market sales barriers. Similarly, the Dakar Integrated SEZ is expected to eliminate all restrictions against local sales.

With the exception of companies in Nigeria's Calabar zone, however, companies surveyed in the zone programs are highly export-focused,

Table 3.5   Export Orientation in SEZs[12]

	Export orientation (% SEZ company production)	Minimum export share (per SEZ regulations)
Bangladesh	95%	90%
Dominican Republic	81%	90%; no minimum in some sectors
Honduras	81%	95%
Vietnam	91%	100% in Export Processing Zones; no minimum in Industrial Zones
Ghana	91%	70%
Kenya	98%	80%
Lesotho	80%	No minimum
Nigeria	25%	No minimum
Senegal	87%	80%
Tanzania	77%	80%

Sources: SEZ investor surveys and individual country SEZ laws.

reflecting the traditional emphasis on economic zones as export platforms and the relatively limited local market sales potential in many countries. Although we have very limited data on the destination markets of exports from the African zones, anecdotal evidence suggests they are relatively dispersed (as was the case with investment sources). Only Lesotho operates as a true export platform, serving mainly the U.S. garment sector market. While zone-based firms in Kenya also serve the AGOA market, an increasing share of exports is oriented toward Europe, which is also a main destination of exports for firms in Ghana and Senegal. But the area in which many of the African zones stand out from programs elsewhere in the world is their *regional, end-product* export orientation. Zones in Latin America tend to serve the U.S. market almost exclusively, through both end-product assembly (e.g., garments and wire harnesses in Central America and the Caribbean; machinery, electronics, and equipment in Mexico; pharmaceuticals in Costa Rica) and intermediates (e.g., semiconductors in Costa Rica). Zones in East Asia operate as global and regional export platforms for end products such as clothing, footwear, and electronics, and regional intermediates in the electronics and automotive sector. In many of the African zones, particularly those in West Africa, there appears to be substantial production of end products destined for both consumers and business, such as metals, building products, chemicals, and food to neighboring countries that have very little global or regional value-chain-based production outside of the garment sector in Lesotho and Kenya. There are a number of possible explanations for this pattern of activity, including the fact that, given the small-scale activity in the zones and the failure of these countries to compete more effectively as export platforms, the export patterns reflect specific, opportunistic investments. On the other hand, bearing in mind the challenges of scale in most African countries and the significant transaction costs of production and cross-border trade, the regional trade observed through the zones might give some indication of what efficient patterns of regional specialization and trade would look like (see Box 3.3).

Employment

As discussed earlier in this chapter, while SEZs are often major contributors to FDI and exports in a country, their overall impact on the labor market tends to be rather less. That is not to say that economic zones are not often a major generator of employment; rather, it reflects the relative share of the export sector in a most countries' economies. In small countries, SEZs are often large contributors to employment. As can be seen

Box 3.3

Selling to the African Regional Market

Nigeria
Several companies operating in the Calabar Free Zone sell largely to the West African regional market. For example, Combination Industries, an affiliate of Geekay International Exports (USA) was the first company to set up in the Calabar zone in 1999, introducing a new snack product (cheese balls) into the local Nigerian market, where it has become the market leader. It is now exporting from the Calabar Free Zone widely throughout the region (Ghana, Ivory Coast, Liberia, Cameroon, Sudan, Sao Tome and Principe, Togo, Mali, Burkina Faso, and Niger).

Tanzania
Most companies operating in Tanzania's EPZ program target the regional African market, particularly because of Tanzania's position as a bridge between the two major regional trading blocs—COMESA (Common Market for Eastern and Southern Africa) and SADC (Southern African Development Community). The largest company in the Tanzanian EPZ program (Vector Health) and its sister company (Net Health) manufacture and sell mosquito nets throughout the region. Two other companies target mainly the Mozambique market: one selling textiles and a second, candles. A recent investment assembles Chinese-manufactured motorcycles for sale mainly into the Democratic Republic of Congo.

Source: Author.

in Table 3.6, the absolute and relative contributions of the SEZ programs to employment in African countries is limited (with the significant exception of Lesotho), even when measured against the limited scale of their industrial sectors. Total jobs supported across all six African SEZ programs under study is equivalent to the employment created in the SEZ programs in Honduras and the Dominican Republic, countries with less than 10 million population. Compared with countries such as Kenya and Ghana, Honduras and the Dominican Republic have generated more than four times as much employment through their zone programs, and 10–15 times as much on a per capita basis. Programs such as the one in Nigeria have created virtually no manufacturing employment.

The data presented in Table 3.6 illustrate one of the weaknesses of Ghana's free zone program: Despite its high level of exports, it delivers only limited employment, with activities concentrated instead in

Table 3.6   Employment Contribution of SEZs

	SEZ employment (2008)	SEZ employment as % of national industrial sector employment
Bangladesh	218,299	3%
Dominican Republic	124,517	30%
Honduras	130,000	30%
Vietnam	1,172,000	19%
Ghana (Tema)	2,025	3.5%
Ghana (single units)	26,534	
Kenya (EPZs)	15,127	15%
Kenya (single units)	15,551	
Lesotho	45,130	>80%
Nigeria (Calabar) (est.)	1,156	<1%
Nigeria (Onne, oil & gas)	20,000	N/A
Tanzania	7,500	2.5%

Sources: SEZ employment based on data from individual country SEZ authorities; national industrial employment from various sources.

resource- and capital-intensive sectors. Indeed, Kenya's EPZ program creates nearly 3.5 times more jobs per US$ of exports; and Lesotho's is nearly five times more labor-intensive, owing to its nearly exclusive concentration in the garment sector.

Again, the bigger concern about the African zones is not so much the scale of their programs at this stage but the evidence that their growth may already be slowing. Vietnam and Bangladesh have managed to shift to exponential job growth over the past decade; but for African zone programs, the story of jobs is similar to that of exports: rapid growth in the first half of the decade followed by stagnation. Indeed, for African zones that depend on the garment sector (Kenya and Lesotho), it is not a question simply of failure to shift to an exponential growth path or even just of slowing growth, but of absolute and relatively acute decline in employment. Employment in Lesotho's export garment sector is down 15 percent from its 2004 peak. In Kenya's EPZ program, the decline is more than 20 percent from the 2003 peak. Even in Ghana, where exports have risen rapidly under the single factory free zone program, job growth was weak (only 4.5% since 2004); at the end of 2008, free zone employment in Ghana stood at virtually the same level as in 2005, despite reported exports from the program growing by 2.5 times.

Additional issues related to the nature and quality of jobs created in the SEZs are discussed later in this chapter.

Results—Dynamic Outcomes in African Zones

In analyzing the success of African economic zones against dynamic outcomes, we will focus on two questions: (1) To what extent have the zones played a role in supporting industrialization or diversification of the host country's exports? and (2) To what extent have the zones contributed knowledge and technology spillovers to local markets? The first question can be explored through sectoral patterns of exports and by analyzing the inter- and intrasectoral adjustments in the zone programs over time. The second question measures an intermediate-level outcome—one that, if achieved, should lead the country down the path toward diversification. This outcome can be analyzed by looking at the main sources of spillover between zones and local economies; that is, product markets and labor markets.

Figure 3.8 maps the broad structure of national exports in each of the 10 countries under study over a period of several decades to see what, if any, connection might exist between structural change in export patterns and the establishment of SEZ programs.[13] Obviously, this analysis provides only a basic picture of coincidence and says nothing about causality. There are many reasons why a country might have experienced a shift in its economic base from agriculture to manufacturing, even in the absence of an SEZ or any proactive industrial policies. Indeed, in most successful zone programs, it is recognized that the SEZs is only one of many tools in a broader program to effect structural change. If nothing else, such a broad analysis may at least identify which countries have managed to adjust their export structure over time and which have not.

All four of the non-African zones show quite dramatic structural changes in export patterns toward greater manufacturing. In the case of Vietnam, the data show virtually no change in manufacturing shares of exports until the zone program was established (along with a range of other policy initiatives linked to the opening of Vietnam's economy), followed by a radical shift in export structure toward manufacturing. Bangladesh experienced a similarly large shift, which only became apparent 5–10 years after its EPZ program was launched. This shift was driven almost entirely by the growth of the garment sector, which had no more than 50 firms in the early 1980s and grew to more than 4,500 firms employing more than 2 million workers by 2009. In the Dominican Republic and Honduras, the structural changes were equally dramatic, although they occurred after the programs had been operational for 10 years.

The African country data tell a very different story. Countries such as Lesotho (a garment export mono-economy) and Nigeria experienced no change in their national export structures. Export structures in Senegal and Ghana have fluctuated somewhat over recent decades, with no clear patterns discernable (at least none that appear to have any relationship to their zone programs). Only Kenya and Tanzania show a broad pattern of sectoral adjustment over time. In Tanzania's case, it is a story of increasing growth of nontraditional exports, particularly services and minerals; again, with no real link to the EPZ program. Kenya is the only country to

Figure 3.8   Comparison of Long-Run Sectoral Changes in Exports with SEZ Program Establishment

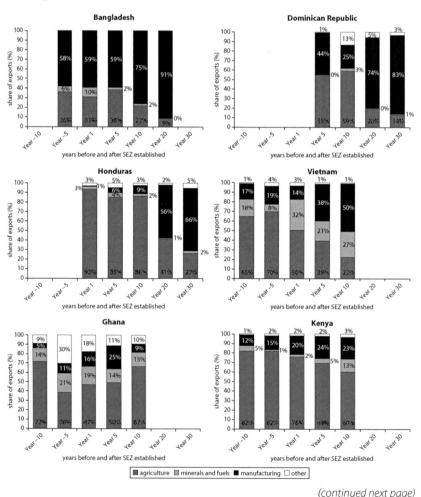

(continued next page)

Figure 3.8 *(continued)*

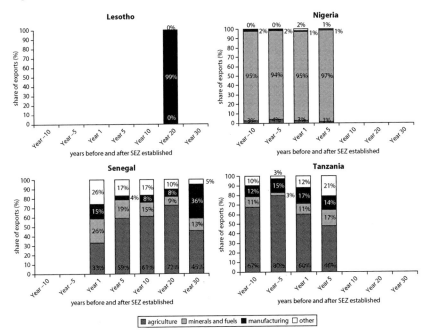

Source: UN COMTRADE via WITS.

have shown a steady rise in manufacturing exports with a corresponding decline in agricultural exports. However, most of this adjustment appears to have taken place before the establishment of the EPZ program, and, in fact, manufacturing share growth appears to have stagnated in the years following the launch of the program.

One factor at play here may be the timing of the launch of SEZ programs in the context of global trends in trade and investment. With the exception of Senegal and Lesotho, the African programs in the study were only operationalized well into the 1990s—probably too late to take advantage of the massive globalization of manufacturing that accelerated during the 1980s and 1990s. One hypothesis is that the structural adjustment seen in Honduras, the Dominican Republic, Vietnam, and Bangladesh is not a story of economic zones but rather of broader macro trends, which African countries were unable to tap into for various reasons (e.g., weak micro competitiveness, lack of fiscal and political stability). An alternative hypothesis is that Africa missed the boat on these opportunities *precisely because* most African countries lacked an effective instrument like SEZs through which to channel trade and investment.

Analyzing structural changes within the SEZs may provide a measure of the extent to which the zone programs facilitate sectoral adjustment, or hinder it. It is instructive to look at how SEZ programs have responded to changing competitiveness in the garment sector, particularly in the post-MFA environment. In Jayanthakumaran's (2003) seminal study on EPZs, the author concludes that there is "a strong correlation between the growth of EPZs and the Multi-Fibre Arrangement in general" and that the phasing out of MFA and guaranteed market access "will eventually result in lower rates of return and will be a possible threat to the existing and new EPZs" (p. 64). Figure 3.9 illustrates clearly, at a broad regional level, the winners and losers in the garment sector since the expiration of the MFA at the end of 2004. In terms of exports to the U.S. market, East and South Asia (particularly Bangladesh) have grown rapidly at the expense of Central America, the Caribbean, and Sub-Saharan Africa, which has experienced declines of up to 40 percent over just four years. More recent trade data suggest that the crisis has further accelerated the changing patterns of competitiveness in the sector.

For SEZ programs that rely on the garment sector, the impact has been significant. While the Bangladesh and Vietnam programs have experienced rapid growth in exports (16% and 34% per annum, respectively) and employment (12% per annum in each country), programs in Latin America and Africa (especially Kenya and Lesotho) have suffered. In

Figure 3.9   Index of Garment Sector Exports to the United States by Region

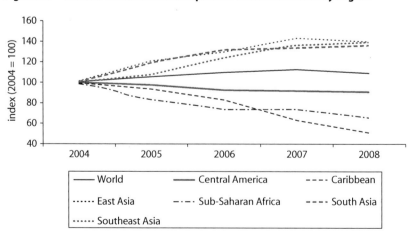

Source: U.S. Office of Textiles and Apparel, Major Shippers Report (http://otexa.ita.doc.gov).

Lesotho, exports are down 25 percent since 2004 and although employment has held firm since 2006, at least 8,000 jobs have been lost since 2004. In Kenya, job losses in the SEZs are nearing 10,000 from their peak. Tanzania was unfortunate in launching its program just as the MFA was being phased out. The program originally had commitments from a significant number of garment manufacturers, almost all of whom eventually decided against investing or have closed down. Despite the success of Ghana's free zone program in other sectors, it has been unable to rescue the apparel sector (see Box 3.4).

But in the face of these competitiveness challenges, some zone programs have been successful in at least beginning the process of adjustment. In the Dominican Republic, for example, the flat export picture since 2000 masks substantial sectoral shifts. As shown in Figure 3.10, textile exports declined by more than half between 2000 and 2008, but this was offset by 60 percent growth in nontextile exports.[14] Sectors such as jewelry, electronics, pharmaceuticals, and even call centers are taking over from the traditional garment sector. This shift has contributed to rapidly increasing value added in the zones (value added per worker grew nearly 12% annually between 2004 and 2008). But it has come at the cost of the SEZs maintaining their traditional role as a generator of large-scale employment: Employment in the free zones declined by more than 70,000 (36%) from its peak of over 195,000 in 2000.

Kenya has also shown some evidence of shifting sectoral structure inside the zones. While apparel exports declined some 10 percent between 2004 and 2008, nonapparel exports more than doubled during this period, contributing to steady overall export growth in the program. Indeed, while apparel accounted for 84 percent of Kenya's EPZ exports in 2003, by 2008 it represented less than half. Other sectors—such as horticultural and food processing, call centers, and human and veterinary pharmaceuticals—have emerged in the zones. Productivity is rising steadily in Kenya's EPZ program, in part owing to a shift toward higher value production but also to growing price competition within the apparel sector, which is forcing the remaining apparel companies to maintain volumes with fewer workers.

We now turn to intermediate measures of zone outcomes; specifically, the extent to which SEZs are facilitating spillovers of knowledge and technology to the local economy. The first channel through which these spillovers may occur is through product market links between SEZ firms and firms in the domestic economy. These links can be either forward or

Box 3.4

The Decline of Ghana's Apparel Sector: Limits to Free Zones in the Face of Global Competition

According to figures from the Ministry of Trade and Industry, Ghana's textile and apparel export sector, which once employed 25,000 workers across 24 factories, now employs just 4,000 people in only 4 factories. Several companies in the apparel sector grew in the early 2000s, thanks to the free zone regime and the Presidential Special Initiative (PSI), which provided grants for management and worker training, renting production space, and equipment purchase. Investment also increased after the launch of AGOA incentives in 2002. But those efforts were quickly reversed following the end of the MFA; exports to the United States from Ghana's main sector—cotton apparel and household goods—collapsed between 2004 and 2008, from US$ 6.8 million to US$0.6 million. This collapse was due to a number of macro and business climate factors, including the following:

- The limitations of Ghana's overall business environment.
- The elimination at the end of 2004 of quantitative import restrictions under the World Trade Organization (WTO) Agreement on Textiles and Clothing (ATC), accelerated by illegal imports of cheap Chinese-made clothing, counterfeit Ghanaian fabrics, and secondhand garments.
- The scarcity of skilled labor; for example, one of the apparel companies that survived had to import all its production staff from Sri Lanka.
- Low productivity (the same company noted above estimates that productivity in Chinese garment factories is 120% that of factories in Ghana).
- The fact that some Economic Community of West African States (ECOWAS) countries, notably Nigeria, have banned the importation of certain textile goods.

While the free zone program has been a great success in attracting FDI in a number of sectors, it has been unable to sufficiently offset the declining competitive position of Ghana in the global textile and apparel sector. Ghana attempted to maximize the advantage of quota/duty-free access to the U.S. market under AGOA with the creation of a 72-hectare Textile and Garment Village within the Tema FZ. This project, part of the PSI program, was developed in 2005 with the aim of attracting 112 companies into the zone over three phases. However, only five companies established operations in this section of the zone and, as of July 2009, only one remained.

Source: Author.

Figure 3.10   Index of Free Zone Exports in the Dominican Republic: Textile versus Nontextile

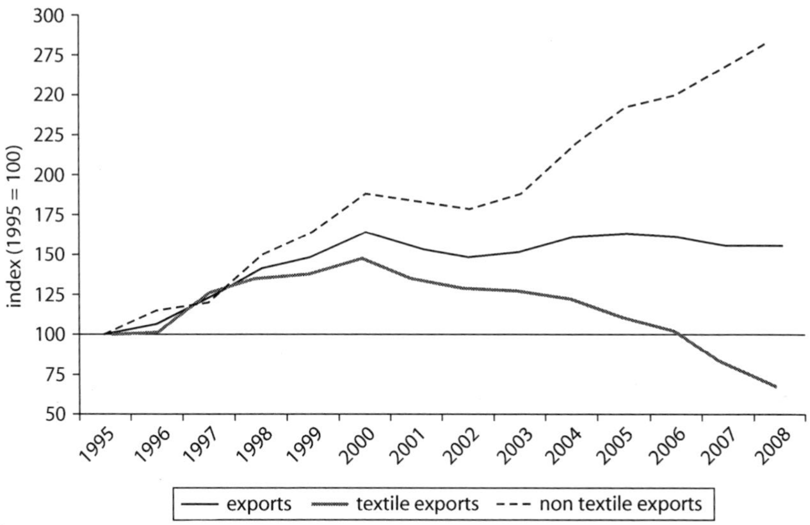

Source: Author's calculations based on data from *Consejo Nacional de Zonas Francas de Exportacion* (CNZFE).

Table 3.7   Share of Materials Inputs in Each Sector Sourced from the Domestic Market

	Garments	Food/ agriprocessing	Other manufacturing	Services	TOTAL (mean)
Bangladesh	17%	—	17%	30%	18%
Dominican Republic	16%	—	17%	19%	17%
Honduras	44%	—	9%	43%	37%
Vietnam	16%	58%	24%	—	23%
Ghana	5%	60%	15%	—	40%
Kenya	17%	84%	34%	41%	34%
Lesotho	9%	35%	25%	18%	14%
Nigeria	—	—	29%	—	29%
Senegal	20%	27%	43%	—	41%
Tanzania	—	55%	26%	—	33%

Source: SEZ investor surveys.

backward. As discussed previously, forward links are limited by zone regulations in most markets, so we will focus on supply links.

Table 3.7 shows the share of raw material inputs sourced from the local market by main sector, as reported in our SEZ firm surveys. The average reported in the African zones is higher than in the non-African zones, primarily because of the relatively larger share of agriprocessing activity in the African zones. Comparing within the garment sector only, the African zones show relatively limited sourcing of local inputs. This is in line with the experience of most zone programs around the world (with the notable exception of Honduras, where the woven garment sector has integrated backward into textiles). Kenya appears to benefit from its status as the industrial and commercial hub of the region, which enables its zone-based firms to source more inputs locally. While African SEZ programs may be struggling to expand local sourcing, establishing better local links appears to have long been a challenge for zone programs worldwide. Data from Jayanthakumaran (2003) on the East Asian SEZ success stories indicates that, with the exception of relatively large markets like Korea and Indonesia, which sourced 34 percent and 41 percent, respectively, from the local market, most zones struggled; by the mid-1980s, Malaysia sourced only 4 percent of inputs locally; Sri Lanka, 5.3 percent; and the Philippines, 6 percent.

A second channel for transmitting spillovers occurs via the labor market—through the free movement of skilled workers across firms. Figure 3.11 combines two measures. The first is the relative share of management of SEZ-based firms that are nationals of the SEZ host

Figure 3.11   SEZ Labor Market Integration

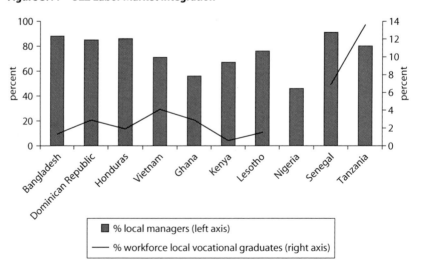

country. With the exception of Nigeria (46%) and Ghana (56%), the large majority of managers in all the zones studied are locals. In general, the African zones appear to rely somewhat more heavily on foreign management than the non-African zones—one-third of managers in the surveyed firms in Kenya were foreign, as were one-quarter in Lesotho. In Senegal, by contrast, foreign share of management is reported at below 10 percent.

Another measure used in Figure 3.11 is the share of the workforce sourced from local vocational training programs. This measure is designed to capture the extent to which zone-based firms hire locally trained skilled workers; these are the workers who are most likely to be in a position to transfer knowledge across firms (inside and outside the zones) or to employ their knowledge in an entrepreneurial venture. Results from the surveys show no clear pattern, with most firms reportedly sourcing only a very small share of workers through such programs. The stand-out situations here are Tanzania (14%) and Senegal (7%) at one end, and Kenya (less than 1%) at the other end. It is important to note that the use of workers from vocational training programs depends on many factors, including the sector, the nature of firm activities, the availability of vocational training programs, and any specific initiatives and incentives available to zone-based firms to employ vocational workers.

Such measures may give some indication of the availability of skilled local workers, but they say little about whether this will actually lead to an effective transfer of knowledge and technology between the SEZ-based firms and the local economy. This transfer depends on many complex factors, including the nature of the technology deployed by the firms, the nature of local labor markets, and the culture and policies with regard to entrepreneurism. All these factors can be affected by policy decisions made by national governments, as well as by the policies and practices of zone authorities. On the issue of labor markets, wide variations exist across the studied zone programs in terms of the extent to which local labor markets help or hinder the potential for spillovers. In some programs (e.g., Lesotho and the Dominican Republic), entire sectors are essentially controlled by foreign-owned firms or within the zone enclaves. In others (e.g., Bangladesh and, somewhat less so, Kenya), workers move relatively fluidly between zone-based and local firms. In Senegal and Tanzania, rigid labor markets seriously restrict the movement of skilled labor across firms, possibly choking off the potential for an SEZ to deliver spillovers to the local economy.

Results—Socioeconomic Outcomes in African Zones

Both measures of success discussed in this chapter—static and dynamic—are concerned only with economic efficiency, but the impact of SEZs on their host societies goes further. Much (mainly critical) documentation exists on the social and environmental impacts of zones but, like most research on zones, it is largely based on single country or small-sample case studies. In this section, we will focus primarily on the employment-related social effects of zones. Specifically, we will focus on African SEZ program outcomes in terms of (1) the quality of employment generated; (2) the extent to which workers' rights are protected in the zones; and (3) the gender-differentiated impacts of zones (given that a large majority of workers in most zone programs are female).

These social issues should not be viewed as completely segregated from the economic issues discussed earlier; over time, social and economic outcomes are closely entwined. Zone programs that fail to offer opportunities for high-quality employment and upward mobility of trained staff, that derive their competitive advantage from exploiting low-wage workers, and that neglect to provide an environment that addresses the particular concerns of female workers are unlikely to be successful in achieving the dynamic benefits possible from zone programs and are likely to find themselves in a "race to the bottom." By contrast, zone programs that recognize the value of skilled workers and seek to provide the social infrastructure and working environment in which such workers thrive will be in a position to facilitate upgrading.

In this section, we focus mainly on outcomes, from a quantitative perspective. For additional discussion of operational practices for establishing and enforcing labor standards in SEZs, see Chapter 7.

Quality of Employment and Protection of Workers' Rights

Figure 3.12 compares the relative wages received (factoring in differences in national purchasing power) for unskilled production workers in each of the 10 countries under study. Overall, workers in the African countries receive relatively higher wages than those in Bangladesh (and, for some countries, more than those in Vietnam) but substantially lower wages than workers in the two Latin American countries. The monthly wage (adjusted for purchasing power) ranged from a low of US$232 in Kenya to US$371 in Senegal; for the sample overall, it ranged from US$124 in Bangladesh to US$675 in Honduras.

Actual monthly wages received by workers in Kenya were reported to average just US$96. This is less than half the average wage reportedly paid

Figure 3.12   Average Monthly Wages plus Benefits (Converted at Purchasing Power Parity [PPP])[15]

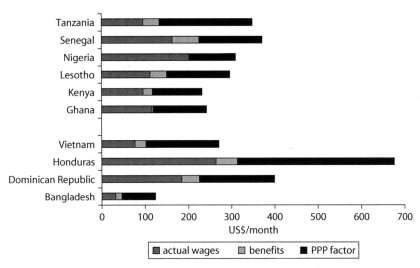

Source: SEZ investor surveys.

by firms in Nigeria. On the other hand, it is three times the actual wages received by unskilled workers in Bangladesh's SEZs (US$32, or little more than US$1 per day). Overall, the purchasing power parity adjustment is much lower for the African countries in the study, reflecting an average 20 percent higher cost of living. This situation may place significant limitations on African zones' ability to balance the pressures of competitiveness and paying a living wage. Indeed, in many of the zones studied—particularly those that depend on labor-intensive global sectors such as garments—extreme competitive pressure on wages appears to have given rise to a debate over whether a living wage is a reasonable objective.[16]

Another way of looking at wage rates in the zones is to compare them with national minimum wages or, better, with comparable sector- and task-specific wages outside the zones. Table 3.8 includes data on how the base wages in Figure 3.12[17] compare with national minimum wages. In almost all countries, unskilled wages inside the zones are substantially higher than the minimum wage. The main exception is in Honduras, where the *maquila* sector lobbied successfully to be exempt from a large increase in the national minimum wage in 2009. A similar lobbying effort in Tanzania exempted large exporters from a minimum wage increase.[18]

Table 3.8   Labor Quality and Workers' Rights: Summary Statistics[19,20]

	Unionization rate (as reported from investor surveys)	National unionization rate	Wages relative to national minimum	Temporary share of SEZ workforce
Bangladesh	60%	<5%	+25%	4%
Dominican Republic	1%	8%	+50%	2%
Honduras	0%	8%	−9%	1%
Vietnam	83%	40% (est.)	+10%	2%
Ghana	35%	42%	+135%	27%
Kenya	14%	38%	+22%	20%
Lesotho	42%	42%	+17%	16%
Nigeria	14%	10% (est.)	+300%	7%
Senegal	52%	27%	+75%	84%
Tanzania	25%	36%	−13%– +60%[21]	22%

Sources: SEZ investor surveys; various sources for national unionization rates and minimum wages.

And, in the Dominican Republic, firms inside the zones have a lower pre-scribed minimum wage than the national minimum wage. In all three zones, unskilled workers typically receive wages above the minimum when benefits and bonuses are taken into account. For the African zones in particular, the SEZ wage premium over the minimum wage is very significant. Whether this is a reasonable comparison, however, is questionable. In the case of Nigeria, for example, the national minimum wage of US$50 is considered to be far below a living wage; the same is true in Kenya, Tanzania, and probably Ghana. We have not, as part of this study, undertaken a quantitative comparison of wages for comparable jobs inside and outside the zones. However, anecdotal evidence from most countries indicates that the total of wages and benefits received by workers inside the zones is generally equal to or slightly higher than that for a comparable job outside the zones (with the exceptions of the Dominican Republic, Honduras, and possibly Nigeria). Indeed, for most unskilled workers in the SEZs, the alternative is employment in the informal sector, where wages are lower, risk is high, and benefits are nonexistent.

Another measure of the quality of employment is its security. The last column of Table 3.8 shows the average share of the workforce that was reported to be temporary in the SEZ firm surveys. Temporary workers not only have less job security but are not likely to receive the full range of benefits available to permanent staff. Here, the African zones (except for Nigeria) stand out as making substantial use of temporary labor. Whether this is linked to the SEZs specifically, however, is difficult to say. Many

African countries struggle with highly inflexible labor markets, which causes firms to make greater use of temporary workers. Thus, the levels of temporary workers reported in Table 3.8 may reflect, more than anything, that the African zones have not resolved the problem of rigid labor markets. In the case of Senegal, for example, an SEZ-specific relaxation of the rules for hiring temporary workers[22] has led many firms to rely almost exclusively on temporary workers.

The first and second columns of Table 3.8 show the SEZ and national unionization rates. Overall, union participation in zones (as reported by the surveyed firms) is somewhat lower than the national rates, with the exception of Senegal and Bangladesh. Within the African programs, union membership is particularly low in the Kenyan and Nigerian programs. This is perhaps not surprising, given the historical legal treatment of unions in these zone programs. The Nigerian free zone law prohibits strikes and lockouts for a period of 10 years after a company begins its activities in a given EPZ. The law also states that employer-employee disputes are not to be handled by trade unions but rather by the authorities who manage these zones.[23] In Kenya, until 2005, workers in the EPZs were prohibited from joining unions or engaging in collective bargaining.

A wide range of negative work quality and social consequences are common across many of the zones under study, including the following:

- *Lack of job advancement opportunities*: A common problem across most zone programs is the lack of mobility of production workers into supervisory positions. This is particularly true for women, who dominate the production workforce in many SEZ companies but are poorly represented in supervisory and managerial positions (see below).
- *Difficult work hours and shift structures*: In Honduras, for example, workers in the *maquila* factories typically work 11–12 hours a day, four days in a row, before having four days of rest. This scheme has led to some adverse social implications as many *maquila* workers, lacking a living wage, take a second job for the days they have off.
- *Lack of social infrastructure*: Most of the large zones locate in or near major metropolitan areas but attract their workforces from distant rural communities. This has led to large-scale migration in some countries (e.g., Honduras and Lesotho) and put significant pressure on the already weak social infrastructure, particularly regarding the provision of as decent housing, education, and health services. It has also contributed to health problems such as HIV (in Lesotho, an estimated 40% of the apparel workforce is affected by HIV).

Perhaps the single biggest concern identified across the zones is poor enforcement of agreed-upon labor standards, working conditions, and pay and benefits. Although most zone programs have made significant progress in the past decade in terms of meeting international standards on a de jure basis, de facto enforcement lags considerably in many programs.

Gender-Differentiated Impacts

Several studies of employment in SEZs have found that firms located inside zones employ more women than firms in the rest of the country (ILO-UNCTC 1988; Kusago and Tzannatos 1998; Cling and Letilly 2001; Milberg and Amengual 2008). In this regard, zones have created an important avenue for young women to enter the formal economy at better wages than in agriculture and domestic service, their main alternative occupations (ILO 2003). Table 3.9 presents 2005 and 2006 data on the share of female workers across a number of major global SEZ programs.[24]

The results from the SEZ survey support these findings across most of the 10 countries studied (Figure 3.13). With the notable exception of Ghana and Nigeria, the share of the workforce that is female is larger in the SEZ firms than in firms in the rest of the nonagricultural economy. In most cases, the relative female share of employment in the zones is at least 50 percent higher than outside the zones; in Senegal and Bangladesh,

Table 3.9   Share of Female Workers in Economic Zones, 2005–06

Madagascar	71%
Mauritius	62%
Malawi	51%
Jordan	33%
Morocco	20%
Sri Lanka	77%
Korea	70%
Malaysia	54%
Philippines	74%
El Salvador	85%
Guatemala	70%
Nicaragua	90%
Honduras	75%
Mexico	60%
Dominican Republic	53%

Source: Boyenge (2007).

Figure 3.13   Share of Females in the SEZ Workforce Compared with the Overall Nonagricultural Workforce

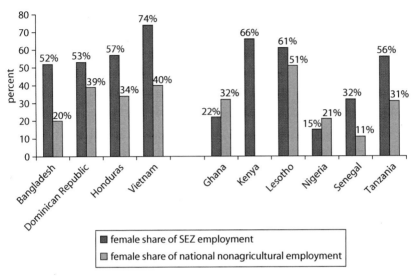

female share of SEZ employment

female share of national nonagricultural employment

Source: SEZ surveys.

SEZ employment is more than twice as female-intensive as employment in the nonagricultural economy overall. In Senegal and Nigeria, female participation in the overall nonagricultural economy is substantially lower than in the other countries surveyed.

These findings are broadly in line with the sector specialization in the zones. In fact, the link between female workers and SEZs is not a direct one. SEZs do not attract female workers per se, but they do attract firms in sectors whose basis of competition is highly dependent on the available supply of low-wage, flexible, and unskilled/semiskilled workers, a set of requirements that often results in female workers. These firms are most likely attracted to economic zones in part because they (1) minimize costs (e.g., through tax incentives and administrative efficiencies); (2) provide access to serviced land and more reliable infrastructure; and (3) reduce the investment requirement, lowering risk and providing operational and strategic flexibility. So it is probably more appropriate to refer to sectors and tasks that are gender-concentrated rather than zones. Although female share of the labor force for a particular industry varies by country, some general patterns become clear by pooling the data from all 10 countries in the survey (see Table 3.10).

Table 3.10   Female Share of SEZ Labor Force, by Main Sector

Garments	61%
Electronics	59%
Other manufacturing	43%
Textiles	36%
Food and beverages	35%
Metal and metal products	31%
Wood, paper, and wood products	22%
Chemicals	14%
Services	34%

Source: SEZ investor surveys.

Indeed, evidence from countries such as Costa Rica (Jenkins 2005) and the Dominican Republic (USAID 2007) shows that as zones move away from a concentration on the garment sector or even upgrade within the sector, the gender mix usually changes toward much greater male participation. This change is driven by changes in production technology that are not accompanied by an equal upgrade in the skills of female workers, as well as the competitive pressure that results when males are attracted to previously overlooked sectors by the higher wages prevalent inside SEZs.

Another important issue is the extent to which female workers have opportunities to move up to supervisory and management positions. Outside the zones, gender bias in relation to certain tasks or positions often undermines the potential of female workers to move up the ladder. Figure 3.14 compares the share of female workers in the surveyed zone programs with the share of female managers. With the exception of Ghana, there is a clear gap in the number of females at the managerial level in SEZs relative to their participation in the overall workforce. The largest gap is in Bangladesh, where female workers represent more than half the workforce but account for only 14 percent of managers. The African zone programs show, on average, much lower ratios of overall to management staff, but we do not know whether this reflects less bias in the firms based in Africa. It may simply be sector differentiation and the fact that the African zone programs are, overall, less reliant on the garment sector. However, the ratio in Kenya, which has a strong garment sector, is substantial; while in Lesotho, which is dominated by the garment sector, 44 percent of all managers are reported to be female.

Other issues that relate specifically to female workers in the zones are the structure of shift work, the availability of onsite medical care, and

Figure 3.14   Share of Management Positions in SEZs Held by Females

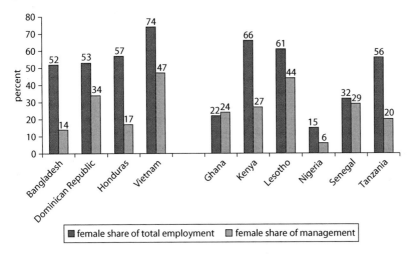

Source: SEZ investor surveys.

how employers address pregnancy and family-related issues. (See Chapter 7 for details on the policies and practices implemented in the zones under study.)

Conclusions

This chapter has shown that, taken as a whole, the African zones included in this study have underperformed, against their own goals and in terms of their relative progress against objective measures of success. However, the data show heterogeneity among the countries. Ghana's free zone program has seen a steady increase in investment and exports, although the main beneficiaries have been capital- and resource-intensive firms based outside the flagship Tema zone. And the rapid growth of the apparel sector in Lesotho cannot be dismissed, although sustaining export growth in the country will likely rely on diversifying market reach in the garment sector (beyond the heavy reliance on the U.S. market under AGOA) and attracting a wider range of light industrial activities into the country.

Most African zones are in the very early stages of their development and in most cases there is some evidence of progress: growth rates since 2000, although from a low base, are fairly strong across most zones. It is true that even highly successful zone programs have usually taken 5–10 years to settle in before beginning to achieve rapid growth. However, assuming that the African zones will fall into this pattern eventually would be a mistake. The evidence presented in this chapter suggests that, rather than moving toward an exponential growth path, African zones may already have peaked and may be starting to experience slowing growth and stagnation (with some exceptions, particularly Ghana and possibly Tanzania, whose program is not yet fully established). As this chapter has shown, a slowdown is evident across investment and exports, and is particularly acute in terms of employment.

Perhaps most importantly, none of the African zones appears to have made any significant progress toward taking advantage of the dynamic potential of economic zones as an instrument of sustainable structural transformation. None of the African countries in the study have managed to achieve a significant, lasting change in export structure, in stark contrast to the four non-African countries. Moreover, African zones—and, in fact, all the zone programs included in this study—are still failing to provide good quality, upgradeable job opportunities, although there have been some improvements.

This leaves us with two important questions: (1) Can the performance gap we observe in the African economic zones be addressed within the zone programs and in the related trade and economic policy arenas? and (2) If so, how? If the answer to the first question is no, then the investment and opportunity cost of pursuing zone programs as policy is wasted, and they should be abandoned in favor of alternative policy actions. Whether the performance gap can be addressed depends on the main reasons behind it. On the basis of the evidence presented in this chapter, three possible hypotheses for the gap might be considered: (1) bad timing or, more specifically, a missed window of opportunity; (2) a fundamental competitiveness problem; and (3) poor planning and implementation. If the performance gap can be explained by timing, economic zones may be an insufficient instrument in the current environment. If the issue is a fundamental competitiveness gap in the African economies, economic zones may or may not play a role, depending on whether the gap is comprehensive or sector- or task-specific. If African countries can achieve a competitive advantage in another sector or task and economic zones can play a relevant role in facilitating or sustaining that advantage, then zones would still be relevant. Finally, if the performance gap is primarily a function of poor planning and management, the focus should be less on policy and more on implementation of the existing zone programs.

On the question of timing and whether African countries have missed a window of opportunity in which zones could have played a catalytic role, we put forth several arguments to suggest that this may be one part of the story. The successful economic zone programs in Latin America and East Asia were established before the rapid growth in global trade and investment spurred, in part, by the spread of global production networks (GPNs) during the 1980s and 1990s. GPNs tended to make significant use of economic zones as locations for investment, particularly in labor-intensive assembly and light manufacturing. In the absence of economic zones to provide infrastructure and a policy environment conducive to GPN investment, African countries may have missed a real opportunity; by the time zone programs were launched in countries like Nigeria, Ghana, and Tanzania, many of the nodes of production networks were already well-established. Moreover, by the late 1990s, China and other East Asian producers had become major global manufacturing forces, with labor costs and economies of scale with which few African countries could compete. Finally, the expiration of the MFA at the end of 2004 dramatically changed the playing field in the global garment sector (where economic zone investment has traditionally been concentrated), making it much more difficult for African countries to attract the type of large-scale investment that fueled the growth of economic zones elsewhere in the world.

But this argument about timing is limited to a narrow conception of economic zones as bases for low-wage assembly operations. So, while it may explain in part why African zones have not been successful in traditional EPZ activities, it should not preclude the use of zones in sectors such as agriprocessing and services, among others, which are now in earlier stages of significant globalization of trade and investment. Newly established zones in the Middle East, South Asia, and Latin America are growing on the basis of these sectors rather than traditional assembly. For Africa, then, the question may be less about timing per se and more about comparative advantage and competitiveness.

Competitiveness—at least in labor-intensive manufacturing sectors—is clearly a problem for the African zones. As shown in Figure 3.15, wages and benefits in the lowest cost African country in our survey (Kenya) are 15 percent higher than in Vietnam and 2.5 times higher than in Bangladesh. Labor costs in the African zones remain much lower than those in the Latin American zones in the study; however, productivity lags far behind that of the Dominican Republic and Honduras. Moreover, investors based in zones in these countries have established a strong track record of serving the U.S. market: They have access to specific services and materials inputs (including textiles) in the region, and benefit from a location that enables them to serve the U.S. market quickly. None of the

Figure 3.15   Unskilled Labor Costs (US$/month)

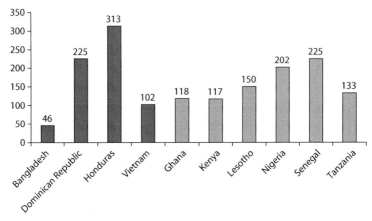

Source: Author's calculations based on data from SEZ investor surveys.

African zone programs surveyed have similar access to the benefits of a true local industry cluster, and they face significant challenges of remoteness from markets, which are generally aggravated by poorly performing internal and gateway transport systems.

These findings are in line with much recent research on Africa's poor manufacturing competitiveness (World Economic Forum 2009; Collier and Page 2009). The factors that contribute to the competitiveness gap are many, including high transport and transaction costs, and high costs imposed by risk. These costs add to the already high wage bill and price African producers out of global markets. They also contribute—along with a poor policy environment, limited local competition, and protection—to raising the cost of living and so inflating wages, creating a vicious circle.

Addressing the competitiveness challenge will require a comprehensive approach that goes well beyond what economic zones can deliver. Some (cf. Collier and Page 2009) argue that economic zones can play a role in improving manufacturing competitiveness by creating the conditions for achieving scale economies, allowing some African industry sectors to reach thresholds after which benefits of scale can be realized. However, the question remains as to whether African zones can be more successful in the short and medium term by focusing on sectors in which they are in a position to develop competitive advantage. The evidence presented in this chapter suggests that, in many countries, will mean adding value to regionally available natural resources, including minerals and, most importantly, agriculture.

This brings us to the third hypothesis—that the performance gap is a function of ineffective strategy and planning (e.g., focusing on sectors in which the country lacks a comparative advantage) and poor implementation of the zone program in terms of regulations and operating practices, infrastructure, and service delivery. These issues were not addressed in this chapter but have certainly contributed to the success of many zone programs in Asia (through a strong developmental state) and Latin America (through a dynamic private sector). To assess the effect of planning and implementation on performance, we first need to determine which of these factors influence zone outcomes, and how. We turn to these questions in the next chapter.

Notes

1. Gross exports relative to total manufactured exports.

2. Both the Liberian and Senegalese programs became dormant and are in the process of being overhauled and relaunched.

3. Data in columns 2 and 3 are the average over the period 2005–2007.

4. In the case of Senegal, data were made available only on the number of newly established EFE firms each year; no data were made available on the number of firms that are operating at any one time; thus, the actual number of active firms is somewhat smaller than the number reported here.

5. In some other cases—such as Mauritius, Honduras, and El Salvador—local investors played a critical role from the start, catalyzing FDI.

6. The data shown are percentages of firms, not of investment value. The difference can be significant; for example, according to data from the Ministry of Planning and Investment, local investors accounted for more than half of all firms in the industrial zones in 2009 but only 26 percent of investment by value.

7. One exception is the share of local versus foreign ownership in Vietnam, which is based on 2009 data from the Ministry of Planning and Investment that takes into account firms in both export processing zones and industrial zones. The surveys were carried out only with firms in the export processing zones, which are almost exclusively foreign-controlled.

8. The data shown are percentages of firms, not of investment value. The difference can be significant; for example, according to data from the Ministry of Planning and Investment, local investors accounted for more than half of all firms in the industrial zones in 2009 but only 26 percent of investment by value.

9. In fact, some of this activity is actually re-exports: According to data from the Ghana Free Zones Board, in many years, exports from the free zone program are actually higher than reported production.

10. Unfortunately, we have insufficient time series data on Senegal and Nigeria to include them in the analysis, and the Tanzania program has too little history to be useful for this analysis. It is worth noting that based on what we know anecdotally about the Nigeria and Senegal programs, had their data been available, they would likely strongly support our conclusions.

11. Note that we have data on Lesotho only from 2000.

12. Data based on results from firm surveys (weighted average).

13. Sectoral share of exports are author's calculations based on data from UN COMTRADE. "Year 1" represents the year in which the SEZ program was established in the country; thus, "Year 5" would be five years after the establishment of the program and "Year –5" would be five years before the establishment of the program. Data are available only from 1976 through 2008. For programs established in the 1970s or earlier, no "pre-SEZ" periods are available to study; for programs established later, "Year 10," "Year 20," or "Year 30" data may not be available.

14. However, the global financial crisis has caused widespread and steep decline throughout all FZ manufacturing sectors. During the first six months of 2009, exports of apparel and shoes continued to decline (at –18% and –12%, respectively); even faster decline was experienced in jewelry (–59%) and electronics (–51%).

15. Wages and benefits are based on the average reported by firms in the surveys undertaken as part of this study. They are converted to a "PPP wage" based on a 2009 PPP deflator (Source: World Development Indicators).

16. The concept of a "living wage" is defined in various ways; according to the ILO, it refers to wages sufficient to meet the basic living needs of an average-sized family in a particular economy.

17. Before the inclusion of benefits and the PPP adjustment.

18. This exemption was not designed specifically to protect zone-based firms but should benefit many of them.

19. Refers to unionization rate reported by exporter firms in the most recent World Bank Enterprise Survey, unless otherwise indicated.

20. Data for Onne Oil and Gas Free Zone; no data available from Calabar Free Zone.

21. Average wages reported for unskilled workers in the zones is 13 percent below the level established for manufacturing workers in 2009. However, recent legislation allows for a lower level of minimum wage for exporters that meet certain requirements on export intensity and employment. Relative to this level, average zone wages are 60 percent higher.

22. Firms operating in the free zone were given extra flexibility to hire workers on temporary contracts for a period of up to five years, to avoid the rigidities in hiring and firing that are in place to protect permanent workers.

23. EPZ Act, Article 4(e).

24. Note that the female share of the workforce as reported here from the ILO's database (data from 2005–2006) is higher in some cases than the share reported to us in our firm surveys (from 2009). For example, in Honduras, our surveys indicate that 57 percent of the workforce is female, compared with 75 percent reported by ILO; in Bangladesh, our survey indicates only 52 percent female compared with 85 percent in the ILO database. However, the ILO database includes the huge workforce in the industrial zones outside the EPZ regime.

References

Aggarwal, A. 2005. "Performance of Export Processing Zones: A Comparative Analysis of India, Sri Lanka and Bangladesh." Indian Council for Research on International Economic Relations, New Delhi.

Arce-Alpazar, G., R. Monge-Gonzalez, and J. Rosales-Tijinero. 2005. "Cost-Benefit Analysis of the Free Trade Zone System: The Impact of Foreign Direct Investment in Costa Rica." *OAS Trade, Growth, and Competitiveness Studies* (January).

Boyenge, J.P.S. 2007. *ILO Database on Export Processing Zones, Revised.* Geneva: ILO.

Cling, J. P., and G. Letilly. 2001. "Export Processing Zones: A Threatened Instrument for Global Economy Insertion?" DT/2001/17. Developpement et Insertion Internationale (DIAL), Paris.

Collier, P., and J. Page. 2009. *Industrial Development Report 2009.* Vienna: UNIDO.

FIAS. 2008. "Special Economic Zones. Performance, Lessons Learned, and Implications for Zone Development." World Bank, Washington, DC.

Ge, W. 1999. "The Dynamics of Export-Processing Zones." Discussion paper no. 144. UNCTAD, Geneva.

ICFTU (International Conference of Free Trade Unions). 2003. "Export Processing Zones: Symbols of Exploitation and a Development Dead End." ICFTU, Brussels.

ILO (International Labour Organisation). 2003. "Employment and Social Policy in Respect of Export Processing Zones." ILO, Geneva.

ILO/United Nations Centre on Transnational Corporations. 1988. "Economic and Social Effects of Multinational Enterprises in Export Processing Zones." ILO, Geneva.

Jayanthakumaran, K. 2003. "Benefit-Cost Appraisals of Export Processing Zones: A Survey of the Literature." *Development Policy Review* 21(1): 51–65.

Jenkins, M. 2005. "Economic and Social Effects of Export Processing Zones in Costa Rica." Working Paper 97. ILO, Geneva.

Kaplinsky, R. 1993. "Export Processing Zones in the Dominican Republic: Transforming Manufactures into Commodities." *World Development* 21(11): 1851–1865.

Kusago, T., and Z. Tzannatos. 1998. "Export Processing Zones: A Review in Need of Update." SP Discussion Paper 9802. World Bank, Washington, DC.

Milberg, W., and M. Amengual. 2008. "Economic Development and Working Conditions in Export Processing Zones: A Survey of Trends." ILO, Geneva.

Rolfe, R. R., D. P. Woodward, and B. Kagira. 2003. "Footloose and Tax Free: Incentive Preferences in Kenyan Export Processing Zones." Paper presented at the Biennial Conference of the Economic Society of South Africa, Somerset West, South Africa, September 17–19.

Sadni-Jallab, M., and E. Blanco de Armas. 2002." A Review of the Role and Impact of Export Processing Zones in World Trade: The Case of Mexico. Post-Print halshs-00178444_v1, HAL.

Schrank, A. 2008. "Export Processing Zones in the Dominican Republic: Schools or Stopgaps?" *World Development*, 36(8):1381–1397.

UNCTAD. 2003. *World Investment Report 2002: Transnational Corporations and Export Competitiveness.* United Nations, Geneva.

USAID (United States Agency for International Development). 2007. *Dinamicas recientes de la produccion, el comercio y el empleo en las zonas francas de exportacion de la Republica Dominicana.* USAID Greater Access to Trade Expansion Project. Arlington, VA: Development and Training Services, Inc.

U.S. Office of Textiles and Apparel. 2010. Major Shippers Report. Accessed via: http://otexa.ita.doc.gov

Warr, P. 1989. "Export Processing Zones: The Economics of Enclave Manufacturing." *The World Bank Research Observer* 9(1): 65–88.

Watson, P. L. 2001. "Export Processing Zones: Has Africa Missed the Boat? Not Yet!" Africa Region Working Paper Series No. 17. World Bank, Washington, DC.

Willmore, L. 1995. "Export Processing Zones in the Dominican Republic: A Comment on Kaplinsky." *World Development* 23(3): 529–535.

World Economic Forum. 2009. *Global Competitiveness Report 2009.* Geneva: World Economic Forum.

Zhao, M., and T. Farole. 2010. "Partnership Arrangements in China-Singapore (Suzhou) Industrial Park." Mimeo (March). World Bank, Washington, DC.

CHAPTER 4

Which Factors Matter for the Performance of SEZs?

Introduction

As discussed in Chapter 2, debate has raged for some time over the effectiveness of economic zones as a policy instrument, and many recommendations have been offered on whether and how zones should be implemented. However, much of the advice about SEZs has not been grounded in strong evidence, either in support of broad conclusions or on the specific direction policy should take. A wide range of factors may determine whether or not an SEZ program is successful; in addition to the investment climate, the incentives offered to investors, and the quality of program design and implementation, these factors may include broader issues such as wages and productivity, trade preferences, market prospects, government policies, and the macroeconomic environment.

But which of these factors matter? Answering this question requires some comparative, large-sample, quantitative analysis to test hypotheses and complement the existing anecdotal evidence. But SEZs are notorious for failing to track and publish consistent and comprehensive data, which has severely restricted the prospects for rigorous quantitative analysis (Kusago and Tzannatos 1998; Cling and Letilly 2001). Limited data exist on the structures, practices, and performance of economic zones around the world, and most research has been limited to single-country and a few comparative case studies. Given the large investments and high opportunity costs[1] of SEZ programs, however, a better understanding the factors that contribute to success is very important. Moreover, the increasing competition for foreign direct investment in the wake of the global economic crisis may accentuate the differences between SEZs that perform well and those that do not. For African countries—in need of FDI to contribute to industrialization, technology access, and learning— getting SEZ investments right is critical.

This chapter aims to contribute to overcoming the research gap on the factors that determine SEZ performance by assessing the relationship between SEZ program outcomes and several factors, including the investment climate, wages, incentives, location, management, and market access. It is based on a database of SEZs in more than 70 mainly low- and middle-income countries, complemented by an in-depth survey of SEZ investors in 10 countries with a specific focus on the Africa region (see Appendix C for details on the methodology). While data limitations restrict the analysis to simple correlations, the findings are clear. The investment climate in SEZs—specifically, infrastructure and customs clearance—is strongly correlated with SEZ program outcomes as measured by exports, investment, and employment. But the wider national investment climate and competitiveness are also strongly correlated with SEZ outcomes, as is the scale of the accessible local market. In contrast, the traditional sources of competitiveness for export processing zones— low wages, trade preferences, and fiscal incentives—are generally not found to be correlated to SEZ outcomes. We also find no quantitative evidence of a systematic difference in outcomes between publicly and privately run SEZ programs in our large-country sample.

These findings suggest that the emerging policy consensus that recommends focusing on the SEZ investment climate is well-founded. And it underscores the importance of a comprehensive approach to the investment climate, with particular attention to delivering high-quality infrastructure (especially reliable power) and facilitating efficient import and export transactions, along with regulatory and business licensing issues. The findings also suggest that governments must focus their efforts beyond the gates of the zones to ensure that wider aspects of the national business environment are also addressed.

The Investment Climate, FDI, and Trade

The investment climate describes the risks, opportunities, and transaction costs involved in investing in and operating a business. It is determined by a complex interaction among laws, policies, and their implementation. Firms decide where to invest, how and how much to invest, and how to operate based (explicitly or implicitly) on the perceived and experienced investment climate, including such factors as finance (access and cost), infrastructure (cost, availability, and reliability), labor (cost and quality), the regulatory environment, taxation, corruption, and the wider policy environment. These investment climate factors also determine export outcomes, both indirectly through their impact on FDI and directly through the way they shape the opportunities and constraints of domestic producers. In export-led growth models, FDI tends to play a particularly crucial role in catalyzing export activity, so the relationship among the investment climate, investment, and exports is strong.

FDI is often categorized by its objectives as either market-seeking or efficiency-seeking (Helpman 1984; Markusen 1984). For market-seeking (horizontal) FDI, investment climate certainly matters; however, factors such as market access and the size of the market opportunity that the investor seeks to exploit are critical determinants that may act as a counterbalance. This explains why large markets like Brazil and China attract large FDI despite not ranking highly on many indicators of investment climate. A similar situation may hold when investors seek access to precious material inputs or particularly low-cost or high-skilled labor. But in most cases, efficiency-seeking (vertical) FDI, which aims to make use of a country's factors of production to establish a platform for regional or global exports, is strongly determined by the investment climate.

The relationship between investment, particularly FDI, and the broad investment climate has been widely studied. The literature linking investment climate to trade and investment outcomes is extensive, and the findings show consistently that a better investment climate is associated with higher levels of productivity, exports, and investment.[2] Much of the empirical research equates the investment climate with institutions; for example, the quality of the bureaucracy, levels of corruption, and meta-institutions such as property rights and the rule of law (Knack and Keefer 1995; Acemoglu et al. 2001). For example, Benassy-Quere et al. (2007) find an association between good institutions and FDI. A number of studies show that higher levels of corruption are associated with lower levels of FDI than would otherwise be expected (Drabzek and Payne 1999; Smarzynska and Wei 2000; Wei 2000). Stein and Daude (2001) use a broad mix of institutional indicators and conclude that good institutions have a positive effect on FDI.

Another set of literature focuses more on what can be called "micro features" of the investment climate, including infrastructure, trade facilitation, and business regulations. Empirical studies in this area have tended to focus on trade rather than investment as the outcome, although at least for vertical FDI, one can assume a strong correlation. Djankov et al. (2006) highlight the importance of trade and transport facilitation on trade outcomes, particularly for time-sensitive products, such as those that are physically perishable or operating in global just-in-time production networks. Recently, Portugal-Perez and Wilson (2010) assessed aggregate indicators of hard and soft infrastructure in 101 developing countries and found a strong correlation between infrastructure quality and export outcomes. Eifert et al. (2005) show the effect of investment climate on firm-level productivity and exports in Africa. Drawing on firm-level surveys in eight developing countries, Dollar et al. (2004) find that the investment climate—as defined by customs clearance times, infrastructure reliability, and access to financial services—is associated with firm-level productivity and export propensity as well as with inward FDI flows. Finally, studies of tax rates and incentives (Head et al. 1999; Wei 2000; Bobonis and Shatz 2007) suggest that while lower tax rates are associated with higher levels of FDI, incentives have a limited effect.

The findings from this broad research support the strong relationship between the investment climate and firm productivity. This translates into trade outcomes, although foreign investors tend to outperform domestic producers in export markets even in poor investment climates (Eifert et al. 2005). While the relationship may be somewhat weaker in terms of attracting FDI, the research to date suggests that the investment climate is a critical determinant of location for multinational investors. This presents a challenge for low-income countries, whose investment climates are typically much poorer than those in middle- and high-income countries; who have limited resources and capacity to quickly implement major investment climate reforms; and who face political economy barriers to such reforms. It is an even greater challenge in regions such as Africa, where markets are mostly too small and poor to attract market-seeking FDI. In such environments, targeted FDI regimes—like SEZs—are seen as one instrument for overcoming these constraints.

SEZs and the Investment Climate

Several specific aspects of the investment climate are usually targeted for improvement inside special economic zones. First, SEZs are designed to overcome *serviced land and infrastructure constraints* that may hinder investment in the national economy by providing investors with access to long-term leases, prebuilt factory shells, and reliable utilities (electricity, water, and telecommunications). Second, SEZs usually aim to improve the overall *administrative environment*, particularly with regard to the procedures required to register a business, acquire licenses, obtain visas and work permits, and access key services, such as utilities and construction. SEZs often establish "single window" or "one-stop" services, in which the SEZ authority is the single point of contact to arrange the delivery of these administrative services, coordinating with the relevant government agencies. Finally, an important component of the administrative services offered in zones is a privileged and expedited *customs administration*. This often involves stationing customs officers inside or at the gate of the free zone to offer onsite clearance to speed up import and export procedures. It is usually combined with other privileges, including the ability to move and hold goods in bond, and the removal of financial requirements for bonded and duty-free inputs.[3]

But despite the relative orthodoxy in the approach to SEZs—at least in terms of addressing these issues—it is far from clear which, if any, of these factors has a bearing on the success of SEZ programs in meeting short-term objectives of attracting investment and longer term objectives of generating quality employment and sustainable, diversified exports. Empirical studies of SEZs have been limited primarily by the poor availability of consistent, reliable data (Kusago and Tzannatos 1998; Cling and Letilly 2001). And most quantitative analysis has focused on single country or small-sample analysis of the welfare contribution of SEZs, mainly through cost-benefit studies (c.f. Warr 1989; Jayanthakumaran 2003). Johansson and Nilsson (1997) test the catalytic contribution of SEZs on the export supply response of domestic producers, using a sophisticated cross-country analysis; but while their conclusions provide important evidence on the potential role of SEZs, they do not discuss the factors that contribute to the observed outcomes. Similarly, recent research by Tyler and Negrete (2009)—which provides one of the first large-scale, cross-country quantitative studies on SEZs—focuses on the macro impact of zones on GDP growth but does not contribute to a better understanding of what determines how well zones perform.

A few studies in the past decade have provided some initial insight on these questions. Schrank (2001) conducts a cross-country quantitative analysis testing the variation of national SEZ outcomes against measures of national institutions the size of the local market. He concludes that both measures play an important role in determining the success of SEZs and their ability to act as catalysts for industrial upgrading and economic transformation. Rolfe et al. (2003) use a survey-based experiment conducted with investors in Kenya's export processing zones to determine investor incentive preferences. The findings suggest the importance of upfront corporate tax holidays and infrastructure to investors over longer term lower taxes, location, and local market access. Whether this expressed preference translates into improved SEZ performance in terms of exports, employment, and economic transformation, however, is untested; indeed, it conflicts with most of the outcomes-based findings in the FDI literature. Finally, in a study covering India, Bangladesh, and Sri Lanka, Aggarwal (2005) finds that infrastructure, good governance, and the overall national investment climate contribute to the success of SEZs.

We follow in the vein of the research of these three papers, particularly Aggarwal (2005), and attempt to identify the factors that may play an important role in determining how well SEZ programs deliver on their aims of attracting investment, facilitating exports, and generating employment.

Hypothesis, Data, and Approach

Hypothesis

The aim of this research is to identify the factors that affect the outcome of SEZ programs and, specifically, to test the hypothesis that the investment climate inside SEZs is an important determinant of success. We limit our choice of outcomes to three main proximate results: exports, investment, and employment. These are our dependent variables. The objectives of most SEZ programs go well beyond these to embrace dynamic outcomes such as technology absorption, skills development, industrial upgrading, and economic diversification. However, most of these objectives can only be observed in the medium and long term, and SEZs are only be one of many factors that contribute to achieving these aims. Given the limited data availability in terms of both country observations and time period, testing for success against these wider objectives is not possible.

We take as a starting point for our analysis the general export platform FDI model developed by Ekholm et al. (2007), a three-region model (two identical large, high-cost countries in the North and one small, low-cost country in the South) designed to analyze the conditions under which a firm would establish export platform production in the South to serve either its home market or a third-country market. In their basic model, firms in the North choose to establish plants in the South as global export platforms when the South has a large cost advantage and trade costs are low. In our case, we take the export platform situation as given: We simplify the use of SEZs in this case to assume that all investment is for the purpose of export platform production (i.e., it is efficiency-seeking rather than market-seeking). We are concerned not with how conditions motivate firms to choose export platform production but rather, given the choice of export platform production, what conditions in the potential host countries would lead a firm to choose one location over another.

On the basis of this model, we assume that these factors are principally the cost of production and the cost of trade. But for the purposes of understanding why one SEZ location would be chosen over another, we also assess the factors that may contribute to production and trade costs. Here we make use of Aggarwal's (2005) model, which hypothesizes specifically on SEZ performance: We assume that SEZ performance is a function of the extent to which the SEZ minimizes production and trade costs for firms based in the zone (for all potential global markets served from the zone). As per Aggarwal, in our empirical analysis, we test the impact of our independent variables directly on SEZ program outcomes, not on the performance of firms within the SEZs. We do this, in part, because we lack sufficiently detailed firm-level data, but also because it might not be possible to accurately judge the success of an SEZ program on the performance of the individual firms operating within it.[4]

We identify four categories of independent variables that we hypothesize contribute to explaining the performance of an SEZ program:

1. *Traditional factors*—the trio of fiscal incentives, low wages, and trade preferences. These factors are the basis on which most EPZ programs have been designed and positioned. The first two affect a firm's cost of producing (directly or indirectly), while the third affects trade costs.
2. *Zone investment climate*—the infrastructure and administrative environment for firms operating in the zones, which will affect net production costs.
3. *National investment climate*—the infrastructure, administrative, and governance environment at the national level, which will also affect net production costs.
4. *Market access*—the position of the SEZs relative to national, regional, and global markets, which will affect trade costs.

We also assess the management structure of the zone; specifically, the existence of public or privately operated zones. This is slightly outside the model, but given the debate over public versus private provision of zones, we include it to test whether zone management has any effect on outcomes.

Of course, other factors may shape SEZ program outcomes; for example, global macroeconomic dynamics and political economy factors that may not show up in the measures of national investment climate. Another factor we would like to have tested if better data had been available is the impact of local agglomerations or clusters.

Data

The empirical analysis relies on a two-stage approach and uses two datasets: (1) a database of global SEZs, and (2) primary survey data from 10 countries. We will refer to these as the "large-sample" and "small-sample" datasets, respectively.

The large-sample dataset of global SEZs was developed during the second half of 2008 by the World Bank's International Trade Department. This dataset is based on the most recent version of the ILO-EPZ database (Boyenge 2007), complemented with data obtained through extensive secondary research . During the second half of 2008, a detailed zone-level survey was e-mailed to the national authority responsible for SEZ programs in all the countries identified as having had one. This survey asked questions related to zone outcome variables as well as zone location, sectoral mix, ownership and management (public versus private), basic infrastructure, incentives, wages, and labor force profiles. The response rate to the supplemental survey was only 5 percent, which severely limits the availability and value of the dataset and introduces a serious risk of sample bias. Most importantly, the lack of data on the SEZ-level investment climate makes this dataset unsuitable for testing our main hypothesis. Thus, no variables that rely on data from the large-scale survey have been used in the analysis presented in this chapter. All data from the large-sample database refer only to those countries covered by the ILO dataset, with supplemental data collected through secondary research. (See Appendix B for a list of the 77 countries included in the dataset.) The dataset broadly reflects the overall global mix of countries in terms of income levels, with a slight overrepresentation of middle-income countries (53% of the dataset countries are classified as middle income compared with 46% of countries globally; 49% of the dataset countries are classified as low income compared with 42% of countries globally). In terms of regional coverage, the dataset is somewhat skewed toward

Latin America (30%) and Africa (23%), while East Asia (10%) is somewhat underrepresented.

The second source (the small-sample dataset) is based on enterprise-level surveys conducted during the second half of 2009 specifically for this project with investors in SEZs in the six African countries and four non-African countries covered in this report. (Details on the methodology are covered in Chapter 3 and in Appendix C.) The surveys provide a profile of the nature of investment in the zones and the expectations of investors, then explore issues that may determine the extent of success of SEZ programs. While the results from the analysis using the first dataset might be generalizable for global SEZs in developing countries, results based on the second dataset are not, because of the bias toward low-income African countries and the small sample size. (Again, Appendix C provides details of the surveys, including sample selection, completion rates, dates, and locations where the surveys were carried out.)

Data on our dependent variables—*exports, investment,* and *employment*—are from both datasets (see Table 4.1).

Data on *wages* come from the survey results; for the large-sample dataset, we take the log of GDP per person employed as a proxy for average wages. Trade *preferences* are based on the Market Access Tariff Trade Restrictiveness Index (MA-TTRI) available from World Trade Indicators (WTI). For the small-sample dataset, *incentives* are based on an analysis of the relative benefits of the corporate tax incentive offered in the SEZ program (see Figure 5.7); for the large-sample dataset, we take the relative corporate tax break given.

Our variable for zone management (*private*) is measured as the share of zones in each country that are privately operated (available from the dataset).

Zone investment climate variables are available only in the small sample dataset and derive from the surveys. They include an *infrastructure* variable, which measures the monthly downtime caused by electricity outages (taken both as a nominal measure and relative to the downtime experienced by firms outside the SEZs[5]). A *customs* variable measures the average clearance time reported for imports and exports by sea; again, this is taken both nominally and relative to non-SEZ-based exporters. A *logistics* variable measures respondents' perceptions of the logistics environment based on several factors, modeled from the World Bank's Logistics Performance Index (World Bank 2009). A *setup* variable measures respondents' indications of the total days required to establish their operations in

Table 4.1 Summary of Variables Used in the Analysis

Variable	Description	Source	# observations
export	Log of 2008 (or latest year) exports from the national SEZ program overall	Large-sample dataset	55
invest	Log of cumulative investments in the national SEZ program in 2008 (or latest available)	Large-sample dataset	49
employ	Log of 2008 (or latest year) employment in the national SEZ program overall	Large-sample dataset	65
incent1	Ordinal code based on nature and extent of corporate tax incentive offered	Large-sample dataset	64
wage2	GDP per person employed	World Development Indicators	58
tradepref	MA-TTRI	World Trade Indicators	58
private	Share of zones that are privately run	Large-sample dataset	52
gciscore	Global Competitiveness Index score	World Economic Forum "Global Competitiveness Report 2009"	59
dbrank	Global rank in Doing Business Indicators (overall rank)	World Bank "Doing Business 2010"	73
wgiscore	Sum of World Governance Indicators scores across all categories	World Development Indicators	77
fdiattract	FDI Attractiveness Index score	UNCTAD	64
remote	Gravity model calculation based on distance and market size of potential trading partners	Calculated internally based on datasets from CEPII (www.cepii.fr)	72
mktsize	Log of GDP (in US$ purchasing power parity)	World Development Indicators	71
gdpcap	Log of GDP (in US$ purchasing power parity, Atlas Method)	World Development Indicators	71

access	Share of SEZ sales allowed to the local market	Large-sample dataset	75
years	Number of years since SEZ program established (defined as the year in which the SEZ law was implemented)	Large-sample dataset	60
infranom	Monthly downtime resulting from electricity outages	Small-sample dataset	10
infrarel	Percentage reduction in monthly downtime from electricity outages in SEZs versus the national economy	Small-sample dataset	10
customsnom	Simple average export + import clearance time by sea	Small-sample dataset	10
customsrel	Percentage reduction in average export + import clearance time by sea in SEZs versus the national economy	Small-sample dataset	9
logistics	Average rating of logistics performance from World Bank's Logistics Performance Index	Small-sample dataset	10
setup	Number of days it takes to set up a company in SEZ from application to final operating license	Small-sample dataset	10
onestop	Number of respondents that indicate access to single-window service	Small-sample dataset	10
regburden	Amount of time senior managers spend dealing with regulations	Small-sample dataset	10

Source: Author.

121

the zone. Finally, *regburden* measures the amount of senior management time reported to be required for dealing with regulatory issues.

National investment climate variables are taken from standard measures and applied in both datasets. These include the Global Competitiveness Index score (*gciscore*), overall rank in the World Bank's Doing Business Indicators (*dbrank*), sum of scores across the categories of the World Bank's World Governance Indicators (*wgiscore*), and UNCTAD's FDI Attractiveness Index (*fdiattract*).

Market access measures are also applied to both datasets. They include a measure of *remoteness* capturing both physical and economic distance, a measure of local *market size* based on the log of GDP (at purchasing power parity), *GDP per capita*, and a measure of *access* that measures the share of local market sales allowed through the country's zone regime. Finally, we include a control—*years*—that measures the age of the country's SEZ program, reflecting the fact that investment, employment, and exports should be higher the longer a program has been operating.

Approach

Our ability to test this model is restricted by the limited availability of data on individual zone programs. Although we have original survey data on more than 600 firms, we are not able to use firm-level data in measuring our dependent variables, because firm-level outcomes say little about whether an SEZ program has been successful—indeed, they can be misleading. Take, for example, the Calabar Free Zone in Nigeria. It has been in operation for more than a decade and has granted licenses to at least 80 companies. But as of late 2009, only 26 licensed firms remained and only 13 of those were active. Taking outcome measures (including our dependent variables or productivity) and investment climate perceptions of these individual firms as some measure of the success of the free zone program in Nigeria would surely be a case, as described by Haussman and Velasco (2005), of talking to camels in the desert but missing out on the hippos who are not there.[6] Also, we do not follow the approach of Aggarwal (2005), who analyzed data on the zone level. In our case, this would expand the sample available from the rich survey data somewhat (from 10 countries to approximately 30 zones), but it would still be insufficient to carry out robust ordinary least squares (OLS) estimates.

Thus, we are forced to rely on simple correlations, which are clearly not sufficient to test the dynamics of the relationships at hand but at least provide a starting point for future analysis when more data are available. The approach involves a two-step analysis, first testing the data from the large-sample dataset. As noted above, this dataset does not include any information on the SEZ-level investment environment. Therefore, in the first level of analysis, we do not test the main hypothesis on the SEZ investment climate, but we can test the other possible determinants: *traditional factors, the national investment climate, public versus private management,* and *market access.* In the second stage of analysis, we focus on the SEZ investment climate, drawing on the data from the small-sample dataset (10 observations). In all cases, we test against three logged dependent variables: exports, investment, and employment. Because we are only testing correlations, there is no reason to include the full set of variables in the second-stage analysis with the small sample; the relationships have already been tested (more robustly) with the large sample.

Results—What Factors Determine SEZ Performance?

Correlations: Large-Sample Dataset

We start our analysis by looking at the correlations in the large-sample dataset. The results, presented in Table 4.2, indicate that a number of factors are correlated with zone outcomes, and the relationships are all in the direction we would expect. The broad message is that the national investment climate and access to local markets are strongly correlated with zone outcomes, while most of the "traditional factors" do not show significant correlations with outcomes.

Looking first at traditional factors, the results show few significant relationships between SEZ outcomes and wages, trade preferences, and fiscal incentives. And where a significant correlation does exist—between wages and employment and between incentives and investment—the nature of the relationship suggests that low wages and the use of corporate tax holidays do not contribute positively to program outcomes. In the case of wages, they are correlated positively with all outcome measures, significantly so with respect to employment (i.e., higher, not lower, wages are correlated with higher growth and investment). In the case of incentives, the results suggest that reduced tax levels rather than tax holidays or exemptions are correlated with higher levels of investment. These findings support much of orthodox policy advice and are in line with much of the research (Head et al. 1999; Bobonis and Shatz 2007), although recent findings by Harding and Javorcik (2007) suggest that incentives do have some effect on FDI flows.[7]

Table 4.2 Pearson Correlation Matrix from Analysis of Large-Sample Dataset

		Export	Invest	Employ	Incent1	Wage2	Trade pref	Private	GCI score	Dbrank	WGI score	FDI attract	Remote	Size	GDPcap	Access	Years
Outcomes	Export	1															
	Invest	0.526**	1														
	Employ	0.343**	0.295*	1													
Traditional factors	Incent1	0.069	0.424**	-0.072	1												
	Wage2	0.073	0.146	0.289**	0.239*	1											
	Tradpref	-0.022	-0.083	-0.029	-0.146	-0.378**	1										
Management	Private	-0.070	-0.133	0.104	0.066	-0.537	-0.288	1									
National investment climate	Gciscore	0.396**	0.473**	0.486**	0.145	0.498**	-0.250*	-0.135	1								
	Dbrank	-0.214	-0.352**	-0.287**	-0.188	-0.395**	0.182	0.003	-0.625**	1							
	Wgiscore	0.195	0.141	0.155	0.255**	0.509**	0.005	-0.234	0.623**	-0.508**	1						
	Fdiattract	0.354**	0.085	0.439**	0.299**	0.693**	-0.215	-0.133	0.772**	-0.609**	0.596**	1					
Market access	Remote	0.026	-0.158	0.048	-0.101	-0.139*	-0.029	0.1967	-0.031	0.076	0.010	-0.243*	1				
	Mktsize	0.402**	0.654**	0.431**	0.172	0.304**	-0.174	0.175	0.600**	-0.241**	0.056	0.575**	0.005	1			
	Gdpcap	0.100	0.335**	0.331**	0.214	0.841**	-0.390**	-0.125	0.640**	-0.501**	0.573**	0.820**	-0.123	0.352**	1		
	Access	0.165	0.074	0.307**	0.086	0.323**	-0.203	-0.024	0.262*	-0.277**	0.232*	0.485**	-0.073	0.240*	0.393**	1	
Control	Years	0.230	0.175	0.160	0.185	0.119	-0.211	-0.038	0.197	-0.0344	0.012	0.114	0.066	0.307**	0.072	-0.113	1
Observations		55	49	65	64	58	58	52	59	73	77	64	72	71	71	59	60

Source: Author.

Note: * and ** indicate significance at 0.10 and 0.05, respectively.

Although we are unable to test the zone-level investment climate in any detail with the large-sample dataset, we do have data on whether or not the zones have nominal one-stop service for business registration and other licensing procedures. We find no correlation between the existence of a one-stop service and SEZ outcomes. This finding may reflect the popularity of the one-stop concept and the gap that often exists between the claim of having a one-stop and its de facto implementation. It may also reflect the attention that has been paid to addressing licensing issues as the result of such indexes as the World Bank's *Doing Business*. A result of such attention is that this factor has become increasingly less of a differentiator across countries. Another explanation for the lack of correlation between one-stops and SEZ outcomes may be that, while the real and opportunity cost of setup constraints may be large enough to be binding for small local producers, for the larger and mainly foreign investors setting up in SEZs, the impact (good or bad) of setup processes may fade into insignificance before too long.

We find no evidence that zones operated by the private sector have significantly different outcomes than those run by the public sector. While this may reflect a bias in the zone programs covered in the large-sample dataset, those regions known to have particularly successful publicly run SEZ programs (East Asia and the Middle East) are, if anything, underrepresented in the dataset, while Latin America (known for its successful private zones) is somewhat overrepresented. Much anecdotal evidence suggests that private sector operators may be more efficient and effective, and there are many good reasons why it may make sense to have private sector participation in SEZ projects, but the broad international evidence does not provide incontrovertible evidence to support this policy. However, this does not mean that either approach is appropriate in every context. Indeed, in many low-income countries and throughout much of Africa, poor implementation by the state is one of the main barriers to private sector investment and competitiveness. In this context, the development of SEZs by the government risks perpetuating many of the factors that motivate the need for SEZs in the first place.

Turning to the national investment climate, we find evidence of strong correlations between our investment climate variables and SEZ outcomes. The message here is very clear: A better national investment climate is related to better SEZ program outcomes. A country's score in the Global Competitiveness Index is strongly correlated with its level of SEZ exports, investment, and employment. The better (lower) it is ranked in the Doing

Business index, the higher its SEZ investment and employment (the relationship holds for exports as well but is not as significant). And the higher the national investment climate is rated for "FDI attractiveness" overall, the greater its SEZ exports and employment (although, surprisingly, the relationship with actual investment is not strong). The last component of the national investment climate, which measures governance, shows a relationship in the same direction (better governance correlated with better outcomes) but is not significant across any of the dependent variables.

With respect to these findings, the variables for national competitiveness are highly correlated with each other; more important, they are also highly correlated with national incomes. This is not surprising. The literature on institutions and the investment climate always demonstrates clearly that richer countries have better investment climates. What is less clear is the direction of causality. Because we are unable to run regressions, we must be a bit cautious in our interpretation. It may be that what we are reporting as a relationship between investment climate and SEZ outcomes is really just picking up the fact that SEZs perform better in higher income countries. However, this in itself would be an interesting finding and would argue against the widely held belief that SEZs can function as a world-class island in an otherwise unfavorable environment.

The market access picture is somewhat mixed but suggests that, despite the enclave nature of most SEZ programs, the local market matters. Local market size and wealth (per capita GDP) are positively and highly correlated with SEZ outcomes across almost all measures except per capita GDP and exports. We also find some evidence, in line with Schrank (2001), that regulations governing the ability of SEZ-based firms to sell into local markets has a relationship with overall outcomes. There is a positive correlation between the share of local market access provided and all outcome measures, although it is only significant for employment.

Finally, we find a positive but insignificant correlation between the length of time a zone program has been operating and the outcome measures.

We attempted to test the hypothesis by constructing a multivariate regression model using the main categories of explanatory variables discussed in this chapter. However, because of the poor quality of the dataset, we were left with only 20–25 observations in each model, which is insufficient to provide any clear and robust results. The only variable that was significant in any of these regressions was the Global Competitiveness Index rating, perhaps again indicating the importance of the national investment climate for SEZ-level outcomes.[8] This finding indicates that country context is likely to be critical in the outcomes of any SEZ program, so it may be implementation rather than policy and design that is the most critical factor in determining the success of an SEZ program.

Correlations: Small-Sample Dataset

Turning to the small-sample dataset to test the zone-level investment climate, we find strong evidence to support our hypothesis that the SEZ investment climate matters (see results in Table 4.3). In particular, two aspects of the investment climate appear critical: infrastructure and trade facilitation. Our variables measuring utilities infrastructure in SEZs show clearly that poor utilities quality is highly correlated with lower levels of zone exports and employment. While the relationship also holds for investment, it is not significant. This may reflect the sunk costs of investment and the fact that the poor infrastructure affects initial investment more and long-term sustainability less. These findings are in line with previous research on the relationship between investment climate and FDI and trade (c.f. Dollar et al. 2004) and Aggarwal's (2005) study of SEZs in South Asia.

Our findings on customs clearance show a strong relationship across all three dependent variables. Interestingly, for customs clearance, while the nominal variable (measuring actual clearance time) is significant, the relative variable (measuring the relative time advantage enjoyed in the SEZs over firms based outside the zones) is not significant, although its sign is in the direction expected. A strong relationship with zone outcomes is also evident in investors' perceptions of the transport and logistics environment. Again, these findings corroborate the substantial body of empirical research on the relationship between transport and trade facilitation and export outcomes (c.f. Djankov et al. 2006; Freund and Rocha 2010; Portugal-Perez and Wilson 2010).

In line with our findings from the large-sample database, we find no significant relationship between the setup and licensing environment in zones and overall zone outcomes, either with our measure of actual setup times (which is positively correlated but not significant) or with perceptions on the availability and quality of one-stop services. Finally, we find that a higher regulatory burden on firms is correlated with less positive outcomes, but this relationship is not significant.

Table 4.3 Pearson Correlation Matrix from Analysis of Small-Sample Dataset

		Export	Invest	Employ	Infranom	Infrarel	Customsnom	Customsrel	Logistics	Setup	Onestop	Regburden	Years
Outcomes	Export	1											
	Invest	0.646*	1										
	Employ	0.923**	0.583	1									
Zone investment climate	Infranom	−0.654**	−0.145	−0.832**	1								
	Infrarel	−0.772**	−0.620	−0.784**		1							
	Customsnom	−0.698**	−0.654*	−0.579*	0.172	0.725**	1						
	Customsrel	0.359	0.491	0.223	0.467	−0.656*	−0.864**	1					
	Logistics	0.805**	0.103	0.843**	−0.734**	−0.742**	−0.510	0.310	1				
	Setup	0.386	0.053	0.340	−0.419	−0.222	−0.173	−0.097	0.458	1			
	Onestop	−0.314	0.313	−0.233	0.477	−0.066	−0.064	0.277	−0.490	−0.742*	1		
	Regburden	−0.201	−0.310	−0.218	−0.056	0.721**	0.621*	−0.851**	−0.357	0.140	−0.398	1	
Control	Years	0.420	0.273	0.300	−0.176	−0.282	−0.631**	0.619*	0.296	−0.010	−0.258	−0.211	1
Observations		10	8	10	10	9	10	9	10	10	9	10	10

Source: Author.

Note: * and ** indicate significance at 0.10 and 0.05, respectively.

The findings from the small-sample dataset must be viewed with caution, given the limited observations. However, they support the findings from the larger dataset (at least where similar variables have been tested), the broader investment climate literature, and the anecdotal findings from case study research conducted as part of this study. So we have some reason to be confident.

Finally, we attempted to construct a regression model—in this case, using the firm-level responses (approximately 600 observations)—to test the factors that might contribute to SEZ-level investment climate outcomes discussed in this section. We found that variation in outcomes was almost completely explained by the country dummies. No other hypothesized factors—public versus private management, sector focus, foreign versus domestic firms, or size of firms—were significant.[9]

Conclusions

Poor data availability significantly limited the sophistication of the analysis we were able to conduct, but we find clear evidence suggesting that investment climate matters for SEZ performance. Specifically, we find that national investment climate and national competitiveness are strongly correlated with SEZ outcomes. Access to a large local and regional market is also correlated with higher levels of investment, exports, and employment in SEZs. Within an SEZ, transport and trade facilitation and infrastructure quality are the factors that appear to have a strong effect on performance. Finally, we find no evidence to suggest that traditional levers of competitiveness for SEZs—low wages, fiscal incentives, and trade preferences—affect SEZ performance. Indeed, our results indicate that, if anything, the relationship is a negative one.

These findings suggest that the emerging policy consensus to focus on the SEZ investment climate is well-founded. Although business registration and licensing aspects of the investment climate are an important part of the picture, delivering high-quality infrastructure (especially reliable power) and facilitating efficient import and export transactions may have the biggest effect on outcomes. As governments address investment climate issues through their SEZs, long-term success is likely to depend on going beyond the gates of the zones and addressing wider aspects of the national business environment. Our findings suggest that the idea of the SEZ as an oasis in the desert may be a mirage—an SEZ's value appears to be intrinsically linked to the landscape in which it is situated.

Notes

1. Including tax revenues forgone from fiscal incentives as well as the opportunity cost of not implementing alternative policies.
2. Of course, this conclusion is not unanimous. For example, Rodrik et al. (2004) point out that, despite their findings on the importance of property rights, investment levels are higher in China (where property rights are absent) than in Russia (where formal institutions are in place).
3. Many countries offer drawback mechanisms for exporters holding goods in bond or making use of duty-free imported inputs for export production. However, these mechanisms usually require companies to post bonds and then claim refunds, which can tie up considerable capital. Most free zone arrangements allow exporters to avoid such payments.
4. Imagine a zone with an operating environment so bad that 80% of the firms in it went out of business. Analyzing the performance of the remaining firms would give an unfairly skewed view of how effective a zone is.
5. The measure of downtime for firms based outside the SEZs is taken from the World Bank's most recent Enterprise Survey in each country. For comparability, the sample is drawn only from exporters.
6. Referring to selection bias.
7. Their findings on the relationship between investment incentives and FDI flows in a country are ambiguous. When a variable for the existence of an investment promotion agency is excluded from the regression, they find a statistically significant positive relationship between incentives and FDI flows. However, when the investment promotion agency variable is included, the investment promotion dummy is significant (with about the same level of magnitude as the previous results on incentives) and the incentive variable is not. They do, however, find that investment incentives offered by other countries in the region act as a diversion of FDI, a finding that supports the significance of incentives.
8. Details on the regression models and results are not presented in this paper but are available on request from the authors.
9. Ibid.

References

Acemoglu, D., S. Johnson, and J. A. Robinson. 2001. "The Colonial Origins of Comparative Development: An Empirical Investigation." *American Economic Review* 91: 1369–1401.

Aggarwal, A. 2005. Performance of Export Processing Zones: A Comparative Analysis of India, Sri Lanka and Bangladesh." Indian Council for Research on International Economic Relations (ICRIER), New Delhi.

Benassy-Quere, A., M. Coupet, and T. Mayer. 2007. "Institutional Determinants of Foreign Direct Investment." *World Economy* 30(5): 764–782.

Bobonis, G. J., and H. J. Shatz. 2007. "Agglomeration, Adjustment, and State Policies in the Location of Foreign Direct Investment in the United States." *The Review of Economics and Statistics* 1: 30–43.

Boyenge, J.P.S. 2007. *ILO Database on Export Processing Zones, Revised.* Geneva: ILO.

Cling, J. P., and G. Letilly. 2001. "Export Processing Zones: A Threatened Instrument for Global Economy Insertion?" DT/2001/17. Developpement et Insertion Internationale (DIAL), Paris.

Djankov, S., C. Freund, and C. S. Pham. 2006. "Trading on Time." Policy Research Working Paper Series 3909. World Bank, Washington, DC.

Dollar, D., M. Hallward-Driemeier, and T. Mengistae. 2004. "Investment Climate and International Integration." Policy Research Working Paper No. 3323. World Bank, Washington, DC.

Drabzek, Z., and W. Payne. 1999. "The Impact of Transparency on Foreign Direct Investment." Working Paper No. 99–02. World Trade Organization, Geneva.

Eifert, B., A. Gelb, and V. Ramachandran. 2005. "Business Environment and Comparative Advantage in Africa: Evidence from the Investment Climate Data." Working Paper No. 56. Center for Global Development, Washington, DC.

Ekholm, K., R. Forslid, and J. R. Markusen. 2007. Export-Platform Foreign Direct Investment. *Journal of the European Economic Association*, MIT Press, 5(4): 776–795.

Freund, C. L., and N. Rocha. 2010. "What Constrains Africa's Exports?" Policy Research Working Paper 5184. World Bank, Washington, DC.

Harding, T., and B. S. Javorcik. 2007. "Developing Economies and International Investors: Do Investment Promotion Agencies Bring Them Together?" Policy Research Working Paper Series 4339. World Bank, Washington, DC.

Haussman, R., and A. Velasco. 2005. "Slow Growth in Latin America: Common Outcomes, Common Causes." Manuscript (October).

Head, K., J. Ries, and D. Swenson. 1999. "Attracting Foreign Manufacturing: Investment Promotion and Agglomeration." *Regional Science and Urban Economics* 29(2): 197–218.

Helpman, E. 1984. "A Simple Theory of International Trade with Multinational Corporations." *Journal of Political Economy* 94(3): 451–471.

International Labour Organization (ILO). 2003. *Employment and Social Policy in Respect of Export Processing Zones.* Geneva: ILO.

Jayanthakumaran, K. 2003. "Benefit-Cost Appraisals of Export Processing Zones: A Survey of the Literature." *Development Policy Review* 21(1): 51–65.

Johansson, H., and L. Nilsson. 1997. "Export Processing Zones as Catalysts." *World Development* 25(12): 2115–2128.

Knack, S., and P. Keefer. 1995. "Institutions and Economic Performance: Cross-Country Tests Using Alternative Institutional Measures." *Economics and Politics* 7(3): 207–227.

Kusago, T., and Z. Tzannatos. 1998. "Export Processing Zones: A Review in Need of Update." SP Discussion Paper 9802. World Bank, Washington, DC.

Markusen, J. 1984. "Multinationals, Multi-plant Economies, and the Gains from Trade." *Journal of International Economics* 16(3/4): 205–226.

Portugal-Perez, A. and J. Wilson. 2010. "Export Performance and Trade Facilitation Reform: Hard and Soft Infrastructure." Policy Research Working Paper 5261. World Bank, Washington, DC.

Rodrik, D., A. Subramanian, and F. Trebbi. 2004. "Institutions Rule: The Primacy of Institutions Over Geography and Integration In Economic Development." *Journal of Economic Growth* 9(2): 131–165.

Rolfe, R. R., D. P. Woodward, and B. Kagira. 2003. "Footloose and Tax Free: Incentive Preferences in Kenyan Export Processing Zones." Paper presented at the Biennial Conference of the Economic Society of South Africa, Somerset West, South Africa, September 17–19.

Schrank, A. 2001. "Export Processing Zones: Free Market Islands or Bridges to Structural Transformation." *Development Policy Review* 19(2): 223–242.

Smarzynska, B. K., and S-J Wei. 2000. "Corruption and Composition of Foreign Direct Investment: Firm-Level Evidence." NBER Working Paper 7969. National Bureau of Economic Research, Cambridge, MA.

Stein, E., and C. Daude. 2001. "Institutions, Integration and the Location of Foreign Direct Investment." Mimeo. Inter-American Development Bank, Washington, DC.

Tyler, W. G., and A. C. A. Negrete. 2009. "Economic Growth and Export Processing Zones: An Empirical Analysis of Policies to Cope with Dutch Disease." Latin American Studies Association 2009 Congress, Rio de Janeiro, June 11–14, 2009.

Warr, P. 1989. "Export Processing Zones: The Economics of Enclave Manufacturing." *The World Bank Research Observer* 9(1): 65–88.

Wei, S-J. 2000. "How Taxing Is Corruption on International Investors?" *Review of Economics and Statistics* 82(1): 1–11.

World Bank. 2009. "Connecting to Compete: The Logistics Performance Index 2010." World Bank, Washington, DC.

CHAPTER 5

The Investment Climate in Africa's SEZs

Introduction

Failures in individual African SEZ projects can be attributed to a variety of factors, including poor location, lack of effective strategic planning and management, national policy instability, and weak governance (Watson 2001). But one of the main factors contributing to unsuccessful zones may be the failure to create an *investment climate* inside the zone that is substantially better than what is available outside. The investment climate describes the risks, opportunities, and transaction costs involved in investing in and operating a business. It is determined by a complex interaction among laws, policies, and de facto implementation. Firms decide where to invest, how and how much to invest, and how to operate on the explicit or implicit basis of the perceived investment climate. Anecdotal information suggests that African SEZs are too often plagued by the same problems that hinder investment in their wider economies: unstable electricity, lack of water, heavy bureaucracy, and inefficient and corrupt customs. However, so far, no comparative studies exist of the investment climate performance in SEZs, in Africa or elsewhere.

With contribution from Guillermo Arenas, who led the data analysis.

Data and Methodology

The data used for this analysis are primarily based on firm surveys conducted in the second half of 2009, supplemented with key informant interviews and secondary research carried out during the same period. (For details on the survey methodology, see Appendix C.)

In some places, we compare the results of the SEZ surveys with the conditions in the national (non-SEZ) economies, using weighted averages from the World Bank Enterprise Surveys. Although Enterprise Surveys use stratified samples to create an accurate portrait of the business environment in the host economies, they were conducted in different years in the 10 countries in our study.[1] Because some conditions captured by the Enterprise Surveys do not change drastically over short periods, comparisons with SEZ survey data should be valid, especially when the differences are relatively large. However, these comparisons should be viewed with caution.

Although it is possible to compare the business environment inside SEZs with that of only exporting firms outside them (which should offer a more comparable example for SEZs than firms in general) this approach has two problems. First, the Enterprise Surveys were not sampled to be representative of exporting companies, and any comparison would have to perform some sort of poststratification with data not readily available. Second, the sample size for exporters is small in some countries and particularly problematic for some questions in this study. For these reasons, we compare the business environment reported by companies inside the SEZs with Enterprise Survey results from both exporters and nonexporters. For the issues compared in this analysis—utility setup times, outages, and customs clearance—we have no reason to believe that any systematic differences in response exist between exporters and nonexporters.

Because of the nonrandomness of the sample and the different coverage strategies described above, the results reported for the SEZ surveys are simple unweighted averages. In addition, the small sample size of respondents and some item nonresponse issues in certain countries prevented the use of more sophisticated statistical analysis. Finally, the small sample size of SEZ firms in some countries and enclaves makes our averages sensitive to the presence of outliers and firm and item nonresponse. In the most extreme case—Tanzania, with only 17 operational SEZ firms—a relatively small number of outliers or refusals to respond can significantly bias our estimates.

SEZ Investors and Their Investment Criteria

What do investors want from SEZs? What are the criteria on which they decide whether and where to invest? Understanding this is the first step to assessing the effectiveness of the investment climate performance of the countries in our survey. Before we look at these criteria, however, we should have an understanding of the investors in the survey sample. Figures 3.3 and 3.4 in Chapter 3 summarize the sources of investment in survey samples from each country. Globally, SEZs have a high share of FDI, although successful zones tend over time to attract substantial domestic investment. African zones surveyed have, on average, a much higher share of local ownership, with the majority of SEZ investments controlled domestically in three countries: Senegal, Tanzania, and Nigeria. While the four non-African countries in the survey received the majority of their investment from regional sources (the United States for Latin America and East Asia for Asia), the pattern of investment into African zones was less clear-cut, with European, East Asian, and Indian sources predominating in different countries.

The second investor characteristic that may be relevant in determining investment requirements is the sector in which they operate; these data are also shown in Chapter 3 (Figure 3.5). Again, the African zones differ somewhat from the global picture, with much less focus on investment in the garment and textile sector (with the exception of Lesotho). The food and beverage (agriprocessing) sector is particularly important in the African zones.

Table 5.1 summarizes investors' ranking of the relative importance of 11 criteria for selecting an investment location.[2] Among the African countries surveyed, the respondent rankings were remarkably similar, particularly for the top three factors: cost and quality of utilities, access to efficient transport, and business regulatory environment. These three factors are issues over which the SEZ program and individual zone management should have some control. The other two factors rated as highly important by investors are tariffs and duties and the level of corporate taxes; the latter can also be controlled by zones through incentives. Factors such as labor, technology, and markets—which are linked to wider issues of national competitiveness—were ranked lower in importance by investors in African zones. An optimistic conclusion is that zone programs have significant power over the issues that matter most to investors. A more pessimistic view is that the results reflect a selection bias; that is, investors in the African zones have already discounted

Table 5.1   Criteria for Selecting an Investment Location according to Surveyed SEZ Firms (Rankings by Country, Top Five Highlighted)

Investment criteria	African zones	Non-African zones
Cost and quality of utilities	1	3
Access to transport infrastructure	2	2
Business regulatory environment	3	5
Tariffs, duties, and rules of origin	4	8
Level of corporate taxes	5	6
Access to highly skilled labor	6	4
Access to suppliers	7	7
Access to low-cost labor	8	1
Availability/cost of land and buildings	9	10
Access to local and regional markets	10	9
Access to technology	11	11

Source: SEZ investor surveys.

deeper sources of competitiveness, and their responses suggest they are likely to be footloose.

Respondents from the non-African zones surveyed also identified utilities and transport as among their most important investment criteria. However, they place much greater emphasis on access to labor of both the low-wage (ranked as the most important criterion by investors in the non-African zones and eighth by investors in the African zones) and high-skill variety, and are much less concerned with tariffs and market preferences. Across countries, criteria were not ranked significantly or consistently differently by foreign and domestic investors. However, in several countries, local investors ranked access to technology as significantly more important than did foreign investors; this most likely reflects the expectation of benefiting from technology spillover effects from multinationals.

In the sections that follow, we assess the investment climate performance of the African SEZ programs on the five most important issues identified by investors. Our hypothesis is that if African zones can ensure a high-quality business environment relative to these issues, they should be successful in attracting and retaining investors and should have improved outcomes in terms of employment and exports.[3]

The SEZ Investment Climate—Utilities

Access to reliable, competitively priced utilities[4] was ranked as the most important investment consideration by firms in African SEZs. Where high-quality, reliable utilities are available, companies can deploy modern production techniques and ensure the efficient use of resources; where they are absent, costs rise, productivity suffers, and output is inconsistent. Overall, African countries generally fare poorly in the provision of basic utility services. For example, according to data from the World Bank Enterprise Surveys, electricity-related downtime costs African businesses almost 6 percent of sales, more than 2.5 times the average in OECD countries. Africa is the second-worst-performing region after South Asia—nearly 26 percent of all electricity in the region depends on generators, 40 percent more than in the next-worst-performing region (Latin America and the Caribbean). Thus, SEZs could offer a substantially improved operating environment to investors by providing additional infrastructure (e.g., electricity substations, reservoirs) or by ensuring dedicated or prioritized utility supplies.

The results of the survey are mixed. In most African countries surveyed, locating inside an SEZ offers much improved reliability of utilities compared with what is available in the domestic economy. However, because the quality of the national utilities infrastructure in most countries is so poor, the relative improvement in the SEZ setting is still well below what would be required to establish a globally competitive environment for investors. The survey results for electricity are presented below; the pattern for water is similar.

For most manufacturing and services companies operating in SEZs, electricity is the most important utility consideration—both reliability and cost are critical. Figure 5.1 shows that all African SEZ programs offer more reliable electricity than is available to investors in the domestic market. In most cases, the difference is substantial; however, with the exception of Lesotho and possibly Kenya, SEZs have not been able to provide a globally competitive environment. Indeed, for an investor looking for reliable electricity in Africa, locating in an SEZ in Ghana, Nigeria, Senegal, or Tanzania would not even put them in the top half of locations in Africa (see Table 5.2). The relative improvements inside the SEZs were greatest in Lesotho and Kenya—whose national environments for electricity reliability are significantly better than those in the other African countries— as well as in Ghana (although in the case of Ghana, several "outliers" that reported extremely high levels of outages were excluded from the analysis, which has as significant impact on the results). The non-African countries in the sample far outperform most of the African countries. For example, although electricity reliability in Bangladesh is as poor as in the average African country, SEZs in Bangladesh have managed to establish

Figure 5.1   Average Downtime Monthly Resulting from Power Outages

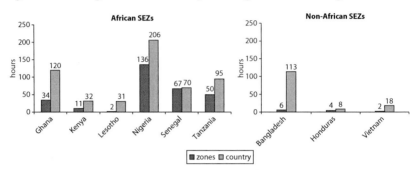

Sources: "Zones"—SEZ investor surveys; "Country"—World Bank Enterprise Surveys.

Table 5.2   Power Outages—Ranking of Surveyed African Countries and SEZs

	Countries		Countries and six SEZs	
	Rank (39)	Times top performer (Botswana: 3.8 hrs)	Rank SEZ (45)	Times top performer (Botswana: 3.8 hrs)
Lesotho	17	8.1	1	0.5
Kenya	18	8.3	9	2.9
Ghana	32	31.6	24	9.0
Tanzania	28	25.0	26	13.2
Senegal	26	18.3	30	17.7
Nigeria	38	54.4	39	35.9

Sources: SEZ investor surveys and World Bank Enterprise Surveys.

an environment that is competitive with countries like Vietnam and Honduras.

What is behind these results? SEZs have attempted to address the problem of frequent power outages by establishing dedicated substations in the larger zones. However, because many African zone programs are characterized by single factory units rather than enclaves (e.g., Ghana, Senegal, and Tanzania), the potential to extend a quality infrastructure environment to all investors is extremely limited. It is not surprising that programs such as those in Lesotho and Kenya are in the best position to deliver an improved environment to their SEZ investors. Differences between countries in how the strategy is implemented may also influence the success of these initiatives. Lesotho, for example, not only provides dedicated substations in its main industrial parks but prioritizes power to industrial areas to minimize downtime when power shortages occur nationally. Bangladesh and Vietnam follow similar strategies. The Tema zone in Ghana and Calabar in Nigeria also have dedicated substations, but reported problems with investment and maintenance lead to frequent power cuts and force most firms to rely on generators. Finally, all the non-African SEZ programs offer the possibility for private companies to purchase electricity from the grid at wholesale rates and provide services into the zones. Such deregulation or demonopolization of utilities services can be a significant advantage in SEZs. But despite the huge problem with reliable electricity, this approach does not appear to be in practice in any of the African SEZs.

The SEZ Investment Climate—Transport and Trade Facilitation

The second most important criterion noted by all SEZ investors in both the African and non-African countries is access to reliable transport infrastructure. This relates not only to issues of location and hard infrastructure (e.g., roads, rail, ports) but also to the soft infrastructure of customs and trade facilitation. The overall efficiency of the transport environment has a substantial impact on the competitiveness of exporters—it affects their ability to access markets cost-effectively, quickly, and reliably, and to access critical inputs to the production process.

SEZs should ensure quality transport access between the zones and key trade gateways, but this happens only occasionally and is an expensive proposition. Thus, the investment climate performance of an SEZ with respect to transport is likely to be determined, more than anything, by where the SEZ is located. The closer SEZs are to the main trade gateways (ports, airports, borders), the more likely they are to offer an effective transport and logistics environment for investors. Most of the African countries in the survey have located their main zones near the main trade gateways or major cities. However, a number of zones are located in peripheral regions, including some in Nigeria, Bangladesh, Vietnam, the Dominican Republic, and Lesotho. These SEZs have struggled to attract more than a handful of investors.

The importance of access to quality roads and port infrastructure is especially clear in contrast to poor conditions in the overall economy. Table 5.3 shows the ratings from the 2009 Global Competitiveness Index (World Economic Forum 2009) on the quality of road and port infrastructure in each country in the study. It shows a high correlation between the rankings on road and port infrastructure. Problems with road

Table 5.3   Quality of Roads and Port Infrastructure in Selected Countries (Country Ranking)

	Quality of roads	Quality of port infrastructure
Ghana	76	69
Kenya	91	84
Lesotho	113	114
Nigeria	112	122
Senegal	78	54
Tanzania	108	120
Bangladesh	95	113
Dominican Republic	70	58
Honduras	74	36
Vietnam	102	99
Correlation	0.9272	

Source: World Economic Forum (2009).

infrastructure tend to be compounded by poor access to and quality of ports, as in the cases of Nigeria, Tanzania, and Lesotho. The countries that experienced the biggest problems with low-performing zones in peripheral locations (Bangladesh, Nigeria, Lesotho, and Vietnam) are ranked in the bottom half in terms of transport infrastructure.

Equally important to road, rail, and port access is ensuring that exporters have access to efficient soft infrastructure to facilitate trade—primarily customs clearance but also other procedures that affect trade logistics (e.g., other border-related agencies). Because SEZs cater to exporters, they have substantial potential to deliver improvements in import and export clearance procedures. Indeed, this has always been recognized as a critical requirement and source of differentiation for SEZ programs.

The survey results are mixed. While respondents in Nigeria, Senegal, and Kenya report clearance times that are faster, on average, than those reported by exporters in the national economy, respondents in Ghana, Lesotho, and Tanzania report clearance times that suggest that the environment inside the zones is actually worse than that in the wider national economy (see Figure 5.2).[5] But the most striking difference is between the African and non-African SEZs. The average reported clearance times in the non-African SEZs are much faster than those in the African zones, and the difference in performance compared with the wider economies is substantially greater than what has been achieved in Africa. Across the four non-African SEZs, the reported clearance times

Figure 5.2   Average Time Needed for Imports through Main Seaport to Clear Customs

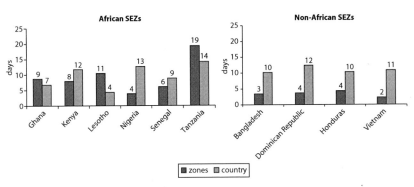

Sources: *"Zones"—SEZ investor surveys; "Country"—World Bank Enterprise Surveys.*

inside the zones averaged more than five times faster than those outside the zones; only one SEZ in the African sample (Nigeria) reported such a difference, while the remainder offered only marginal improvement or even worse times.

A number of factors likely contribute to these results. First, while most SEZ programs implement onsite customs clearance services, not all the African programs offer this amenity across all their zones. Where single factory units proliferate, it is particularly difficult to extend privileged customs clearance services. Second, the availability of a special administrative regime for customs clearance does not necessarily guarantee its effectiveness. For example, in Tanzania, many investors complained that while clearance procedures for SEZ firms were established by law, many customs agents working at the port or airport were unaware of the system. Finally, the effectiveness of onsite clearance cannot be separated from the efficiency of the ports; many of the African SEZ programs (e.g., Tanzania and Kenya) suffer from serious port-related delays that undermine the potential value of the privileged customs administration in the zones.

Figure 5.3 suggests a relationship between the availability and quality of onsite customs services in the zone and the SEZ's performance on clearance times. The best performing SEZs in terms of clearance time also had the highest share of respondents who reported that they have access to onsite clearance services. SEZs that offered less or no perceived access to onsite customs (Ghana, Lesotho, and Tanzania) had long average clearance times.

Figure 5.3   Relationship between Access to Onsite Customs Clearance and Average Import Clearance (Days)

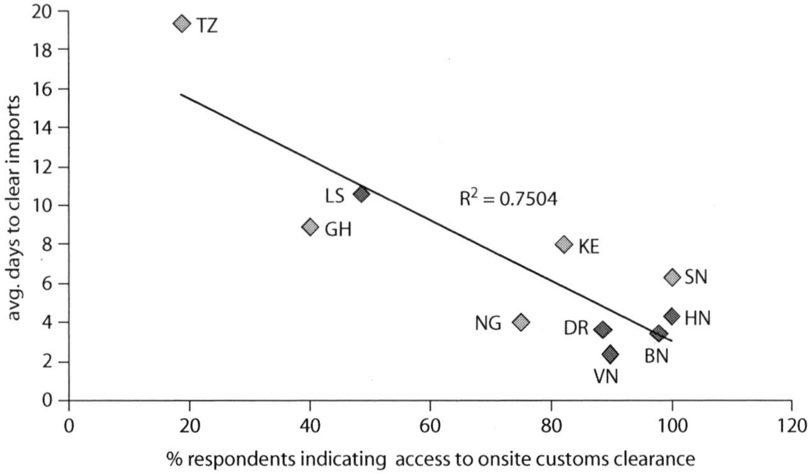

% respondents indicating access to onsite customs clearance

Source: SEZ investor surveys.

The SEZ Investment Climate—Business Regulatory Environment

The business regulatory environment encompasses a wide range of issues that affect the ease with which firms can set up businesses and operate on a day-to-day basis. It describes the relationship between the private sector and the institutions of the state (i.e., the bureaucracy). In most countries in Africa, excessive and poorly administered regulation undermines competitiveness by raising the costs and risks of doing business, consuming substantial management time, and distorting the incentives that are the basis of competition. In particular, the process of setting up a business—including obtaining licenses and permits, preparing facilities, and getting access to utilities and other services— can be time-consuming, costly, and susceptible to rent-seeking by government officials.

One of the principal nonfiscal benefits of SEZs is their potential to streamline this process; in part, by reducing the regulatory burden on companies that operate in the zone (e.g., not requiring compliance with certain regulations and not requiring certain permits and licenses). Most SEZs also try to shield investors from direct interaction with the bureaucracy by setting up one-stop services and coordinating all regulatory requirements between the investors and the various ministries and agencies.

Figure 5.4 shows a strong relationship between access to such services and time required to set up a business in an SEZ[6] (although the country with the second fastest reported setup time, Tanzania, did not have a one-stop facility in place). In Figure 5.5 we see that the African SEZs in the survey generally outperformed the non-African SEZs. No direct comparison can be made between the start-up times in SEZs versus those for investors outside SEZs, because the procedures are different. In fact,

Figure 5.4   Relationship between Access to One-Stop Services and Average Time from Application to Start-Up (Days)

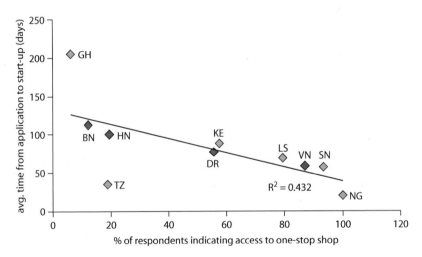

Source: SEZ investor surveys.

Figure 5.5   Average Time to Obtain an Electricity Connection (Days)

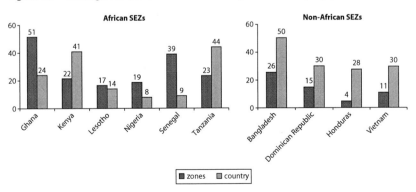

Sources: "Zones"—SEZ investor surveys; "Country"—World Bank Enterprise Surveys.

across all countries in the survey, average start-up times were significantly longer inside the SEZs than outside. This is not surprising, as the limited space in zones and the incentives available to zone companies require an application and a fairly rigorous selection process that is not necessary outside the zones.

In terms of applying for basic services such as electricity and water, most of the African SEZs have not been successful in substantially improving the investment environment relative to the national economy (see Figure 5.5). In fact, only in Kenya and Tanzania do investors in the SEZs report a shorter waiting time to establish an electricity connection than the average firm in the domestic market. In Senegal, Ghana, and Nigeria, the experience of zone investors is actually worse than that reported in the domestic market. Again, the results are significantly different in non-African zones, where waiting times inside the SEZs are usually half or less than outside. One of the determining factors is the existence of zone enclaves (industrial parks) and prebuilt factory units. Investors in these areas tend to obtain utility connections quickly, whereas single unit investors generally face longer time frames and much less predictability.

The SEZ Investment Climate—Tariffs and Preferences

The fourth most important criterion noted by survey respondents relates to tariffs and trade preferences, and the associated rules of origin. On the import side, all SEZs in the survey offer virtually the same preferences to companies operating in the zones: the use of duty-free import materials, components, and capital equipment in production. The administrative regimes differ somewhat from country to country, but the investment climate is fairly standardized in this respect across zones. Where SEZs (or, rather, the countries in which they are based) offer greater potential competitive differentiation is in the markets to which they have preferential access. Indeed, a large share of FDI that has gone into SEZs worldwide has been driven by quota-hopping or other methods to ensure preferential access to key export markets.

Table 5.4 lists the main vehicles through which investors in the SEZs can access export markets. Most of the African zones are in an enviable competitive position, especially with regard to their access to U.S. markets through the African Growth and Opportunity Act of 2000 (AGOA). For all countries surveyed, AGOA access allows manufacturers to use fabric from third countries.[7] This is a significant advantage over SEZs located in other

Table 5.4 Market Access from SEZs

	Preferential trade access			Local market sales restrictions
	United States	*European Union*	*Regional*	
Bangladesh	N/A	Everything But Arms; no third country fabric derogation	SAFTA	10%
Dominican Republic	DR-CAFTA; no third country fabric derogation	EPA w/ third country fabric derogation	CACM	10% (100% in some sectors)
Honduras	DR-CAFTA; no third country fabric derogation	N/A	CACM	5%
Vietnam	Generalized System of Preferences (GSP), but restrictions and tariffs on clothing, footwear, etc.	GSP	Association of Southeast Asian Nations (ASEAN)	No local sales in EPZ; no restrictions in industrial zones
Ghana	AGOA w/ 3rd country fabric derogation	Interim EPA	ECOWAS	30%
Kenya	AGOA w/ third country fabric derogation	EPA w/ third country fabric derogation	EAC, COMESA	20% in practice; none in law
Lesotho	AGOA w/ third country fabric derogation	Everything But Arms; no third country fabric derogation	SADC/SACU	None
Nigeria	AGOA w/ third country fabric derogation	N/A	ECOWAS	Unclear: Law states 25% maximum local sales, but NEPZA indicates 100% local sales possible
Senegal	AGOA w/ third country fabric derogation	Everything But Arms; no third country fabric derogation	UEMOA, ECOWAS	20% in DIFZ; none in DISEZ
Tanzania	AGOA w/ third country fabric derogation	Everything But Arms; no third country fabric derogation	EAC, SADC, COMESA	20%

Sources: WTO national Trade Policy Reviews; individual country SEZ laws.

regions, including even Central America. Access to the European Union is relatively less favorable with regard to rule of origin; but again, the situation in the African zones is relatively attractive. Preferences available through regional trade are also a significant potential source of advantage, particularly because access to many of the regional African markets is restricted from outside the region. However, in the regional trade context, some of the African SEZs are at a disadvantage compared with other locations in their country, because regional trade agreements may not give full preferences to exports from SEZs. For example, in the Economic Community of West African States (ECOWAS), SEZ exports are not considered to originate from within the trading bloc and are not given preferential access.

Finally, access to local markets is an important consideration for many investors, particularly local and regional investors. The African SEZs in this survey are somewhat less restrictive than the zones located outside the region; however, in Ghana, Kenya, and Tanzania, significant restrictions exist. The growth of regional trade agreements is a potential threat to SEZ competitiveness, especially combined with local market restrictions. For example, under the new EAC agreement, all sales to any country in the bloc are considered local. For an investor looking mainly to serve the regional market, the local market sales restrictions (e.g., in Kenya and Tanzania) would make SEZs less attractive.

The SEZ Investment Climate—Level of Taxes

The provision of corporate and other tax incentives is a long-established practice in SEZs worldwide. Many SEZ regimes become overly reliant on granting general tax incentives rather than addressing other aspects of the investment environment, raising the risk of a race to the bottom with other zones. On the other hand, incentives have played an important role in catalyzing investment in some SEZ programs,[8] particularly in the early stages of their development. Our survey respondents confirm that incentives are an important consideration for investors. The headline incentive normally involves corporate taxes.[9] Standard corporate tax rates do not vary enormously across countries—most are in the range of 25 percent to 30 percent. All the SEZ programs (except Senegal and Vietnam) offer substantial exemption periods, and Nigeria, the Dominican Republic, and Honduras offer permanent tax-free status to SEZ investors.

Do the tax incentives have a significant effect on the economics of an SEZ investor? We developed scenarios based on a "typical" large and small SEZ investor and analyzed the implications of the tax incentives

Figure 5.6   Impact of SEZ Corporate Tax Incentives on a Simulated Large Investor

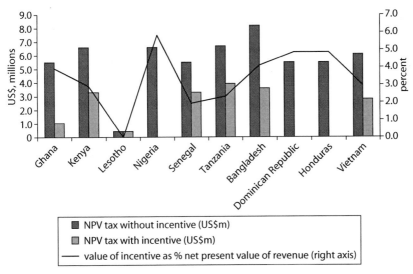

■ NPV tax without incentive (US$m)
□ NPV tax with incentive (US$m)
— value of incentive as % net present value of revenue (right axis)

Sources: Author's calculations based on data from individual country SEZ authorities and World Bank Doing Business data (www.doingbusiness.org) for national corporate tax rates.

based on net present value (NPV) of cash flows over a 20-year period[10] (see Figure 5.6). The NPV of the tax incentive for a large SEZ investor could be up to US$20 million and for a small investor, up to US$6.6 million. This is equivalent to 4 percent of revenues for a large investor and nearly 6 percent for a small investor. With the exception of Nigeria, the average benefit of the tax incentive offered in the African SEZs was lower (1%–3%) than in the four non-African zones in the survey (2%–3.5%).

Conclusions

In this chapter, we summarized the results of a 10-country survey of investors in special economic zones, with a specific focus on SEZs in Africa. The main purpose was to understand how SEZs are performing in addressing the investment climate issues that matter most to investors. We focused on the five issues that investors said were the most important criteria in making investment location decisions: (1) cost and quality of utilities; (2) access to transport infrastructure; (3) business regulatory environment; (4) tariffs, duties, and rules of origin; and (5) level of corporate taxes. The first three criteria are critical components of the "doing business" agenda; thus, SEZ programs—and even individual zones—should have a degree of control over them. This suggests the importance of SEZ policy and management, and the potential for zones to play a significant role in influencing investor location decisions.

Several findings emerge from the survey. First, on most of the criteria assessed, SEZs in Africa offer an improved business environment compared with what is available outside the zones; however, they do not seem to go far enough. The investment environment in most of the African countries surveyed is particularly poor at the national level, and the scale of the improvements offered in most SEZs is not enough to make the zones competitive on a global or even a regional basis. A related finding is that the non-African SEZ programs in the study make investment climate improvements over their domestic environments on a much greater scale. This suggests that the African SEZs can take investment climate reform much further.

One of the reasons African SEZ programs may be restricted in the improvements they can make is that many of the programs are managing a large number of single factory units. The cost and logistical challenge of addressing investment climate challenges (e.g., by offering special customs clearance regimes, one-stop service, and reliable infrastructure) for a dispersed set of companies is a serious constraint to the resources and capacity of SEZ administrators. The African zone regimes that perform best across the board—Kenya and Lesotho—and the four non-African regimes in the study are characterized mainly by zone enclaves (industrial estates), most of which make significant use of prebuilt factory units.

The survey results illustrate the critical importance of addressing the day-to-day challenges investors face inside the zones so they can get on with their business. This means ensuring a steady flow of power, avoiding delays in the flow of goods in and out, and addressing any problems that do arise. Access to high-quality facilities, onsite customs, and one-stop services appears to be related significantly to improved investment climate performance in the SEZs.

Notes

1. Enterprise Surveys were conducted in 2009 in Lesotho, Nigeria, and Vietnam; in 2007 in Ghana, Kenya, Senegal, and Bangladesh; in 2006 in Tanzania and Honduras; and in 2005 in the Dominican Republic.

2. The specific question was as follows: "Please rate each of the factors below in terms of their importance to your company in considering a location for

investment (rate each on a scale of 1–5, with 1 being 'least important' and 5 being 'most important')." Average ratings for each factor in a country were then converted into a rank.

3. Meeting investor needs on their main criteria may contribute to meeting some, but not all, of the objectives of government (e.g., investment, exports, and possibly employment). On issues such as technology transfer, industrial upgrading, and domestic market links, meeting investor criteria may be necessary but not sufficient conditions.

4. The focus of the survey was on electricity and water. Although questions were asked about telecommunications (phone and Internet) availability and setup, the survey did not ask about the reliability of telecommunications.

5. However, there may be explanations related to the biases in the samples. For example, the volume of imports and exports or the nature of the goods may be different inside and outside the zones. Moreover, there is a lag between when the Enterprise Surveys and the SEZ surveys were conducted; for some countries, this is a year or less, but for others it is two or three years. Some changes could be due to improvements or deterioration in the national port and customs environment since the Enterprise Surveys.

6. The survey question asked respondents whether they had access to a one-stop service for setting up and getting permits. If they responded that they did, they were asked to rate the quality of the service. In some zones, the authorities advertised or officially offered a one-stop service, but the respondents said it was not actually available.

7. Under the original AGOA provisions, duty-free access for garments required that the fabrics used in their production come from either the Africa region or the United States. Later, most low-income countries were permitted to source fabric from anywhere in the world. Similar rules of origin and local value added provisions are part of most preferential trade agreements.

8. We are not aware of any successful SEZ program that never offered tax incentives to investors.

9. Many companies argue that corporate taxes are not a major consideration, because multinational corporations (MNCs) often treat their affiliates based in SEZs as cost centers, so profits are kept to a minimum. The incentive structures in many global tax and trade regimes favor minimizing profits for such affiliates.

10. The scenarios were for a large SEZ investor (revenue of US$110m after 20 years) and a small SEZ investor (revenue of US$28m after 20 years). Revenues were grown from a small base to reach 10 percent annual growth after five years and then 5 percent annually from year 10. Steady-state operating profits for both companies were around 25 percent, with losses during the first few years of operations. Accrued losses were assumed to be carried

over and withheld against subsequent year obligations. The NPV of revenues, profits, and taxes was calculated based on an annual rate of 10 percent.

References

Watson, P. L. 2001. "Export Processing Zones: Has Africa Missed the Boat? Not Yet!" Africa Region Working Paper Series No. 17. World Bank, Washington, DC.

World Economic Forum. 2009. *Global Competitiveness Report 2009*. Geneva: World Economic Forum.

WTO Policy Reviews. http://www.wto.org/english/tratop_e/tpr_e/tpr_e.htm.

Zone Practices: Policy, Planning, and Strategy

Introduction

The previous chapters have outlined the progress and performance gaps in the African zones and identified some of the investment climate and strategic factors that determine these outcomes. In this chapter and Chapter 7, we focus on analyzing the policies, strategies, and operational practices behind the observed performance. Drawing on the results of the case study research in our six African and four non-African countries, and from other global economic zone programs (including China, Costa Rica, Jordan, Malaysia, and Mauritius), we document the current/prevailing strategic approaches taken in the zones and the day-to-day implementation of the programs. Our aim is to identify good practices in the planning and implementation of zone programs, particularly those that show a clear link with improved performance and positive socioeconomic outcomes. We also identify lessons that can be learned from poor strategy, planning, and operational practices.

This chapter and the next cover a wide range of issues. To avoid a meandering discussion, we use a fairly rigid structure in both chapters— each section covers a specific strategic or operational issue for effective functioning of economic zone programs. We have organized the issues in two groups: those that are strategic or planning-oriented and those that are more operational.

Organization of Chapters 6 and 7

Chapter 6. Policy, planning, and strategy	Chapter 7. Operations, management, and learning
1. Introduction	1. Introduction
2. SEZs in the national trade and industry policy framework	2. Marketing and investment promotion
3. From policy to practice: strategic planning in SEZs	3. Location, land, and development
4. The SEZ legal and regulatory framework	4. Registration, licensing, and administrative procedures
5. Institutional framework and the SEZ regulatory authority	5. Infrastructure
6. Partnerships and private sector participation	6. Customs, trade facilitation, and transport
	7. Promoting linkages with the local economy
	8. Monitoring, enforcement, and learning

Within each of these sections, we organize the discussion around summaries (i.e., reflecting the prevailing situation across the zones studied) or normative statements (i.e., identifying good practice). Each section contains two to five such statements, which are designed to address different facets of the main issue in the section. We go into significant detail on many issues, but the discussion is not intended as a step-by-step guide on how to plan and implement a zone program.[1] Rather, we wish to highlight the most important policy and operational considerations. The two chapters do not end with a specific set of policy conclusions. Instead, the conclusions should be clear in of each of the 45 or so individual statements and in the details that follow each statement. We provide higher level policy conclusions on the nature and role of economic zone programs in Chapter 8.

SEZs in the National Trade and Industry Policy Framework

Consistent political leadership at the highest levels is critical to the success of SEZ programs.
One of the most important success factors for SEZ programs in East Asia was strong support and active commitment to the program at the highest levels of political leadership. In addition to supporting the programs, senior political leaders had a very clear vision of the development path they

were targeting and the specific role of SEZs on that path. Successful industrializers in East Asia—including China, Malaysia, and Singapore—developed clear long-term economic growth strategies based on a realistic assessment of strengths and limitations. Common to all these countries' approaches was the recognition of the need to shift away from existing, inward-looking development paradigms and embrace the learning opportunities available through integration into global markets. The SEZs were seen as an important instrument for achieving this, through their ability to promote export-oriented investment and to attract FDI. Deng Xiaoping made specific reference to the SEZs as an instrument in this outward-looking transformation strategy, describing them as "a window of technology, a window of management, a window of knowledge as well as a window of international policy."

Singapore's long-term growth strategy also focused on SEZs as an instrument of global economic integration and was embraced by Prime Minister Lee Kuan Yew as part of an outward-oriented growth strategy. Similarly, Vietnam gave its economic zone program the highest level of political attention. Particularly during the early years of its development, it was championed by the prime minister and came directly under his purview. This signaled to officials that the economic zone program was deemed to be a central instrument in the government's industrial development strategy. But the program was also an important signal to foreign investors of the government's commitment to outward-oriented growth and foreign investment, thus lowering the perception of risk on the part of FDI.

In almost all the classic success stories, a senior politician or business person—often both—champions the SEZ program and helps ensure continued government support. In Mauritius, for example, these champions were Swiss-Mauritian entrepreneur José Poncini and Gaëtan Duval, who was foreign minister in a coalition government when the decision was made to launch the export processing zone program (see Box 6.1). Critically, high-level political commitment went beyond words, strategies, and planning into ensuring the successful implementation of the strategies. For example, Costa Rican President Jose Maria Figueres played a prominent and active role in attracting Intel into its free zone program. And senior Chinese politicians, including the president, have been involved in efforts to move projects forward and to overcome problems in partnership projects; for example, with the government of Singapore (in Suzhou) and recently in projects in Africa.

In many programs, the political importance of the zone program is reflected in its institutional design; specifically, by locating the program in

Box 6.1

Evolving Economic Zone, Trade, and Investment Policies to Meet Changing Needs in Mauritius

Mauritius strategically aligned its diversification and industrialization strategy with the international trading regime, capitalizing on its labor costs and its cultural proximity to European markets to create a specialized, attractive investment microclimate in its EPZ. However, this trade and investment strategy has not been static. Initially, the EPZ was a liberal enclave inside a highly protected economy. Over time, in parallel with the erosion of preferential trade access, the country's own trade and investment regimes were progressively liberalized, and the EPZ became less of an enclave and more of a catalytic exclave. The EPZ has retained much of its focus on the garment sector—it is the world's second largest producer of knitwear, the third largest exporter of pure wool garments, and the fourth largest supplier of T-shirts to the European market. But liberalization in the trade and investment regime has allowed for diversification outside the EPZ in line with the island's evolving comparative advantage, including the launch of the offshore financial sector and the free port in the early 1990s, the Cybercity/ICT initiative in the early 2000s, and the integrated tourism resort scheme in the mid-2000s.

Source: Author.

the office of the prime minister or head of state. The African programs in our study show some evidence of having been given institutional prominence and of leaders periodically promoting the programs in public. However, consistent personal championing of a zone program is rare in the African context. Two exceptions are Ghana (where the free zone program was a personally championed, at least in its early years, by President Jerry Rawlings) and Senegal (where Karim Wade, a politician and son of the president, is one of the leading figures involved in implementing the Dakar Integrated SEZ).

Institutionally and strategically, successful zone programs have been an integrated component of a long-term national growth (trade and industry) policy framework. Thus, the policy instruments must be flexible enough to adjust to the evolving needs of the country.
The successful East Asian countries situated their zones within a clear industrial policy framework, which had two important implications. First,

it meant that the zones were understood as an instrument to achieve wider national economic development objectives, which helped ensure long-term political support and resource commitments. Second, it meant that—in addition to narrow policies aimed at the zone itself, such as infrastructure provision and business licensing reform—the zone programs benefited from interventions to promote clusters, provide supporting trade and social infrastructure, improve trade facilitation, and address the flexibility and quality of the labor market. In Mauritius, the government's trade policy was closely linked to its objectives in the EPZ program. Understanding the importance of preferential trade agreements to the success of the program, successive governments defended the country's trade position aggressively in bilateral and multilateral arenas to ensure continued preferential access to key markets. When this was not possible, the government secured significant compensation and specific industry support to assist in productivity upgrading and diversification. In Malaysia, the EPZs were linked directly to the national industrialization program through five-year industrial master plans. At the outset in 1969, Penang's chief minister, Lim Chong Eu, declared that the Penang Development Corporate (PDC), which was responsible for the EPZ program, was expected to spearhead economic development within the framework of the national economic policy (Lim 1971).

The experience of the African programs is somewhat mixed. Nominally at least, the establishment of most of the programs was part of a shift from policies of import substitution toward export-led policies of growth. Kenya's EPZ program was launched as part of a wider export development program. In Ghana, the development of the free zone program was part of a well-integrated strategy to position the country as a regional and global export platform. But the problem with many of the African zone programs has been the failure to maintain consistent policy links between the programs and wider strategies of trade and industrialization. For example, in Tanzania, little effort has been made to align the investment in EPZs in the zone programs with the sectors or tasks identified in the national strategies (e.g., services, agriculture, agriprocessing).

The policy framework of the zones should be flexible, so that they can deal with the fact that they may need to attract different types and mixes of sectors, firms, and investment sources as they evolve. Legislative regimes that impose narrow restrictions—such as allowing only processing or manufacturing activity, restricting domestic investors, or limiting local sales—threaten the long-term competitiveness of zone programs.

Predictability and transparency in the government's support for the SEZ program, in the strategic intent for zones, and in the broad approach to the program are critical to attracting high-quality long-term investors. But within the broadly predictable policy environment, successful zone programs ensure some flexibility and seek to experiment with alternative policies. Pragmatism and flexibility are the most commonly cited features in countries where zone programs have been successful. Another feature of the East Asian countries that has contributed to the success of their zone programs is long-term political stability. Stability has enabled the governments to focus on addressing their defined economic objectives without the need to shift policies in response to real or perceived crises. And stability in the policy process itself means that it does not rely on the government remaining in power but rather on effectively functioning institutions, a high-quality civil service, and a political process that favors evolutionary change.

Many African zone programs undermined investor confidence by failing to deliver a predictable policy environment. Senegal is a prime example (see Box 6.2). Nigeria, too, has suffered from inconsistency in its trade and investment policies; for example, attracting FDI in the apparel and furniture sectors and allowing them to export output into the domestic market, then later imposing a ban on all imports of these products, including those from zone-based firms. Nigeria has also suffered from a significant gap between de jure and de facto implementation of SEZ-related laws. Tanzania is a third example of a country that failed to provide a clear and consistent zone policy. In 2006, Tanzania finally operationalized its EPZ program under the stewardship of the Ministry of Trade and Industry; that same year, Parliament established another SEZ under the Ministry of Planning, Economy, and Empowerment. The existence of parallel programs contributed to investor confusion and triggered internal uncertainty over implications of their inevitable consolidation.

Policy consistency in zones should be balanced with the need for programs to evolve to meet the changing needs of investors and governments, and to experiment with different approaches to identify the most effective ones. For example, Vietnam implemented its zones on a pilot basis, maintaining regulatory flexibility (particularly in the early days) and testing alternative models, approaches, and policies in different zones, often with different foreign partners.[2] This flexibility allowed Vietnam to learn and adopt good practices through an informal process that could later be formalized in its national zone policy.

Box 6.2

Policy Reversals in Senegal's Economic Zone Program

In Senegal, weak policy design in the zone program resulted in unintended consequences when it rolled out. Often, the reaction to problems was to abruptly cancel policies, initiate new ones, or return to old ideas, creating an unpredictable environment for investors. Senegal's policies flipped on many issues, including these:

1. *Eligibility requirements:* Under the initial 1974 law, strict requirements on capital investment and employment creation and an explicit exclusion of domestic investors limited investment to large foreign direct investors. This policy was amended in 1983.
2. *Corporate tax exemption:* The 1974 law offered 100 percent exemption from corporate tax; under the 1995 law, a 15 percent corporate tax was applied; under the 2007 law for the Dakar Integrated Special Economic Zone (DISEZ), 100 percent exemption is also offered. The 1974 and 2007 laws relate to specific enclaves, but the 2007 law brings back the distinction between enclaves and the national territory that the 1995 law attempted to eliminate.
3. *Access to local market:* The 1974 law allowed 40 percent of output to be sold locally; under the 1995 law, this was reduced to 20 percent; the 2007 DISEZ law places no restrictions on local market sales, which face a 2 percent tax.
4. *Enclaves versus national territory:* Under the 1991 law creating the "points francs," the government attempted to extend benefits beyond the Dakar Industrial Free Zone (DIFZ) enclave to the national territory. As a result of poor controls on eligibility, the entire program had to be cancelled. The 1995 law effectively reextended the benefits beyond the enclave; however, as noted above, the 2007 DISEZ reestablished the distinction between exporters in the national territory and those in the free zone enclave.

Source: Author.

From Policy to Practice: Strategic Planning in SEZs

A critical foundation for SEZ programs is thorough strategic planning based on a rigorous assessment of demand. Development of an individual zone should be guided by the market demand study for location, investment phasing, and marketing and promotion.
One of the striking features of many SEZ programs in Sub-Saharan Africa (with exceptions such as Mauritius, Madagascar, and Kenya) is that the

few investors they have managed to attract are spread across a wide range of manufacturing sectors. In contrast, many zones in Latin America, South Asia, and East Asia have established themselves as industry clusters. One possible reason for the lack of a noticeable investment focus in the African zones is insufficient attention to strategic planning and positioning.[3] For example, in Tanzania (the program launched most recently among the countries in our study), the overall EPZ and SEZ programs result from government strategies—the export development strategy and the Mini-Tiger Plan 2020, respectively. However, the actual development of the programs has not included any obvious strategic planning process,[4] and the government of Tanzania has not undertaken any formal analytical studies to assess the country's competitiveness as an investment location, its main sources of comparative advantage, or the optimum opportunities and strategic positioning of the SEZ program.

The situation is similar in many of the African zone programs. The lack of strategic planning is particularly problematic because these programs have been launched relatively recently—late on the world stage and in a highly competitive globalized market for foreign investment. It is critical that zone programs are market-tested and that they respond specifically to investor needs. A "build it and they will come" approach only works when there is huge pent-up demand for investing in the country/region (with or without an economic zone), which was probably the case in China and in the United Arab Emirates during the 1990s and 2000s.[5]

In addition to the analysis discussed in Box 6.3, which helps determine the strategic positioning of a zone, a critical success factor is to undertake a rigorous demand planning assessment. Senegal's original DIFZ program provides a cautionary tale of the risks of disconnection between planning and demand (or perhaps between potential demand and delivery). The zoned site covers some 600 hectares, but only 69 hectares have been developed, and even this limited area is much more than required by the companies operating there. Similarly, the Calabar Free Zone in Nigeria was designed to cover 200 hectares but has never filled more than a quarter of its space with active companies.

Successful zone programs focus on activities that align well with their comparative advantage and develop clear sources of competitive differentiation.

Zone programs that focus on comparative advantage can quickly attract investment. For example, Bangladesh has a very clear comparative advantage in labor, in terms of both extremely low costs and large supply, so it is attractive as a low-cost manufacturing location. Unlike many zone programs

Box 6.3

Key Elements in the Strategic Planning Process for Economic Zones

Key components of the SEZ strategic planning process include the following:

1. *Analysis of trade data and trends:* Looking at patterns of global and regional trade and investment flows will give a sense of the sectors that are receiving the bulk of investment in the region and in similar countries, and of emerging trends. For example, in recent years, some global buyers have shifted their approach to garment sector investment; there has been a notable trend in South-South trade and investment in many product sectors; and the growth of FDI in IT-enabled services has accelerated. Taking account of such trends is critical to shaping the ongoing strategic positioning and marketing strategy for the SEZ program. For example, in response to the growth of call center investments, zone programs in the Dominican Republic, Ghana, and Honduras have all initiated targeted efforts (including adjustment of zone regulations where necessary) to position themselves to attract investment in this area and have begun targeted marketing.

2. *Assessment of sources of comparative advantage:* What industries are you in at the moment? What industries are nascent? Where do you have comparative advantage (e.g., labor costs, natural resources, location, market access preferences)? The primary sources of comparative advantage for an SEZ will derive from the sources of comparative advantage in the country overall and in the region in which the zone is located. Most traditional export processing zones (EPZs) have focused on light assembly operations (especially garments) and have thrived where a country had large pools of low-cost labor combined with preferential access to key markets. SEZ programs in countries such as Bangladesh, Vietnam, and many in Central America (e.g., Honduras, Haiti, the Dominican Republic, El Salvador) grew rapidly by targeting these preference-driven, labor-intensive sectors.

3. *Input from investors:* Best practice in strategic planning for SEZ investment also involves approaching the process from the standpoint of the investor; that is, thinking about the investment location decision-making process and the criteria that will drive it. If possible, this process should involve direct input from existing and potential investors, through surveys, focus groups, interviews, and so on. This input will reveal important sector-level variations in investor requirements. The questions then are (1) How effectively does your SEZ meet these requirements? and (2) How does your zone compare with alternative locations that these investors will likely consider?

(continued next page)

Box 6.3 *(continued)*

4. *Benchmarking:* The second question should be addressed through a benchmarking process—comparing your SEZ against alternative location options, normally including other SEZs in the region as well as locations in the country that may be outside an SEZ.

This strategic planning process should result in a prioritized list of broad industries in which the SEZ is likely to be in a strong position to attract investors and of the markets that can be most competitively served. This outcome should highlight the clear value proposition of the SEZ program.

Source: Author.

(and even the Bangladesh Export Processing Zones Authority's [BEPZA] own stated intentions at times), Bangladesh has not attempted to use the EPZ program to defy its comparative advantage and, as a result, has managed to attract investment on a large scale. Of course, challenges of upgrading and diversification arise, but at least the program is in a position of strength (having proven its capacity to deliver against objectives and having established its financial sustainability) from which to consider the next stages of its evolution. The same can be said for the programs in the Dominican Republic and Honduras (see Box 6.4). The successful development of the Jebel Ali Free Zone in Dubai highlights the value of focusing on comparative advantage—with limited industry and labor, Dubai recognized the significant opportunity of its geographic location and deepwater port, and designed the zone as a regional logistics hub. The developers successfully applied the same concept in Djibouti, a country with a similar geographic advantage.

The experiences of Ghana and Nigeria with their free zone programs offer another case in point. Although Ghana has attempted to attract investment in labor-intensive garments (through its Textiles Village project) and in the human-capital-intensive ICT sector (through an IT park initiative), its relatively high levels of free zone investment and exports have come from sectors that actually align much more closely with the country's comparative advantage in natural-resource-intensive sectors. In fact, around 80 percent of exports from Ghana's free zones in 2008 came from the cocoa and wood processing sectors. In Nigeria, the original free zone program, designed to attract labor-intensive manfuacturing, has largely failed (firms in the free zones tend to be more capital-intensive

Box 6.4

Strategic Evolution: Changing Comparative Advantage and Competitive Differentiation in Honduras

The zone program in Honduras was designed to take advantage of its location relative to the North American market, preferential market access under the Caribbean Basin Initiative, and comparative advantage in low-cost labor in order to serve as a base for outsourcing apparel manufacturing. Its success was primarily due to the labor advantage, along with having a local entrepreneurial base with some experience in the sector. After major growth during the 1990s, some of these comparative advantages began to erode in the 2000s—particularly the labor cost advantage, because of the emergence of competition from Asia. Honduran exporters reacted by building competitive advantage in several other ways:

• Diversifying by attracting investors in other light manufacturing activities (e.g., wire harnesses) and services.
• Moving upstream in the garment sector by becoming full package suppliers.
• Backward integrating through investment in textile manufacturing.
• Building on the geographic advantage to become a preferred location for serving the U.S. market quickly for products with short lead times.

In the last area, Honduras invested in improving its main port (Puerto Cortes) and worked with the United States to make it one of the few Latin American ports certified by the U.S. Container Security Initiative. In addition, many of the Honduran-owned *maquila* subcontractors are establishing relationships with Chinese producers to partner with them to become a base for product lines and specific runs that require short lead times to the U.S. East Coast.

Source: Author.

than their peers outside the zones), but the country managed to quickly attract large-scale investment into its oil and gas free zones. For example, the Onne zone at Port Harcourt has attracted at least 80 international investors and created more than 20,000 jobs.

Targeted zone strategies are most effective; this requires some sector and market focus, as well as a limit on the number of objectives a program seeks to achieve.
All the African zone programs under study are small and in need of a growth strategy. But, as mentioned previously, they face a highly

competitive global environment, and most African countries have not yet established credibility as locations for FDI, either inside or outside the zones. This challenge is aggravated by the limited resources available in most programs to invest in marketing and promotion. For example, Tanzania probably entered the SEZ market too late to achieve substantial growth in traditional labor-intensive manufacturing such as garments and textiles. In the absence of labor cost or scale advantages (e.g., Bangladesh, China, Vietnam), the tax and infrastructure incentives available in the EPZs are unlikely to be sufficient to carve out a major competitive advantage. This all points to the critical need to develop a targeted positioning strategy, most likely focused on specific product-market combinations.

African zone programs also should consider limiting the number of objectives they seek to achieve, at least in the initial years. This could help ensure a more targeted strategic approach, and a more realistic one, given resource limitations. As Table 6.1 shows, most programs have a wide range of objectives, including attracting FDI and creating jobs but also supporting technology access, skills transfer, uprgading, and foreign exchange earnings. While all these objectives are relevant and important, they can lead to competing priorities and a lack of focus, especially during the early years, when it is critical to attract good investors to form a base for the program. Vietnam, for example, has focused on attracting FDI, with only two main objectives for the short term: employment and technology transfer. The government has tried to maximize FDI by not imposing constraints on enterprises, such as local content requirements (with some industry-wide exceptions). The Vietnamese government understood that the country's location and low labor costs were comparative advantages but that they might be insufficient if taxes were too high or additional costs were imposed on investors. Kenya initially limited its objectives to three but later added several others.

Despite the need for focus, zone programs that become overly reliant on a single product or market are vulnerable to changing global economic circumstances and evolving competitiveness.
The downside of specialization is vulnerability. Even many zone programs that have been successful in generating large-scale investment, employment, and exports (e.g., the Dominican Republic, Kenya, Lesotho) have been hurt by excessive sector (or even product) and market reliance. Specifically, many zone programs have focused entirely on labor-intensive assembly. While programs such as the one in Vietnam have managed to attract a wide range of sectors in virtually the same task-based

Table 6.1 Summary of Stated SEZ Program Objectives

	Jobs	Exports	FDI	Technology	Diversification	Upgrading	Foreign exchange	Other
Bangladesh	✓	✓	✓	✓	✓	✓		✓
Vietnam	✓	✓	✓	✓				
Ghana	✓*		✓	✓	✓		✓	✓
Kenya	✓		✓	✓	✓	✓*	✓*	✓
Nigeria	✓	✓	✓	✓		✓	✓	
Senegal	✓	✓	✓				✓	
Tanzania	✓	✓	✓	✓	✓	✓	✓	✓

Source: Author, based on review of individual country SEZ laws.
* Original objectives (others added subsequently).

163

activities—including electronics, automotive, and footwear—others have failed to pursue anything beyond garments. The combination of the global downturn and declining competitiveness compared with low-wage Asian manufacturers (particularly in the post-MFA context) has ravaged the SEZs in Lesotho, Kenya, and elsewhere, as is documented in this report.

Similarly, reliance on single end markets through trade preferences has been a source of growth but also of vulnerability for zone programs. Lesotho and Kenya, whose garment sectors rely almost exclusively on the U.S. market, are examples of this risk (see Box 6.5). Honduras and the Dominican Republic exhibit the same overreliance, but they at least have

---

Box 6.5

The Price of Concentration: Ups and Downs in Lesotho's Garment Sector

Lesotho's export textile and garment sector (which is virtually all accounted for by FDI supported through the industrial parks) is a primary driver of economic development in the country. It contributes 18 percent of GDP, accounts for more than 90 percent of total exports, and employs more than half of the country's labor force (employment in the sector peaked at over 53,000 in 2004). Among African countries, Lesotho stands out in its ability to attract FDI into the non-natural-resource sectors: Since 1980, FDI inflows have averaged 15 percent annual growth, and the rate has increased to 26 percent annually since 2000.

However, Lesotho is mostly in the business of cut, make, and trim (CMT); as a result, the only value added comes in terms of labor input. Furthermore, Lesotho's textile and clothing volumes are heavily concentrated in specific products: men's woven cotton trousers and cotton pullovers, virtually all of which go to the U.S. market. Lesotho's over-reliance on the U.S. apparel market has had a significant effect on its exports in recent years. Since the MFA phaseout at the end of 2004, Lesotho has suffered, although it has performed better than many African countries. We can observe five stages over the past decade: (1) massive growth from 2000 through 2004 following the introduction of AGOA; (2) a major drop-off in 2005 following the expiration of MFA; (3) stabilization after the imposition of safeguards against Chinese imports; (4) another major drop-off in 2008 following the expiration of safeguards; and (5) continuing decline in 2009 owing to the economic crisis.

Source: Author.

a geographic advantage for serving the U.S. market, with or without preferences. The limits of the preference advantage to African countries, in the
absence of competitive production, is clear from the fact that they are losing U.S. market share to countries such as Bangladesh, Vietnam, and
China, which do not have preferential access. In contrast, one factor in
Mauritius' early success with its EPZ garment activities was the cultiva-
tion of supply and market relationships across a number of locations,
including Asia, the United States, and Europe.

The SEZ Legal and Regulatory Framework

*The SEZ law and accompanying regulations are the critical foundation
for any zone program. They must be comprehensive and transparent,
with unambiguous ground rules established for all actors. While this
may not be sufficient to guarantee success, the absence of good laws and
regulations almost inevitably leads to failure.*
Particularly when zone programs are not controlled top-down by national
governments (when local governments and the private sector are involved
in planning and implementing projects), it is critical that the legal framework establish an unambiguous set of rules and procedures guiding the
entire process of site selection, investment, development, licensing, and
operations. Licensing regimes should ensure that private developers
adhere to specific criteria in terms of the locations in which they develop,
the nature of physical development, and environmental practices, among
other things; they should also ensure that developers are vetted in terms
of their financial capacity and record of experience. Many zone programs
experience delays because developers run into difficulty accessing the
necessary finance to carry out development. Recently, for example, this
problem has delayed high-profile investment by Chinese developers in
Ethiopia and Mauritius. In fact, as a result of similar experiences in the
first round of China's tender process for support of private developers'
international zone projecs, China's Ministry of Commerce now requires
developers to demonstrate an annual turnover of RMB15 billion (about
US$2 billion) for at least the two previous years to qualify for possible
participation in the program.

Linked to this issue is the importance of having a national physical
master plan for zone development. In the absence of a framework guiding development, local governments can overextend themselves in
acquiring land and committing to zone development or, worse, abuse
their takings power to acquire land without due regard for resettlement

and compensation. There is also a risk of local governments competing against each other for investment and inevitably resorting to offering greater and greater incentives. Finally, there is a risk of rent-seeking related to partner selection, procurement linked to zone development projects, and the issuance of licenses to firms that may benefit from the incentives available through the regime.

Several of these issues have arisen in Vietnam, which is by far the most decentralized of all the programs studied for this report. A report (Action Aid Vietnam 2007) estimated that more than 100,000 households had been displaced because of the development of industrial zones and complexes and that less than two-thirds of those households had benefited from enhanced work opportunities, improved social and technical infrastructure, or adequate compensation for appropriated land. However, the 2006 national master plan, which now forms an integral part of the legal framework of the zone program in Vietnam, sets strict criteria for zone development or expansion. Before the 2005 decision to standardize incentives nationally, competition was rife across provinces in discounting land rents and local service charges; this competition has decreased dramatically since 2005.

While SEZ law and regulations should provide a clear and detailed framework, it must be flexible enough to meet local requirements and to evolve to meet changing policy needs.
It is important to have a legal and regulatory framework that can, and does, evolve with changing requirements. Most of the African zone programs established legal frameworks based on traditional export processing zone models, which resulted in fixed rules about the nature of firms that could invest in zones, the locations of investment, the nature of activities that could be performed, and the markets to which production could be sold. These models have proved inflexible in the face of changing requirements, such as the growth of the services sector (as a potential export but also as an input to the goods-producing activities in the zones), regional trade integration, local market integration, and the development of industry clusters. While many countries—including Kenya, Tanzania, and Senegal—are shifting to more flexible SEZ models, such a shift requires not just retooling the existing framework but scrapping it and starting over with new legislation and regulations. Given the competitive challenges of many African zone programs and the limited financial and staff capacity, the process of shifting the legal framework is absorbing critical resources.

A more effective approach is to adjust the legal and regulatory framework in an evolutionary way to reflect ongoing changes in the program. This approach has been taken in Honduras, where the government learned from its early mistakes and enacted several pieces of legislation in the late 1980s and 1990s that added to the existing free zone law to broaden the geographic reach of the SEZ policy to cover the entire country and, most important, extended participation to local investors.

African zone programs should consider carefully before including single-factory schemes in their SEZ frameworks.
As discussed previously in this report, many African countries—including Senegal and Ghana especially, but also Kenya and Tanzania—use single factory free zone or manufacturing-in-bond programs that allow companies to be licensed as free zones regardless of where they are based in the country. While such programs provide substantial flexibility for investors and usually limit the infrastructure commitment of governments, they can also be highly problematic from a service delivery point of view. One of the main benefits of zones with co-located companies is the ability to concentrate infrastructure and services; few low-income countries can deliver effective services (e.g., utilities, licensing and administration, and customs) to firms spread across wide geographic areas.[6] The other major drawback of such programs is that they open up significantly greater scope for existing local foreign firms to "switch in" to the zone program to access incentives. Indeed, in the Senegal program, this is explicitly permitted. In the absence of a physical barrier that forces clear new investment, SEZ regulators face a greater challenge in monitoring and auditing potential new investors.[7]

However, a number of successful zone programs do operate single factory schemes, including Mauritius, the Dominican Republic, and Honduras. Togo is another example of an African country that runs a single factory scheme. A review of successful single factory programs suggests three possible ways they can be relevant as part of the zone framework:

1. The country is developed enough so that high-quality infrastructure is widely available and services can be delivered effectively; for example, through the use of ICT infrastructure.
2. The geographic area of the country or region covered by the zone program is limited, so infrastructure gaps among locations may not be significant, and concentration of service delivery is still possible.
3. The legal framework offers the potential for private sector development of zones, and the private sector supply response is strong. In

this situation (as is the case in Honduras and the Dominican Republic), the spread of small, privately run industrial parks offsets the
need for geographic distribution through a single factory licensing
scheme.

*The legal framework should avoid creating institutional conflict through
overlapping regimes, responsibilities, and accountabilities.*
The operations of many SEZ programs have suffered from overlapping
zone regimes that are not recognized in the legal and regulatory frameworks and that create significant confusion and, in some cases, open institutional conflict. This is almost inevitably the case when the programs are
born through different government ministries. Multiple programs offer
some potential for greater innovation and experimentation, and may be
justified on the basis of specialization if the activities are dramatically different (e.g., a program designed to target high-tech services versus a manufacturing process-oriented program). However, in most cases, they are in
conflict with one another. The result is the atrophy of one program, open
conflict across ministries, confusion, wasted resources, or—in most cases,
as shown in Box 6.6—all of these.

In Senegal, which recently announced the establishment of a new SEZ
regime, institutional conflict has largely been avoided through two actions:
(1) the existing free zone regime at the Dakar Integrated Free Zone has
been suspended, and no new investments are allowed; and (2) the same
authority—APIX (Agence national de Promotion et de Investments du
Senegal)—will oversee both regimes.

*The legal framework should outline clearly and discretely the roles and
responsibilities of key actors.*
The operation of an SEZ program requires four key players: the zone
owner, the zone *developer,* the zone *manager or operator,* and the zone *regulator.* Until the 1990s, most programs remained fully in the hands of the
public sector, and it was common for the same government body to perform all these functions simultaneously. This approach is still common
around the world. However, with the growing participation of the private
sector in zone programs, the traditional structure is increasingly problematic. Specifically, it creates a conflict of interest in which the government
is responsible for regulating and promoting all the zones in a country,
including some zones developed and operated by the private sector and
other (inherently competing) zones developed and operated on behalf of

Box 6.6

Overlapping Zone Regimes

Tanzania: EPZ versus SEZs

The Tanzanian EPZ program was launched on July 1, 2002, with the passage of the EPZ Act; it was initially under the aegis of the National Development Corporation and eventually transferred to the Ministry of Trade and Industry. To expand the potential of economic zones to contribute to the Mini-Tiger economic development strategy for 2020, the government enacted the Special Economic Zones (SEZ) Act in 2006, under the coordination of the Ministry of Planning, Economy, and Empowerment. Thus, two competing programs existed in the country, creating a confusing situation for potential investors. The situation was even more complex because, despite the passage of the SEZ Act, the program was never properly operationalized. No legislation was passed establishing an institutional structure for regulating and managing the program (no SEZ authority was established) and no regulations governing the program were put in place. As a result, the SEZ program ended up coming under the administration of the EPZ authority, which was forced to license investors interested in the SEZ program under the existing EPZ regulatory regime.

Nigeria: manufacturing free zones versus oil and gas free zones

In 1992, the Nigeria Export Processing Zones Decree allowed for the establishment of EPZs by public, private, or public-private entities under the approval and regulation of the Nigerian Export Processing Zones Authority (NEPZA). Just four years later—and long before the first NEPZA free zone was established—the government issued a new act, creating the Oil and Gas Free Zones Authority (OGFZA), a parallel organization to NEPZA with responsibility for developing, regulating, and promoting free zones in the oil and gas sector. This move, described by some as politically motivated, created significant confusion over the roles and responsibilities of OGFZA and those of NEPZA. The two institutions clashed for many years. In March 2008, the attorney general issued a ruling declaring OGFZA responsible for all oil- and gas-related activities in the country. This means that NEPZA not only does not have any authority over the oil and gas free zones, but that oil and gas activities in NEPZA-regulated zones are technically the responsibility of OGFZA. This could lead to even more confusion and overlapping regulations in the existing zones.

Source: Author.

the government. More often than not, the same government agencies are responsible for regulation and development, so they are essentially regulating themselves. This is the case across Africa; for example, in Tanzania, Kenya, Nigeria, and, to a lesser extent, Ghana and Senegal. It can be a significant barrier to attracting private sector developers and becomes a point of contention when private investors run into difficulties or disagreements arise. For example, in Lesotho, where the public developer of industrial parks also acts as the promoter, regulator, and administrator of the licensing regime, provision of land and factory shells and below-market rates has been cited as a key factor undermining investment by private sector developers, resulting in an acute shortage of industrial facilities. Tanzania may face a similar problem, with below-market lease rates being offered in the government-run Benjamin William Mkapa SEZ (BWM-SEZ). In Bangladesh, where the same authority is responsible for zone development, management, and regulation, the first privately developed zone languished for eight years awaiting approval for its operating license and has since struggled to move forward on construction owing to lack of guarantees from the government regarding energy supplies. The initial delays were ostensibly related to environmental clearance, but the situation suggests the existence of a politicized process.

Avoiding this conflict of interest usually involves separating the regulatory role as much as possible from the roles of owner, developer, and operator. Such separation allows the regulator to remain fully independent from an individual zone. As part of the process, SEZ programs need to clearly outline the specific responsibilities of the various actors—see Table 6.2 for a summary of the main roles and responsibilities. It is important to note that the owner of an SEZ may or may not be the developer. Indeed, while it is most often the case that the developer has at least some share (if not the majority) of the SEZ, it is not uncommon, even in privately developed projects, for government to have an equity share.[8] Thus, even where the government is not a lead owner and operator of zones, the regulatory activity of the zone authority should be conducted at arm's length. Another way to avoid this conflict is to allow significant private sector representation on the board that oversees the regulator, so the private sector has a voice in decisions that affect the SEZ program.

The free zone program in Ghana, under the authority of the autonomous Ghana Free Zones Board (GFZB) is a good example of a program that clearly separates these roles. GFZB is responsible for planning, regulation, and promotion of the free zones, and for packaging sites for development

Table 6.2   Summary of Roles and Responsibilities in an SEZ Program[9]

	Primary responsibilities
Government	• Conduct strategic planning. • Select site(s) and package land; establish land use guidelines. • Conduct initial feasibility studies. • Select developer and enter development agreement. • Develop offsite infrastructure. • Training/workforce development and social services. • Regulation and administration of the SEZ program (see below).
Regulator	• *Designate SEZs:* Designate public and private land as SEZs and public or private land owners or their agents as SEZ developers/operators. • *Facilitate government services:* Facilitate licensing, permitting, and regulatory services within the SEZs, particularly relating to land use, business licensing, environmental permitting, building permitting, labor regulation (including foreign work permits), and inspections; may also include business registration, utility regulation, and dispute resolution. The regulator may set fees commensurate with the cost of service delivery in these areas. • *Monitor compliance:* Monitor compliance with the SEZ legal framework, including SEZ policies, standards, and requirements, and enforce compliance through appropriate penalties independently from other public agencies.
Developer	• *Land use planning:* Create a final land-use master plan and prepare the land accordingly (grading, leveling, and other preconstruction activity). • *Provision of infrastructure:* Internal road networks, drainage and sewerage, and conduits and infrastructure for utilities. *Note that in most cases offsite infrastructure is the responsibility of the government.*
Operator	• *Facility leasing:* Manage lease and rental agreements with investors and assume responsibility for main services of the zone (e.g., maintenance, security). • *Utilities provision:* Ensure provision of onsite utilities (electricity, gas, water, telecommunications) through own provision or via domestic providers. • *Provision of other value added services:* May include a wide range of services, such as business and training centers, medical and child care services, transport, and recruiting. • *Marketing:* Experienced private developers often have a network of multinational clients across a range of industries to which they can market new SEZ opportunities. *Note that the SEZ authority/regulator and other parts of government (a national or local investment promotion agency) typically carry out some marketing activities.*

Source: Adapted from Investment Climate Department's *SEZ Practitioners Guide* (forthcoming).

(through leases to private developers). From the outset of the program in 1995, GFZB's role did not include zone development or management. Costa Rica's program, under the authority of the Free Zones Corporation of Costa Rica, operates under a similar framework. In the Dominican Republic, the National Free Zones Council (CNZFE) has similar responsibility for planning, regulation, and promotion of free zones. However, in the Dominican Republic, the government developed a large number of publically owned and operated free zones[10] that are run by an autonomous agency (Proindustria) linked to the Ministry of Commerce and Industry. While CNZFE does not conduct any marketing or planning activities on behalf of the public parks, it is responsible for regulating these parks. Conflict of interest is kept at bay through the institutional structure of the CNZFE board, which legally mandates one seat to the director of Proindustria and two seats to representatives of private free zone operators.

Establishing a sound legal framework is a necessary but not sufficient condition for zone success. The de facto situation matters enormously.
Despite the importance of the issues discussed in this section, the evidence from the research conducted in this study suggests that establishing a clear and sound legal framework is not enough to guarantee the success of SEZ programs. In fact, effective de facto implementation may be more important than the legal framework, and this is where many of the African zone programs fail, owing to poor implementing capacity of the zone authorities or the failure of government agencies to coordinate or deliver on their obligations with respect to the program. In Ghana, for example, the legal framework that guides the free zone program is sound and flexible enough to meet changing requirements and the needs of different stakeholders in the zone development process (e.g., government and private developers). However, disputes between the private developer and the government, and problems with infrastructure delivery in the Tema zone have seriously hindered development of the zone. Similarly, in Senegal, it was not the legal framework of the program but the inability to deliver a decent investment climate that led to failure.

Of course, national competitiveness and market potential matter at least as much and probably more to potential investors than the de jure or de facto environment in the SEZs. It is likely that more investors will set up in China's SEZs even in the absence of a good legal framework than will come to Lesotho, Tanzania, or Ghana, with their watertight frameworks.

Fiscal incentives may play a role in attracting investment in the short term, particularly in new zone programs, but they do not have a positive effect on the long-term success of zones. The evidence presented in Chapter 4 suggested that fiscal incentives are not associated with improved outcomes in zone programs; in fact, where they do show any significant correlation with outcomes, the relationship is a negative one; that is, the provision of significant fiscal incentives (specifically tax holidays) is associated, over the long term, with poorer performance in terms of exports and employment in zones. However, there is some evidence in many programs and in recent research (Harding and Javorcik 2007; Harrison et al. 2010) that fiscal incentives may attract initial investment, particularly from FDI. In fact, we are aware of no zone programs that did not, at least in their initial stages, offer some form of fiscal incentive to attract investors (see Table 6.3). So the bigger issue may not be the availability of fiscal incentives but rather the extent to which programs have managed to carve out sustainable competitive advantage and avoid a reliance on incentives. In this respect, the African programs under study have failed to move beyond incentive-based competition, while programs in other regions— particularly in East Asia but also in Mauritius—have managed to do so. Of course, these programs are the exceptions; in our study, only Vietnam was moving away from heavy use of tax-based incentives. So the African zones are far from alone in their failure to adopt best practices in this area.

Whether or not African zones eliminate fiscal incentives in the short term, the evidence shows that incentives do not compensate for a poor investment climate. Thus, the significant government investment of financial resources, human capital, and time in zone programs should be devoted to delivering quality services to investors and ensuring that the business environment is as competitive as possible—this is the precondition to investment. For example, Senegal's initial zone program relied on the idea of creating a tax-free paradise for foreign investors, but it failed to deliver on the factors that allow companies to operate competitively. If they are not competitive, they will not be profitable; and without profits, there is little benefit in a corporate tax waiver. Ironically, since its 1995 policy redesign, Senegal's program has been one of the few in the world that no longer provides tax holidays, instead offering free zone investors a permanent low-tax option; unfortunately, it appears that only half the lesson was learned, as no significant offsetting improvements to the investment climate followed.

Table 6.3   Summary of Fiscal Incentives Offered in SEZs

	Corporate tax holidays or reductions	*Other fiscal incentives*
Bangladesh	10 years exempt +5 years at 50% of normal rate (v. 35% national rate)	No dividend tax; accelerated depreciation; expats pay no income tax for 3 years
Dominican Republic	Unlimited exemption (v. 25% national rate)	No value added tax (VAT), business tax, or municipal taxes
Honduras	Unlimited exemption (v. 25% national rate)	No local sales tax, excise tax, tax on net assets, or municipal taxes
Vietnam	4 years exempt, 50% reduction for next 9 years, then 25% (v. 28% national rate)	N/A
Ghana	10 years exempt, then 8% (v. 25% nationally)	Permanent exemption from withholding taxes on dividends
Kenya	10 years exempt, then 10 years at 25% (v. 30% national rate)	No VAT or stamp duty (perpetual); 10-year holiday on dividend tax; investment in new equipment 100% deductible
Lesotho	Exempt for sales outside Southern African Customs Union (SACU); 15% inside SACU	No withholding tax on dividends; training deductible at 125%
Nigeria	Unlimited exemption (v. 30% national rate)	Unlimited exemption from local taxes and VAT; rent-free land during construction phase
Senegal	15% rate (v. 35% national rate originally, now 25%)	No withholding tax on dividends, employers taxes on staff, property taxes, licensing fees, or stamp duties
Tanzania	10 years exempt then revert to national rate (30%)	10-year exemption on local taxes, withholding on rents, dividends, and interest; no VAT on utilities or wharfage

Sources: Individual country SEZ authorities and World Bank Doing Business data (online data, www.doingbusiness .org) for national corporate tax rates.

Fiscal incentives are "sticky" and prone to inflation; over-reliance on them distorts investor behavior and can put countries in a "race to the bottom" situation.
Although several of the zone programs under study—including those in the Dominican Republic, Honduras, and Nigeria—offer unlimited tax holidays, most set specific periods, normally 5 or 10 years, after which normal domestic corporate tax regimes return, either immediately or through a staged phase-in. However, the experience in many countries is that

investors come to rely on incentives or at least to expect them. We found countless examples of companies seeking to extend tax holidays—by lobbying for an extension, by lobbying for access to an alternative incentive of equivalent value, or even by closing the business and reopening under a new name. The focus on tax incentives distorts not only the behavior of investors but also that of those responsible for the zone program, leading them to respond to competitiveness challenges with short-term fiscal breaks (e.g., rent reductions) rather than targeting competitiveness more holistically through improved infrastructure and service delivery. This situation also leads to inflation in incentives, part of an inevitable race to the bottom for programs that rely on incentives as their primary basis of competitiveness.

Lesotho, for example, initially offered foreign manufacturers a five-year tax holiday, followed by a standard 15 percent tax rate. This was reduced to 10 percent in 2007, after the post-MFA decline of Lesotho's FDI garment sector. In the wake of continued decline in the global economic crisis, the tax rate has been eroded to zero on all exports outside the Southern African Customs Union (SACU). The fiscal incentives have created major distortions in the market and may put the government in a fiscal bind in the future. First, there is increasing demand from exporters to extend the zero corporate income tax to exports within SACU, because the South African market represents a significant opportunity for export growth. Second, domestic manufacturing firms that primarily supply exporting firms with inputs are subject to the standard (25%) tax regime, which puts them at a disadvantage to foreign suppliers and undermines the potential for domestic links. Third, the general taxation regime—which still applies to investors in other key sectors such as minerals, tourism, and services—is unattractive to foreign investors, leading to increased pressure to offer special incentives to these sectors as well. And it is not just corporate tax holidays that are potentially damaging. Other fiscal incentives—including exemptions from local taxes and VAT, direct subsidies, and below-market rents—can have even more damaging effects on local markets (see Box 6.7).

Finally, generous incentive programs can confer exclusive privileges to certain (sometimes sector-specific) local elites. These elites can then become a powerful force acting against comprehensive reform across the national economy.

Fiscal incentives are problematic in the WTO context.
SEZs are not specifically mentioned in any of the WTO agreements; however, many of the incentives typically offered as part of SEZ policies are

Box 6.7

Distorting Markets through Incentives: Subsidized Factory Shells in Lesotho

There is virtually no private provision of industrial sites for export manufacturing in Lesotho; for almost all foreign investors, the Lesotho National Development Corporation (LNDC) is the industrial landlord. LNDC has invested in speculative development of factory shells for rent to foreign investors. These are normally provided on a five-year lease at subsidized rates—the current charge for serviced facilities is M7.10 per square meter per month (US$0.92–1.32[11]). The availability of these serviced facilities does more than simply overcome the restrictive land laws and provide cheap rent; it also reduces the risk and start-up time for foreign investors, which has been a critical factor in attracting and retaining export manufacturing investment.

However, the sustainability of this traditional EPZ-type model is increasingly being called into question. Because LNDC provides facilities at below-market rents, private Basotho developers have little chance of competing. The few that do enter the market find that foreign investors have little interest in their facilities or make use of them only until a unit becomes available in an LNDC industrial park. And because it subsidizes rents, LNDC cannot recover the costs of development of factory shells, rendering them unsuitable for accessing commercial finance for new developments. The result is that LNDC is highly constrained in its ability to provide new factory shells, which in turn places a major restriction on new investment in the country. Despite a clear demand for new factory units, particularly from South African investors, development is limited by the lack of funding. According to LNDC, 14 definite commitments from foreign investors to establish factories in Lesotho remain in the backlog.

Source: Author.

subject to WTO disciplines, mainly through the Agreement on Subsidies and Countervailing Measures (SCM Agreement). These include direct subsidies, rent subsidies, and tax holidays or reductions in any form of direct tax, with the exception of elimination of import duties, which is not considered an actionable subsidy.

Under the provision of Special and Differential Treatment (SDT), least-developed WTO members and countries whose per capita gross national product is under US$1,000 in 1990 dollars are exempt from the prohibition on export subsidies. Other middle-income countries are also

Table 6.4   Categorization of Sub-Saharan African WTO Members vis-à-vis Article 27 of SCM Agreement

	LDCs	MICs (18)	MICs (23)
Description	Least-developed countries (LDCs)	Middle-income countries, but with per capita income less than US$1,000 in 1990 US$	Middle-income WTO members with incomes above US$1,000 (1990) and with existing SEZ programs at time of accession
Situation	Generally exempt from prohibition on export subsidies	Generally exempt from prohibition on export subsidies until reaching US$1,000 (1990 US$) for three consecutive years, then must phase out	Programs grandfathered in; exemptions expire in 2015
Sub-Saharan African Countries	All others not mentioned in MIC 18 and MIC 23[12]	Cameroon, Congo (DR), Cote d'Ivoire, Ghana, Nigeria, Senegal, Zimbabwe	Kenya, Mauritius

Source: Creskoff and Walkenhorst (2009).

exempt for the time being, but these exemptions will expire by 2015 (see Table 6.4 for a summary). Thus, most African countries are not prohibited from subsidizing exports under WTO, which opens up considerable legal scope for the types of incentives that are normally offered in the free zones. However, there are three important caveats:

1. Exemption does not necessarily prevent another country from bringing a case against an "exempt" country under the SCM Agreement; it simply changes the burden of proof. Thus, a nonexempt country would automatically be found in contravention of WTO if a case were brought against it. An exempt country can still be found in contravention if the complainant can prove that the subsidy was harmful to its exporters.
2. Article 27 includes an export competitiveness clause: If an exempt country achieves 3.25 percent of the world market in any product[13] for two consecutive years, it is no longer exempt and must phase out all subsidies within eight years. This is unlikely to happen in most African countries; for example, even a large and concentrated garment exporter such as Lesotho does not come close to reaching this threshold.

3. Exemption under Article 27 does not extend to a prohibition on the use of domestic over imported goods; that is, measures that promote import substitution or subsidize the use of domestic content. This provision has implications for a number of zone programs,[14] although it does not directly affect any of the programs included in our study. (Nigeria's export expansion grant, which sits outside the zone program, would run afoul of this provision.)

Several of the major African zone programs—including Nigeria, Kenya, and Ghana—will need to shift away from their reliance on tax incentives in the near future. This may be a significant challenge to the competitiveness of these zones. However, other programs—such as those in Mauritius and Vietnam—have managed this transition without too much difficulty. The Dominican Republic is in the process of implementing changes to its regime; for example, eliminating local content requirements, export performance requirements, and restrictions against local market sales.

Successful zone programs are moving increasingly toward removing fiscal incentives and toward integration of zone tax regimes with those of the national economy. They are implementing alternatives to fiscal incentives, such as (1) a greater focus on service delivery in the zones; (2) the development of nonfiscal incentives; and (3) shifting the scope and targeting of fiscal incentives.
Despite the continued importance of fiscal incentives, some programs have managed to move away from them in recent years after having established a position of competitiveness. Perhaps most famously, China went through a process of progressive integration between the tax levels offered to FDI in the SEZs and those of domestic firms; tax breaks for FDI have now been largely eliminated in the coastal regions. Several other countries have also undone the tax subsidies they once offered to foreign firms. Two examples are Vietnam (which followed China's path of progressively adjusting the tax levels in the free zones to match those of the local economy) and Mauritius (which followed the opposite path—extending the free zone benefits to the domestic economy).

An often-overlooked challenge of phasing out fiscal incentives, particularly corporate tax breaks, is maintaining credibility with investors regarding the predictability of the policy environment in the SEZs. Many investors have committed themselves to long-term leases (in the case of Bangladesh, for example, for 30 years). The investors' decisions were based on a package of policy expectations, including a fiscal incentive regime.

Making substantial changes to the regime, such as eliminating tax breaks, would send a message that the government's other commitments on zone policy might no longer be guaranteed. Managing this issue can be a difficult balancing act.

In Vietnam's case, although FDI in the EPZs started off tax-free, the huge growth of these zones over time and the dramatic changes in Vietnam's national economy that resulted from global integration made it necessary to significantly alter the regulatory and incentive regime. Although new master plans, regulations, and incentive structures were introduced every few years, the process followed a relatively predictable path toward greater liberalization and harmonization with the national economy. And companies that had invested in the zones under previous regimes were allowed to keep their agreed-upon tax breaks. Thus, Vietnam managed to integrate the zones with the national economy over a relatively short period, while avoiding substantial revolutions or policy reversals that might have resulted in investor uncertainty. At the level of individual zones, removing the tax incentive has had an enormous effect on the approach of zone developers, who have shifted from incentive- to service-based competition and are now touting how quickly they can process applications rather than how low the tax burden will be.

Vietnam did not completely eliminate tax holidays and other fiscal incentives for foreign investors. Rather, in compliance with WTO, the country separated these incentives from the SEZ program, instead targeting them to specific industry sectors and specific lagging regions. Malaysia is another example of a country that made significant use of fiscal incentives but modified them over many decades to target the specific needs of its industrial strategy (see Box 6.8).

Getting rid of fiscal incentives presents a problem of collective action; institutions of regional integration may offer an effective avenue through which to address this problem.

Addressing the problem of corporate tax incentives in SEZ programs—and, more widely, in investment promotion regimes—is particularly difficult, because it presents a classic prisoner's dilemma: Two neighboring countries would both be better off by cooperating to eliminate or regulate the provision of tax incentives to foreign investors, but each might benefit most from offering incentives while their neighbor does not. In the absence of knowledge of its neighbor's intentions, each country will act in its own self-interest and choose to offer incentives, so they will effectively cancel each other out and transfer rents to the foreign

Box 6.8

Evolving Incentives: Malaysia

Like most developing countries, Malaysia has used a system of incentives to attract investment. However, the structure has been continuously revised to meet evolving national development objectives. By linking the incentives and the provision of specialized infrastructure facilities to skills development and technology upgrading, Malaysia was able to take advantage of global changes to improve its competitive position. The evolution of the Malaysian system of incentives reflects a shift from general investment promotion to a focus on high-tech sectors and industrial clusters.

The Pioneer Industries Ordinance (PIO) was introduced in 1958 to provide incentives and tariff protection for the development of manufacturing industries. These firms enjoyed *tariff protection and tax relief* for two to five years, depending on the level of investment. By the late 1960s, the need to shelter import-substituting industries was overtaken by the need to export. Toward this end, Malaysia passed the Investment Incentive Act (IIA) in 1968 to encourage *employment creation, dispersal of industries, and investment in capital-intensive projects*. The incentives provided under the IIA (Pioneer Status, labor utilization relief, and location incentives) offered tax relief for 2–10 years and tax credits ranging from 25 percent to 40 percent of capital expenditure. These incentives were focused on attracting more labor-intensive and export-oriented industries compared with the import-substituting industries attracted by the PIO.

To enhance the role of the manufacturing sector in the economy, the government introduced several new policies and programs. The most notable was the Free Trade Zone Act of 1971, whose main objective was to attract export-oriented multinational corporations (MNCs) to invest in Malaysia. Industries operating inside the FTZs would enjoy better (and subsidized) infrastructure, expedited customs, and duty-free imports of raw materials, components, and machinery. This approach to promote export manufacturing was very timely and was successful in attracting the first major wave of export-oriented electronics manufacturing, concentrated initially in components. In 1973, to supplement the FTZ program and promote dispersal of industries to the less developed regions of the country, Malaysia introduced the Licensed Manufacturing Warehouse program, which extended similar treatment to individual factories set up outside the FTZs.

(continued next page)

Box 6.8 *(continued)*

In 1985, the industrialization process became more cohesive with the implementation of an Industrial Master Plan (IMP), which identified three policy instruments for increasing technology capability: *research manpower; institutional arrangements, such as industrial parks; and incentives for R&D (research and development)*. Twelve priority sector development plans comprised a comprehensive strategy to lift Malaysia's industrial base. To further boost the IMP, the Promotion of Investment Act (PIA) of 1986 was passed to replace the IIA. Under the PIA, the labor utilization relief incentive was abolished and the Pioneer Status incentives were modified. Promoted industries and projects would enjoy tax relief for up to five years, regardless of the size of the capital investment. Amendments to the Income Tax Act of 1967 provided tax incentives for training, R&D, and reinvestments. Other instruments—including the exemption of import duty on raw materials, tariff protection for selected industries, and financial and credit assistance—were used to promote industrial development. These incentives, along with other moves to create a more liberal investment environment, are recognized as the impetus behind the recovery of the Malaysian economy in the late 1980s and the rapid uptick in manufacturing investment.

The Second Industrial Master Plan, 1996–2005 (IMP2) extended its reach beyond export manufacturing operations toward more *locally integrated clusters* to encourage the growth of supporting industries, including the service sector. The IMP2 focused on deepening the integration of manufacturing operations along the value chain through investments in R&D and design capability and the development of integrated supporting industries, packaging, distribution, and marketing activities to enhance industrial links and increase productivity and competitiveness.

Since the early 1990s, the investment incentives have been tied increasingly to *technological deepening, exports, and domestic sourcing of inputs*. R&D and *training incentives* have also been introduced. In 1991, a broad reform of Malaysia's investment policy regime phased out tax incentives for exports and reduced the scope of the Pioneer Status. With these changes, "ordinary" Pioneer Status would qualify for only 60 percent exemption (instead of a full exemption) for three to six years (instead of 10). However, full tax exemptions were granted to investments in specific high-tech and strategic sectors. Furthermore, the Malaysian Industrial Development Authority announced that it would screen applications for Pioneer Status more rigorously, using four criteria: value added of 30 percent to 50 percent, local content levels of 20 percent to 50 percent, depth of technology, and linkage effects.

Source: This narrative is largely summarized from a background paper prepared for UNCTAD by Lim and Ong (2002).

investors. The lack of collective action is apparent in practice. Tanzania is unlikely to launch a zone program with no tax holidays when all its neighbors are offering them. And unless a country is forced by WTO or has been successful enough in its development (e.g., China and Vietnam), it is unlikely to make a unilateral decision to abandon fiscal incentives. The regional agenda offers a potential venue to address this collective action problem. First, it is at the intraregional (and, in cases of large federal states like Brazil, Nigeria, and the United States, the intranational) level that the most wasteful incentive-based bidding wars for investors tend to take place. But these investors generally look to incentives only *after* they have decided what region to invest in, so the regional level may be the most efficient point at which to control incentive-based spending. Second, the harmonization of regional trade and investment conditions offers the opportunity to establish a common framework for the provision of fiscal incentives. For example, in the case of NAFTA, Mexico was obliged to shift incentives in its *maquiladora* program away from those linked directly to exports to those based on other types of performance, such as investment level or employment generation. The European Union's trade and investment framework has strict rules for the use of fiscal incentives to attract investment, particularly when the funding for subsidies derives from EU sources, such as Cohesion Funds.

Institutional Framework and the SEZ Regulatory Authority

The institutional mechanisms underpinning the SEZ regulatory authority must balance authority and independence with inclusiveness.
The SEZ regulatory authority is the most important institutional actor in any zone program. The authority, quality, capacity, and focus of the SEZ regulator will often make or break a zone program. The authority must have a strong, institutionally founded mandate; at the same time, it must be inclusive and capable of incorporating and coordinating across the many key stakeholders required to make zone programs successful. In many of the African zone programs included in this study, the zone regulatory authority is both institutionally and operationally weak, which affects its potential to plan and implement effectively. Many also suffer from significant capacity limitations.

A variety of institutional arrangements have been adopted in SEZ programs, including government authorities or corporations, departments based in specific ministries, zone-specific management boards, and (less often) investment promotion agencies. Table 6.5 lists examples of countries

Table 6.5   Examples of Zone Administrative Models

Government authorities or corporations	Ministries	Zone-specific management boards	Investment promotion agencies
Jordan	Cape Verde	Vietnam	Sri Lanka
Bangladesh	Taiwan, China	India	Uganda
Thailand	Slovak Rep.	Turkey	Ireland
Costa Rica	El Salvador	Ukraine	Lesotho
Korea	Honduras	Poland	
Zambia			
Kenya			
Ghana			
Dominican Rep.			
Tanzania			

Source: Adapted from FIAS (2008).

that have adopted these forms. Best practice is to establish the regulator as an independent agency under a board of directors that includes both public and private sector members. This makeup helps separate the zone regime from political processes. It may not be feasible to create an independent agency initially because of legacy situations or other political economy factors; however, a timeline should be established to move toward an autonomous or semiautonomous body.

Most commonly, the SEZ regulator, even when operating as an independent agency, reports through a line ministry, typically the ministry responsible for trade and industry. The relevant minister usually chairs the SEZ authority's board. This setup is common in many of the African zones, including Tanzania, Ghana, Nigeria, and Lesotho. Best practice, however, indicates that the regulator is most effective when its board is anchored to the highest possible level of government—a central rather than line ministry, such as the executive or the ministry of finance. In the Dominican Republic, Kenya, and Senegal, for example, the SEZ program reports directly to the president; in Bangladesh, it reports to the prime minister. This reporting relationship is critical to ensure that the regulator has sufficient authority and autonomy, and is in a strong position to coordinate actions with other ministries. In Bangladesh, the prime ministerial leadership of the board was one of the most important success factors in the functioning of the regulator.

The downside to having high-level authority on the board is that, in the absence of delegated decision making, important activities of the regulator can be unnecessarily delayed. For example, in Ghana, all new free zone licenses must be approved by the board of directors. However, this board is appointed by the president and, following a change of presidency in 2009, there was a long delay before the new president reconstituted the board, resulting in delays for companies waiting to have their applications approved. In Bangladesh, to avoid such delays, the prime minister appointed the permanent secretary to sit on the executive board of the regulatory authority (which includes only the senior management team and is responsible for day-to-day management). Most zone programs delegate substantial decision-making power to the regulatory authority.

In most cases, the SEZ regulator is governed through a committee or board of directors. As noted previously, the most important characteristics of this board are that it includes cross-ministerial involvement and significant (ideally, majority) representation from the private sector. Board composition varies from country to country, but an important principle is to balance the involvement of all parties that need to participate in decision making regarding the zones and companies that operate in them with the equally important need to ensure that the board is efficient and governable. While there is no specific best practice in this regard, most boards are relatively small—12 or fewer members. Private sector participation should include an association of zone operators or companies if one exists; if not, it should include a representative drawn from those stakeholders. Figure 6.1 compares the board structures of the zone regulatory authorities in several countries in this study.

The institutional and administrative structures of the regulatory authority play an important role in determining how effectively the authority carries out its critical function of cross-agency coordination.
This role of the SEZ authority in meeting the needs of investors involves a wide range of activities that cross various ministerial domains, including customs, land use and zoning, taxation, business registration and licensing, immigration, and environmental, labor, and social compliance. Delivering effectively on this mandate starts with being empowered through the SEZ law, which should define the mandate of the authority as both a monitor and enforcer of laws and standards and as a one-stop facilitator of investment licensing. It also requires effective coordination across agencies—a strong institutional grounding can play an important role here. In general, African zones have made significant progress in building capable and institutionally sound SEZ regulatory authorities, but they are still not given enough power to deliver effectively on their mandate.

Figure 6.1   Comparison of Zone Regulatory Authority Board Structures

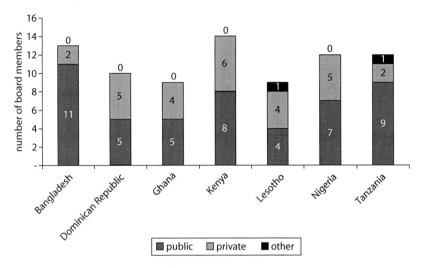

Source: Author, based on information from individual country SEZ laws.

A first-best solution is to provide the regulator with the power to make and enforce decisions on all these issues. This essentially gives it authority over the normally mandated agency or ministry, specifically within the defined SEZs. It is also critical that the regulator's authority extend over not just national but also local authorities, particularly with regard to land use planning and environmental and licensing issues. In some programs where very large-scale SEZs are established (e.g., in China, Jordan, and the new program in Senegal), the SEZ regulator has the power of a governor of a municipality, to which the prime minister or president can delegate the full range of authorities required to enable the regulator to carry out its functions as a one-stop shop. Authority is normally granted either directly in the SEZ law or through the delegation of signature from ministries. Among the African zones in the study, only APIX has this delegation of authority.

In most SEZ programs, delegation of authority for business licensing, issues relating to taxation, and monitoring labor issues is not problematic. However, the majority of zone programs struggle to deliver effective authority to the regulator regarding customs, environmental compliance, and (perhaps most commonly) immigration issues. This is due to political as well as practical considerations. Few SEZ authorities have the capacity to carry out the responsibilities for all of these activities independently, at least during the early stages of their development. This is certainly the case in most African programs, where size, budget, and capacity limitations make this kind of delegation impractical.

Regardless of the institutional arrangements, maintaining good relations with other government ministries and agencies is critical to ensure that the SEZ authority can deliver effectively on its mandate. Such relations must be cemented at both the political and operational (coordination) level. One approach is to have dedicated staff from each of the relevant agencies based at the SEZ authority's one-stop shop and working, at least on a day-to-day basis, under the authority. To be effective, these arrangements normally require a memorandum of understanding (MOU) across agencies on the deployment of staff and a clear delineation of authority. Such a program was put in place in Lesotho a year after the launch of the one-stop center, when management was unable to deliver effectively on its mandate owing to a lack of day-to-day control over staff members from various agencies. In most countries, there are significant political economy constraints to this type of cooperation, with ministries unwilling to give up any authority over their staff members or their domains. Weak interagency coordination is common among the African programs (indeed, among a large share of SEZ programs globally). Lack of coordination contributes to serious inefficiencies in zone program performance; where cross-agency relations are not just poorly coordinated but openly conflictual, they can cripple a zone program (see Box 6.9).

The Nigerian case proves that board representation alone is not sufficient to overcome cross-agency conflict (both the Nigerian Port Authority and Customs sit on the NEPZA board). However, high-level authority at the top of the board, combined with interministerial committees and the establishment of MOUs and service-level agreements across agencies, can certainly contribute to improved coordination.

Most African SEZ authorities suffer from a lack of clear, medium-term predictability in their operating budgets.
A critical principle to ensure effective functioning of the EPZ regulator is autonomy of operation. Beyond an institutional structure that gives the agency independence from any single ministry, true autonomy depends on having a sufficient and predictable budget that is not vulnerable to political influence. This is problematic in almost all the African zone authorities included in the study. First, although significant resources are

---

Box 6.9

Institutional Conflict in Nigeria's Free Zone Program

The underperformance of Nigeria's free zone program can be attributed to a number of issues related to the adverse business environment (nationally and within the zone) and policy instability. Perhaps most important, the zones have suffered from a number of problems related to institutional conflicts:

- *NEPZA versus the Port Authority at Calabar:* Conflict between the port authority (which controlled the Calabar port) and the EPZ authority effectively undermined the potential for integrating the Calabar Free Zone and its adjacent port; this, in turn, severely affected the competitiveness of the free zone.
- *NEPZA versus Customs:* Several years after legislation was passed to allow free zone companies to sell to the local market, customs authorities, who opposed the move, continue to block local market sales.
- *Tinapa/NEPZA versus Customs:* Tinapa Business Free Zone and Resort, designed as an alternative to Dubai and London for shopping and tourism, saw its duty-free allowance reduced from the planned US$5,000 per person to only US$330 per person after US$400 million investment had been sunk into the project.
- *NEPZA versus OGFZA:* Conflict between the two free zone programs (discussed in Box 6.6).

Source: Author.

---

often devoted to SEZ-related capital expenditures, zone authorities appear to struggle with limited budgets to support their roles as promoters, operators, and regulators. For example, Tanzania's new zone authority (EPZA) was forced to operate with a skeletal staff during its first two to three years because of limited resources. A recent organizational study conducted by Tanzania's National Institute of Productivity recommended that EPZA expand its staff to 44. However, owing to funding constraints, the staffing buildup had to be done in stages—as of July 2009, EPZA still had only 17 permanent staff members. In comparison, according to FIAS (2008), the Egyptian General Authority for Investment and Free Zones had more than 4,000 employees at one point. In Kenya, Tanzania, Ghana, and Lesotho, zone authorities expressed concern about their operating budgets and indicated that investment, maintenance, and marketing activities suffered significantly from lack of funds. And not only are budgets small, they are unpredictable. In most of the African zone programs, a ministry or the exchequer allocates the budget to the zone authority on a year-to-year basis.

Best practice is to link the budget in some way to the revenues earned through the zone program. This does not mean expecting the zone authority to be self-sufficient through fees raised for licensing and other services. These fees can be an important revenue source, but they are typically not enough to cover the budget of an authority, and expectations of self-sufficiency can be lead to excessive administrative charges that deter investors. For example, in Ghana, investors complain that they are required to pay the zone authority US$50 for a permit every time they import a consignment. Instead, best practice (as followed, for example, in China) is to set up a formula for establishing the annual budget, including giving the authority a specific share of taxes generated through the zone. This has the added benefit of giving the zone authority an incentive not to compete on tax holidays.

Decentralization of zone authorities presents opportunities for competition and innovation, but in most low-income countries, scale and capacity limitations outweigh the potential benefits.

In some larger countries, particularly those with significant local autonomy, zone programs and regulation are sometimes devolved to the local level. One significant drawback experienced by countries that have followed this approach (aside from duplication of activities) is that inconsistent policies and capacities across regions can result in highly uneven programs that confuse investors. The same problem occurs if a country operates more than one type of zone regime; for example, in Nigeria, where separate zone regulatory authorities have been established for the oil and gas sector (OGFZA) and all other sectors (NEPZA). This led to significant high-level conflict between the agencies that had to be resolved by the attorney general, and has caused confusion for investors, especially for oil and gas companies based in NEPZA industrial zones and services companies based in OGFZA zones (see Box 6.9).

Similarly in Vietnam, different kinds of zones—EPZs, industrial zones, technology zones, and border free zones—are regulated by different agencies linked to different ministries. The result is investor confusion, but the situation also allows powerful investors to negotiate the most favorable terms across different zones and regions. Decentralization of zone decision making authority in Vietnam led to a proliferation of zones and incentive models and, in many cases, poor location and investment decisions made without proper planning. In the absence of regional government in

Vietnam, each province tends to want its own zone. Therefore, the planning process often becomes political, with too many inefficient investments getting approval. Recently, the government addressed the problems by creating a strong centralized framework, while continuing to decentralize investment decision making and to empower provincial authorities to issue investment licenses within a standard framework. Over time, this approach has led to more healthy competition in value added services among provinces and zones without undermining national development objectives.

The benefits and drawbacks of decentralization are well documented in the case of Malaysia (see Box 6.10), where state-level leadership contributed to world-class performance of the zone program in Penang, but institutional and resource challenges created inefficiencies in the program.

Partnerships and Private Sector Participation

As discussed in Chapter 4, no clear evidence exists that, globally, private sector ownership and operation of zones is inherently more successful. However, in the African context there is reason to support private-sector-led zones because of the limited government capacity and the potential to reduce investment outlay and risk.
According to FIAS (2008), approximately half of the world's zones are privately owned and half are publicly owned. This mix varies substantially across regions, as can be seen in Figure 6.2. For Sub-Saharan Africa, the report indicates that 51 percent of zones are in private hands; however, this percentage includes many of Kenya's single factory units.[15] Across most of Africa, the government plays a major role in planning, developing, and operating zones, but it often opens up the market to the private sector.

The following is a brief summary of the arrangements in the six African countries covered in this study:

- *Ghana:* Designed for private participation; implementation is effectively a PPP, with an industrial park owned and operated by government within which land is leased to private developers.
- *Kenya:* Open to private developers, but the largest zone (Athi River) and the zone in Mombasa are run by the government (Export Processing Zones Authority).
- *Lesotho:* All industrial parks are owned and operated by government (Lesotho National Development Corporation).

Box 6.10

The Benefits and Drawbacks of Decentralization: PDC and the Malaysia Case

Despite having a unified legislation for its EPZ program, Malaysia does not have a central body responsible for EPZ development. During the early years of development, the state development corporations were given responsibility for managing the EPZs. In the case of Penang, the Penang Development Corporation (PDC) was established in 1969 as the principal development agency of the state; later, it was appointed FTZ authority.

Despite being a state corporation, PDC has adopted the work ethic and management style of a private sector company. These characteristics evolved in the early years of the corporation, when there was more autonomy and freedom of action. PDC's interactions and relationships with multinational investors in Penang also had a positive effect on its style of operation. Although PDC was involved in various aspects of economic development in Penang, its greatest achievement has been in the industrialization program in the state of Penang, which was initiated through the first EPZ in Malaysia. In addition to the state's good basic infrastructure, Penang offered a young, trainable workforce and relatively inexpensive land. However, PDC also recognized the importance of servicing investors efficiently and effectively. In the absence of a central coordinating body for EPZs in Malaysia, the PDC acted as a one-stop agency for investors, not only helping them obtain all relevant information but also arranging for them to meet with the relevant authorities to obtain clearances and approvals (Singh 2010).

However, while state development corporations could raise funds for capital expenditure to plan, develop, and promote the EPZs, they did not have the powers to collect annual fees. Thus, after the early years of development, many of the state development corporations, including PDC, realized that they could not keep drawing on their other revenues for operational expenses. To resolve the issue of funding for operational expenses, the role of the EPZ authority was transferred from the state development corporations to the respective local authorities in 1983.

Source: Singh (2010).

- *Nigeria:* Open to private participation; the flagship zone in Calabar is owned and operated by the government (Nigerian Export Processing Zones Authority). However, many recent projects are PPPs between government (usually state-level) and private developers (some of which are foreign). Oil and Gas Free Zones are publicly owned but privately operated.

Figure 6.2   Mix of Public versus Private Zones by Region[16]

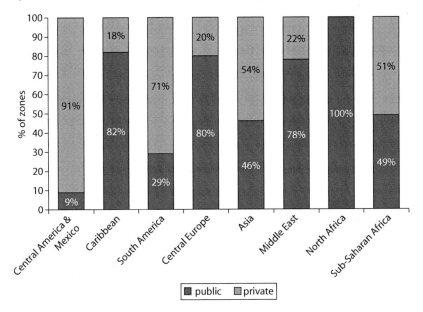

Source: Derived from FIAS (2008).

- *Senegal:* The only existing zone is government owned and operated; an upcoming SEZ will be privately owned and operated (foreign developer).
- *Tanzania:* Government-run (Export Processing Zones Authority) and privately run zones coexist.

While many of the successful East Asian SEZ programs—most notably, China's—were led by the public sector, the situation in Africa (and in most low-income countries) is notably different. In East Asia, the SEZs were primarily needed to overcome a policy problem; specifically, as a mechanism to facilitate a phased program of economic liberalization. The state played a major role in the economy of most of these East Asian countries and, by and large, had strong technical capacity and moderately acceptable governance practices. But in most African countries, the need for SEZs is not primarily to overcome de jure trade and investment policies but rather the de facto situation on the ground; specifically, a poor investment climate and weak governance. The delivery capacity of the state is part of the problem. And where the state is investing in and running zones, the inherent conflict of interest between its roles as developer and regulator can contribute to governance problems.

On the whole, the government-run zones in Africa have not been successful, although the evidence is not clear that this is a function of public sector management. In fact, the success record of private sector zones on the continent does not appear to be any better. Outside of the African zones, the Dominican Republic is the best case for analysis, as it includes a mix of public and private zones.[17] As for the other countries covered in our study, Bangladesh's zones are all government run; Honduras has virtually all private zones (although it retains the original, small government zone in Puerto Cortes); and Vietnam is mainly private, although many of the projects are joint ventures involving provincial governments (but in almost all cases, management is private). An analysis shows no clear pattern of outcomes across the public and private zones in the Dominican Republic in terms of the number of firms and level of investment, employment, or exports. What is clearly different is the service offering across the zones: The privately run zones generally offer higher quality infrastructure and more value added services than the government-run zones, and, accordingly, charge higher rents. The best natural experiments in the Dominican Republic are two cases in which government-owned zones were privatized. In one case (San Pedro de Macoris), zone performance improved substantially when ownership and management were handed over to the association of zone investors. In the other (La Armeria), a similar buyout by the association of investors struggled, and the zone was eventually sold back to the government operator.

There are some reasons to believe that privately run zones would be superior to those owned and operated by government. First, private developers generally choose their zone locations unencumbered by political factors. Second, they generally have a greater financial incentive to deliver a wide range of value added services to their clients. Third, they tend to invest in smaller, more manageable zones, and build out these zones with prefabricated structures, providing greater flexibility for potential tenants. But the real advantage of the private sector is the expertise in planning and developing industrial parks, something that few government operators can match, particularly given the capacity limitations in many African zone authorities.

But private sector operation is no guarantee of success. Ghana's zone program, for example, was a pioneer in Africa for its approach to private sector participation; but the program paid a heavy price for selecting the wrong private partner to lead its flagship free zone project at Tema (see Box 6.11).

Box 6.11

Business Focus at Tema

To drive forward Ghana's vision for the development of its free zone program, the government agreed to a deal with Business Focus Ghana, a company owned by Datuk Shah Omar Shah, a well-known Malaysian businessman with close links to Malaysian Prime Minister Mahathir bin Mohamad and his ruling United Malays National Organization party. Business Focus was involved in a number of other investments in Ghana, including at the port (dry dock) and in real estate—they were part of a major wave of Malaysian investment in the country during the mid 1990s. Business Focus acquired 240 hectares in the Tema enclave on a long-term lease and invested approximately US$10 million in land, internal infrastructure, and the development of prebuilt factory and warehouse units in the enclave. The government and the Ghana Free Zones Board (GFZB) saw Business Focus as a company that could attract tenants from Asia through its strong business networks.

But relations between Business Focus and the GFZB became strained over disagreements on issues related to infrastructure and service delivery, which slowed down investment in onsite infrastructure. In addition, the combination of the Asian financial crisis (along with capital controls imposed in Malaysia) and high inflation in Ghana had a major effect on the company's liquidity. According to other developers at Tema, after a long period of dispute with the government, Business Focus stopped paying rent on the land lease. The company eventually sold most of its investments in Ghana, and the Business Focus enclave at Tema now sits on only eight hectares. The failure of this private initiative set Ghana's free zone program back by many years.

Source: Author.

Even when the private sector leads, government has a critical role to play; therefore, effective structures for public-private partnership (beyond the transactional models) are required. Government always plays a critical role in zone programs, even if it is not leading the zone development and operation. In addition to delivering the necessary offsite infrastructure, government must provide the enabling environment and institutional support for private investments. One important lesson from successful zone programs in East Asia is the importance of partnership between the private and public sectors; private firms are the drivers of growth, but government can play the role of catalyst

and enabler. Thus, governments need to establish good working partnerships with both private developers and the individual firms operating in
the zones.

In Tema (discussed in Box 6.11), neither the private developer nor the
Ghana Free Zones Board delivered on what the other party expected, and
this quickly resulted in finger-pointing. This case study underscores the
importance of a clear delineation of roles and responsibilities between
parties in the partnership, and of a well-developed and legally binding
PPP framework. Service-level agreements and binding MOUs can play an
important role.

*Effective private sector participation requires an institutional mechanism
to enable private sector input to strategic and operational planning.*
With or without private sector development of zones, successful programs rely on an effective partnership between government and the private
sector investors who operate in the zones. An important part of this partnership is ensuring that the private sector has some voice in strategic decisions regarding the zone program. Public-private dialogue is important to
ensure that policies and operational practices in the zones are in line with
the needs of the investors and can be an important mechanism through
which zone-based firms overcome coordination challenges and articulate
their needs for sector-specific public or club goods (Klinger 2010).

The most effective way to institutionalize this input (as discussed
later) is through representation on the zone authority board. Although
Figure 6.1 shows that most programs offer some place for the private
sector on the board, the scale and impact of private sector input on zone
authority boards varies significantly among countries. For example, private sector voice is particularly weak in the programs of Bangladesh and
Vietnam. In the Dominican Republic, in contrast, a close working relationship between the private sector and government has been a mainstay
of the free zone program from the beginning. Unlike the situation in
most countries, the first free zone in the Dominican Republic was set up
by the private sector in 1969. Along with the creation of public zones,
government policies encouraged the private sector to become the backbone of the program. It is an equal partner with the public sector in the
CNZFE—making policies and regulating and promoting the sector. Its
participation in the creation and management of industrial parks has
increased over the years, and it has a majority role on the authorities governing board, giving it real decision-making authority and a meaningful
voice in policy discussions.

While many of the African programs have struggled to develop effective partnerships between the government and the private sector in the zones, Lesotho has been relatively successful (see Box 6.12). This is due to a number of factors, including institutionalized board presence, a proactive government (at least at certain critical moments), and a well-organized private sector.

Beyond the institutional structures established by government, associations and collective action in the private sector also play an important role in zone programs. For example, the success of private sector participation in the Dominican Republic's free zone program is a function of the sector's having organized itself to ensure effective voice and participation in policy discussions with government. This organization has been achieved at the level of the free zone developers—through a strong association, ADOZONA (Asociación Dominicana de Zonas Francas)—and

---

Box 6.12

Effective Public-Private Dialogue in Lesotho

The Lesotho National Development Corporation (LNDC) is one of the few organizations in which the private sector constitutes the majority on the board of directors. This factor, along with a well-established industry association—the Lesotho Textile Exporters Association (LTEA)—has facilitated effective public-private dialogue, leading to practical support from the government for the needs of the textiles and clothing sector.

LNDC and LTEA have worked together effectively to address many challenges in the sector. For example, they partnered to address the skills challenges of the industry by setting up two skills development centers, at Maputsoe and Maseru, to train workers to meet the needs of the sector. The Skills Development for the Garment Industry project was initiated in July 2008 when the Maputsoe Skills Development Centre launched a six-week pre-employment training program on basic sewing skills.

Another project with public-private collaboration is the recent initiative to improve the investment environment in Lesotho. The Private Sector Development Division in the Ministry of Finance and Development Planning is managing and driving a cross-government program of investment environmental reform, while working in collaboration with the private sector to reduce bureaucratic roadblocks and promote business confidence, competitiveness, and job creation.

Source: Author.

through individual firms, which have set up associations in most zones. In Honduras, too, the association of zone developers (Asociación Hondureña de Maquiladores) is well-organized and proactive in its dialogue with government.

Beyond traditional PPP models, governments are increasingly taking advantage of learning through cross-country private and state-state partnerships, the most high-profile of which are the Chinese economic and trade cooperation zones. Such projects could offer significant opportunities for African countries, but they bring their own set of challenges and risks.
China was the pioneer in the use of state-state partnerships in an SEZ program, engaging especially with Taiwan-China, Singapore, and Japan to establish world-class zones quickly while at the same time learning best practices in planning and implementation. Vietnam followed a similar model with the launch of its zone program in the 1990s. Vietnam's first export processing zone, modeled after the flagship Kaohsiung Export Processing Zone in Taiwan-China, was established as a joint venture between the latter's Central Trading and Development Group and the Ho Chi Minh City People's Committee. Linh Trung Export Processing Zone was established in 1992 as a partnership between China's United Electric Import Export Company and the Saigon Industrial Park Development Corporation. By 1994, another four foreign-invested industrial and export processing zones had been established in Vietnam with partners from Japan (Nomura-Hai Phong Industrial Zone in Hai Phong city), Thailand (Amata Industrial Park in Dong Nai province), and Malaysia (Noi Bai Industrial Zone in Hanoi and Da Nang Industrial Zone in Da Nang city).

African zone programs have not taken the partnership approach in their developments during the 1990s and 2000s, with the possible exception of Ghana's partnership with the Malaysian company in setting up Tema.[18] However, a number of examples of this model have emerged in the past few years. In Senegal, the development of the Dakar Integrated SEZ is being led by investors from Dubai. In Ethiopia, Zambia, Nigeria, and Mauritius, Chinese-led economic and trade cooperation zones have been initiated, in some cases with local governments as partners (see Table 6.6 for a summary of these projects). In Ethiopia, projects led by Turkish, Egyptian, and Indian foreign investors have been announced. The main difference between the partnerships in Africa and those in Vietnam and China is that in Asian examples the partnerships were engaged as

Zone (country)	Investment model	Details/comments	Status (June 2010)
Oriental (Ethiopia)	100% Chinese	• Qiyuan Group (steel) • Jianglian and Yangyang Asset Management • Awaiting confirmation of participation from China-Africa Development Fund (CADF)	• In construction • Cement plant in operation
JinFei (Mauritius)	100% Chinese	• Three partners: Taiyuan Iron and Steel Company (50%); Shanxi Coking Coal Group (30%); Tianli Group (20%) • CADF recently announced that it would become an equity partner—it will take 32.5%, diluting other partners' shares	• In planning and construction
Lekki (Nigeria)	Joint venture (JV) (60% Chinese, 40% local) using special-purpose vehicle: Lekki Free Zone Development Co. Ltd	• Chinese partners: CCECC (China Civil Engineering Construction Corporation) Beyond consortium; in 2009, CADF joined as an equity partner • Nigerian partners: Lagos State (20%); Lekki Worldwide Investments Limited (20%). Lagos state received its shares in return for provision of land and a 50-year franchise to operate the zone; it is also expected to contribute US$67m to construction costs. • The Chinese consortium is to invest US$200m.	• In construction
Ogun (Nigeria)	JV (82% Chinese, 18% local)	• Chinese consortium based in Guangdong • Nigerian share owned by state government, which provided land and 100-year concession in return for shares.	• In construction and limited operation
Chambishi (Zambia)	JV (95%+ Chinese)	• China Nonferrous Metal Mining (Group) Company (CNMC) (95%) has provided all the capital • Non-Ferrous African Mining (15%); this is a JV between CNMC (85%) and Zambia Consolidated Copper Mines Ltd., a Zambian government-owned holding company (15%).	• In operation

Source: Brautigam and Tang (2010).

part of a clear strategy not only to attract investment but also to learn the details about implementing zone programs. So far, there is no evidence that the African countries involved in cross-national investments are taking significant steps to take advantage of the learning potential of the partnerships.

Notes

1. For a step-by-step guide, see the World Bank Investment Climate Department's "SEZ Practitioner's Guide," currently available in a beta version on http://ifcsp.ifc.org/icas/sez/guide/default.aspx.

2. Vietnam's strategy involved partnering with zone developers (public and private) from other parts of East Asia, including Taiwan, China, Singapore, and Japan.

3. In some cases, a strategic planning process is followed but its results are not executed or are poorly executed.

4. The Export Processing Zones Authority does have a strategic plan prepared by the World Bank, but this document is more a strategic guide to the institutional direction and the operational approach of the authority; it does not provide insight into the positioning of Tanzanian zones.

5. Here there were large regional markets, as well as resources that were restricted by economic and social policies, and instability in the region. For a time, the United Arab Emirates offered a true enclave opportunity. Its zone programs made investment even more palatable for foreign investors by eliminating tax obligations and substantially lowering risk.

6. The evidence presented in Chapter 5 shows that this holds true across the African single factory schemes studied in this report.

7. Not to mention the moral hazard that stems from the fact that zone authorities are much more likely to be judged on the number of new licenses they issue than on their net contribution to the government's tax base, so they may have every incentive to promote the proliferation of single factory licenses.

8. Most often through their ownership of the land on which the project is developed.

9. May be the same as the developer or under a contractual agreement with the owner/developer.

10. The public zones in the Dominican Republic are generally in more remote locations and provide more basic, low-cost infrastructure and services that are clearly differentiated from those in the private sector.

11. Based on an exchange rate of M7.57 to US$1 as of December 18, 2009.

12. With the exception of South Africa, which is not exempt from Article 27.

13. The definition of "product" is subject to some debate but is generally considered to be at the 4-digit level of commodity classification.

14. For example, India's SEZ program provides tax holidays but requires that companies be "net foreign exchange earners," which implicitly favors local purchase over imports.

15. In Kenya, a number of private firms have licenses as free zone developers; in reality, however, they are operating as single factory units. The FIAS (2008) data do not appear take the single factory licensed firms in Ghana and Senegal into account.

16. Based on approximately 2,500 zones identified worldwide in 2005, excluding zones in the United States and Europe.

17. The Dominican Republic has 31 private zones, 21 public zones, and three public-private joint ventures.

18. The Malaysian company, Business Focus, was not an established zone developer, so this is not the same type of partnership model.

References

Action Aid Vietnam. 2007. *Food Security for the Poor in Vietnam*. Hanoi: Action Aid International Vietnam.

Brautigam, D., and X. Tang. 2010. "China's Investment in Africa's Special Economic Zones." Mimeo (January). World Bank, Washington, DC.

Creskoff, S., and P. Walkenhorst. 2009. "Implications of WTO Disciplines for Special Economic Zones in Developing Countries." Policy Research Working Paper 4892. World Bank, Washington, DC.

FIAS. 2008. *Special Economic Zones. Performance, Lessons Learned, and Implications for Zone Development*. Washington, DC: World Bank.

Harding, T., and B. S. Javorcik. 2007. "Developing Economies and International Investors: Do Investment Promotion Agencies Bring Them Together?" Policy Research Working Paper Series 4339. World Bank, Washington, DC.

Harrison, A., L. Du, and G. Jefferson. 2010. "Firm Performance and Industrial Policy in China." Presentation at World Bank Conference on Growth, Competitiveness, and the Role of Government Policies. Washington, DC, June 16.

Klinger, B. 2010. "(New) Export Competitiveness." Mimeo (February). Center for International Development, Harvard University, Cambridge, MA.

Lim, C. E. 1971. Extract of speech by Dr. Lim Chong Eu, chief minister of Penang, when moving the second reading of the Penang Development Corporation Bill. April 10.

Lim, P. L., and C. I. Ong. 2002. "Malaysian Case Study of the Use and Impact of Performance Requirements." Paper prepared for UNCTAD (December).

Singh, C. 2010. Forthcoming. "The PDC Story as I Know It (1970–1990)." In volume of essays to commemorate 25 years since the founding of ISIS Malaysia, ed. Khoo Siew Mun. Institute of Strategic and International Studies, Kuala Lumpur.

CHAPTER 7

Zone Practices: Operations, Management, and Learning

Introduction

This chapter follows the same structure and approach as that in Chapter 6, with a focus on operational and management practices in the zones, and on monitoring and learning. The following specific issues are covered:

- Marketing and investment promotion
- Location, land, and development
- Registration, licensing, and administrative procedures
- Infrastructure
- Customs, trade facilitation, and transport
- Promoting linkages with the local economy
- Monitoring, enforcement, and learning

Marketing and Investment Promotion

Most SEZ authorities lack the scale and specialization to be effective in investment promotion. Therefore, close cooperation with national investment promotion agencies is often critical; this is usually best achieved through formal institutional links.

In most countries, the SEZ authority has primary responsibility for marketing and promotion, and usually for investor aftercare as well, while a separate national investment promotion authority (IPA) performs these roles for FDI outside the zones. While a separation of these agencies is usually advisable, it can also be a source of operational disconnect between the agencies, resulting in poor coordination of activities. In most cases, it appears that the national IPA does provide some high-level promotional support to the SEZ authority (usually marketing the SEZs as one investment option in the country), but there is generally little coordination of marketing planning and execution, and no formal process for handoff or cross-support of investor aftercare between the agencies.

Other zone programs run into similar challenges at the local level. For example, in Nigeria, much of the investment promotion in support of zones comes through state governments; although they might coordinate with a specific zone in the state, there is little higher level coordination with national SEZ promotion efforts. In Vietnam, there is no national-level responsibility for promoting zones, with (often independent) promotional efforts taking place at the level of provincial government, regional investment promotion centers (linked to the Ministry of Planning), and individual zone management boards.

Coordination of marketing and promotion efforts must go beyond the IPA. Best practice is to have a cooperative approach, involving a coalition of interested stakeholders that includes the zone developer, local business associations and chambers of commerce, and the investors that operate in the zones. In smaller countries or countries with a strong corporatist model (for example, Costa Rica and the Dominican Republic), it may be possible to achieve effective informal coordination among agencies and other stakeholders, but in most cases coordination is best achieved through formal means. In some of the cases assessed in this study (e.g., Tanzania, Nigeria, Kenya, and Bangladesh), the lack of formal institutional links among the agencies is an important source of operational disconnect. In other cases (e.g., Kenya, the Dominican Republic, Ghana), the SEZ authority and the IPA sit on each other's management boards, although this is usually not enough to ensure active, on-the-ground coordination. Other approaches that have been used internationally include signing an MOU, establishing a service agreement, or establishing a marketing and promotion committee or board. The following are some examples of good institutional coordination in SEZ programs:

- *Ghana Gateway:* This project to establish Ghana as a regional export hub (anchored on the free zone program) established a board that includes the Ghana Free Zones Board, the Ghana Investment Promotion Centre (GIPC), and the main stakeholders involved in trade facilitation (ports, airports, customs). Marketing and promotional efforts were coordinated under the authority of this project board.

- *Dominican Republic:* The free zone program has been promoted successfully for several decades through coordinated efforts of the authority (CNZFE), the association of private zone developers (ADO-ZONA), and the Centre for Export and Investment of the Dominican Republic (CEI-RD). While CEI-RD has overall responsibility for investment promotion for the country, primary responsibility for promoting the free zones lies with CNZFE. Complementing CNZFE, ADOZONA plays a major role in promoting the sector, as does Proindustria, which carries out investment promotion related to the public sector zones.

Closely related to the issue of coordination is that of defining clear roles and responsibilities for the various parties involved in the investment promotion efforts, to avoid duplication and eliminate the risk of important activities falling through the cracks between two organizations. Such definition is important not only between the IPA and the SEZ authority but also between the SEZ authority and private developers (assuming that the program includes private developers). In this case, the role of the zone authority is a general one (promoting the overall program), while developers play a more tactical role, promoting individual projects. For example, in Jordan a formal marketing partnership was established for the promotion of the large-scale Aqaba Special Economic Zone (ASEZ); it included the SEZ authority (ASEZA), the investment promotion agency (Jordan Investment Board), the Jordan Tourism Board, the overall developer (Aqaba Development Corporation), and individual real estate developers in the zone. Each partner agreed to specific roles and responsibilities of promoting the SEZ.

The timing of promotional efforts matters—many zone programs promise too much, too soon.
One of the challenges in marketing a zone program is when to start promoting it. There is a natural tendency to want to start marketing immediately once the concept of having an SEZ program has been approved. Brochures and compact discs with mockup versions of the master plan are commonly used as a basis for early marketing efforts. But the long time frame between inception and completion of large

infrastructure projects like SEZs means that it can easily be four or five years or more before a zone is developed to the point that investors can begin operating.

Overhyping a project too far ahead wastes precious marketing resources and can give potential investors the negative impression that the project is proceeding too slowly. For example, an investor in Tanzania recalled being told in 2008 that the country's new SEZ[1] would be ready "in three months"; he was told the same thing in 2010. While there may be some value in limited communications—primarily aimed at national image-building—heavy promotion is unlikely to be effective more than two years before the SEZ is ready to accept investors.

One way to deal with this time gap is to launch something on a pilot basis, to give investors a sense of what is possible through the zone program while the larger infrastructure projects are ongoing. Kenya did this effectively: While the flagship EPZ at Athi River was in development for several years, the authorities allowed an existing small-scale private park (Sameer) to become an EPZ in the meantime. This enabled them to "soft-launch" the EPZ program.

A related issue that has been problematic in some of the African zones is overselling the zone and not having the product to back it up. For example, Nigeria's EPZ program was promoted with the promise of a free zone linked to a deepwater port in Calabar; 15 years later, the port had not been dredged. Nigeria also offered a wide range of attractive incentives, but it turned out that even more lucrative incentives were available to investors outside the zones. Later, Nigeria promoted a change in the regime allowing EPZ companies to sell to the domestic market—a practice that Customs still refuses to acknowledge or allow. One of the most striking features of Senegal's initial EPZ program in the 1970s was the huge amount of resources spent to launch and promote the zone through international offices. The zone benefited from substantial donor funds from the European Development Fund (EDF), which supported promotion offices in Paris, Brussels, Cologne, and New York. Later, UNIDO joined EDF in financing promotion in Paris, New York, and Tokyo. Again in the 1980s, EDF funded an office in Brussels. Although no official figures are available, it is clear that tens of millions of dollars were spent to promote the zone. But the reality for investors was poor infrastructure, few services, and a generally uncompetitive business environment. Using the marketing funds to get the product right from the start would have paid better dividends.

The flip side of exciting investor interest too far ahead is the much greater problem of developing a zone and attracting no response from potential investors. For example, in its first two years of operation, the Zolic Free Zone in Guatemala constructed over 24,000 square meters of factory space, which sat vacant for several years. A similar situation occurred in the government-established Puerto Cortes free zone in Honduras. In both cases, the zone programs lacked adequate marketing support at the outset. But a second reason for the slow start is that the strategic planning process that would have supported the marketing effort was never completed.

Incentive structures within SEZ authorities often result in favoring quantity of investors over quality, which leads to poor realization of stated investment intentions.
One of the problems identified in most of the zone programs under study, but particularly in the African and Asian programs, was a poor conversion rate between promised and actual investment. For example, in Vietnam, only about 50 percent of registered capital investment is ever operationalized. And in the Kano zone in Nigeria, although 25 licenses were issued to firms intending to set up, only three firms are actually operating in the zone.[2] Part of the problem here relates to the functioning of the zone authorities, specifically the rigor with which they review applications for licenses and the strictness with which they enforce rules on investors initiating and completing their investments. In many cases, licenses are given to firms that are not capable of realizing investments or that simply hope to extract some rent from holding the license.

This situation stems, in part, from the incentive structures the zone authorities face: Their performance—and, in many cases, their revenue stream—is often judged on the number of licenses they issue. The problem is also linked to the often misplaced desire to fill up the space in the zone as quickly as possible. But forgoing quality for quantity has several negative implications:

- Investors may pay an initial license fee but never follow through and operationalize their investment (or they may start but go out of business quickly), often because they are unable to obtain sufficient funding or they are not financially stable. This has been a major problem in Nigeria, Senegal, and Bangladesh. While the application approval process may be partially at fault, the root of the problem is often that the programs are not marketing proactively to targeted investors but instead simply responding to whoever shows an interest.

- Space in the zone may get filled up with investors who are unlikely to meet the program's objectives in terms of employment and exports or unlikely to deliver sufficient revenue (e.g., through service fees) to the operator to cover operating costs. Again, this problem is linked to regulatory and operational issues such as criteria for entry and pricing models, but it also stems from the upfront marketing strategy.
- A disparate set of companies and industries may set up in the zones, limiting the potential for establishing clusters and linking with local suppliers. With the exception of Mauritius, Madagascar, and Kenya, this has been a problem in most African SEZ programs.
- Finally, low standards send the wrong signal to important foreign and domestic investors about the quality of the zone. High-profile investors are unlikely to want to participate in a zone full of unknown companies or companies of questionable quality.

On the other hand, some zone programs go too far in setting strict criteria on size, investment level, or job creation to ensure that they fill the zone with the right kind of investors. In most cases, the result is that too few companies, rather than too many, register. For example, in Senegal, strict criteria established at the launch of the program not only prevented many local companies from participating but, in stipulating a large investment requirement, raised the risk level for foreign investors. A more effective approach might be to target key anchor investors who match the desired profile.

Targeted marketing and anchor investor strategies have proved highly effective in many zones.

Bearing in mind the challenges noted above and the limited capacity and resources of most SEZ authorities, they should target their efforts to the sectors and markets defined in the strategic planning process. Most successful zone programs follow an anchor investor strategy, in which they put substantial effort into attracting specific, targeted high-profile investors at the outset of the SEZ program. These anchor investors play an important signaling role to other potential investors and often bring with them a network of suppliers and partners. In many cases, specific incentives are provided to attract these anchors, but this is by no means always the case. For example, in Costa Rica, although great personalized effort went into the negotiations with Intel, none of the incentives were company-specific; rather, they were part of wider programs available in the country and its free zone regime. Evidence from successful anchor investor strategies like Costa Rica's suggests that facilitation and aftercare matters as much or more than individual incentives. The following SEZ programs have implemented successful anchor investor strategies:

- *Vietnam:* Vietnam actively pursued and created favorable conditions for high-profile anchor investors such as Canon, Samsung, Panasonic, and Intel, all of which brought with them their own supporting investors. The successful attraction of these companies signaled the competitiveness of Vietnam's EPZs as an investment location, resulting in many of their competitors also investing.

- *Honduras:* When Honduras stepped up efforts to attract investment in the free zone program in the late 1980s, it targeted North American garment companies, with a focus on high-profile anchors such as Sara Lee Knit Products (Champion and Hanes brands) and Arrow. These companies became the foundation for the growth of the free zone sector, attracting suppliers and competitors, and expanding their own operations many times over.

Although most anchor investor strategies focus on attracting well-known multinationals, local investors can play a catalytic role. Indeed, domestic investors can play the role of anchors, signaling marketing opportunities to foreign investors, who may be unaware or uncertain. Particularly in new markets or those that have experienced instability in the past, large multinationals are seldom willing to take the risk of being the first to invest.[3] In both Honduras and El Salvador, for example, domestic entrepreneurs in the garment sector invested in the development of industrial zones, using their own factories as anchor tenants. This was a signal to foreign investors regarding the potential of the market and helped catalyze FDI into the SEZ program.

Successful investor targeting in zones is not only grounded in a strong demand and comparative advantage analysis but is also opportunistic. Timing has been critical to the success of many SEZ programs. But timing is not an issue of luck: Some programs have clearly been much more effective than others in aggressively exploiting specific market opportunities and targeting their promotional efforts. A good example is the targeting of investors based on the availability of export market preferences. Honduras and the Dominican Republic targeted U.S. garment sector investors on the basis of opportunities available through the Caribbean Basin Initiative (CBI) and the Central American Free Trade Area (DR-CAFTA). Lesotho did the same when it exploited AGOA preferences. Vietnam's EPZs took advantage of its own integration into the WTO, growing ASEAN free trade, and the trend toward integrated production networks in "factory Asia" to target Asian manufacturers that participate in global manufacturing value chains. Other programs have exploited their position as an oasis of stability or freedom in a region that was financially attractive but otherwise inhospitable to investors. The Dubai-based free zones and the Chinese SEZs are good examples of this.

Location, Land, and Development

Zones can play a valuable role in overcoming land access constraints in African countries. However, comprehensive national and regional master planning is critical to ensure that infrastructure integrates effectively with the domestic economy and national trade gateways.

One of the fundamental benefits of SEZs is their ability to overcome land and infrastructure constraints by concentrating infrastructure investment and making land plots (and, in many cases, prefabricated industrial or office units) available to investors. In densely populated, land-scarce countries such as Bangladesh and Vietnam, it is no surprise that zones can overcome land access problems. It is perhaps more surprising that this also seems to be of greatly value in the African countries studied, despite their relative abundance of land. The main reason is that, although there may be plenty of undeveloped land, securing it is highly problematic in most countries. This is due to a number of factors, including communal ownership or rights over land, poor land tenure law, weak property rights protection, and the risk of claims being raised during and long after purchase and development. In addition, the bureaucratic process of purchasing land and securing development permits is problematic in many countries. Figure 7.1 shows the performance of the African countries under study (and in comparison with the OECD) against the World Bank's Doing Business measure for registering a property.

With the exception of Ghana, which ranks at or ahead of the average OECD level of performance, property registration is a long and costly affair in most African countries. The situation is particularly bad in Nigeria, Senegal, and Lesotho, where it can take more than 100 days to complete registration, at a cost of up to 20 percent of the value of the property (versus just 20 days and 5 percent cost, on average, in the OECD).

Figure 7.1   Time and Cost of Registering a Property
(Doing Business 2010 rank for each country in parentheses)

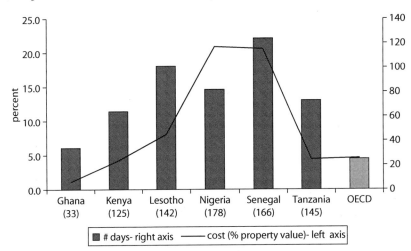

Source: World Bank (2009).

Again, it may be worth considering these issues in the context of the substantial use of single factory zones in African countries. The data shown in Figure 7.1 suggest that, for Ghana and Kenya at least, land access is not so problematic; thus, on this factor, single factory zones may be a realistic consideration, although both countries struggle with significant infrastructure issues that would be a major barrier to dispersed investment. But given the land access constraints in Senegal, a single factory model is difficult to understand.

In the successful East Asian programs, detailed and comprehensive national and regional master planning was used to integrate the zones physically into the local and national economies. Indeed, a primary factor in the East Asian success story was the use of large-scale zones that linked zone-specific activity with the wider trade gateways, sources of labor, and social infrastructure. In contrast, in many of the African and Latin American zones, development planning has been limited to standalone industrial parks.

Location is a critical determinant of zone success; however, most countries attempt to use their zone programs as instruments of regional development policy. With almost no exceptions, this approach has failed.

As discussed in Chapters 4 and 5, the location of an SEZ in a country—in particular, its proximity to major trade gateways (ports and airports) and the country's largest metropolitan areas—is critical to its success. This is particularly important for zones that depend on manufacturers who require access to imported inputs, business services, large pools of labor, and transport networks. But it also holds true for knowledge-based zones (e.g., IT parks), which may have less need to access ports but require proximity to population centers to access specialized labor and business services, as well as high-quality backbone services (utilities). Still, most countries continue to use SEZs to try to attract investment and create employment in remote and lagging regions. In just about every case, these efforts have failed:

- *Lesotho:* In an effort to support development in the southern areas of the country, LNDC established industrial parks in Mafeteng and Mohales Hoek. To date, only two companies are based in Mafeteng. In Mohales Hoek, LNDC built eight factory shells, all of which sit idle. Despite the incentive of cheaper rents, investors have shown that they prefer to be located near the labor and supply markets around Maseru and Maputsoe. Moreover, transport costs from the southern part of the country are substantially higher—road and rail networks are much better around Maseru—and the border post closest to Mohales Hoek cannot handle 40-foot containers, forcing exporters to drive all the way back through Maseru to use the border post there. Finally, LNDC has found that foreign managers have little interest in these remote locations, preferring to be based where they have access to a better quality of life for their families, especially good schools.

- *Bangladesh:* While the first two EPZs—in the main cities of Dhaka and Chittagong—and the recently established zones along the Dhaka-Chittagong corridor have been successful in attracting investment, BEPZA also has three zones in the northern (Uttara EPZ) and western (Ishwardi and Mongla EPZs) parts of the country that are almost empty, despite significant additional incentives offered to investors, including a 50 percent subsidy on the already below-market land lease and factory rental rates and a 30 percent cash incentive for investing in agricultural-based industries. These three zones are all located more than 600 kilometers from the international port[4] and hundreds of kilometers from Dhaka; the poor transport infrastructure makes it difficult to get goods in and out. In addition, availability of reliable electric and gas supplies is a major problem, and these remote locations lack manufacturing clusters, making access to supplies problematic.

- *Dominican Republic:* The Dominican government has long attempted to promote investment in the depressed regions along the Haitian border and has provided a number of investment incentives through the FZ program. First, the free zone law extends the normal fiscal incentives to 20 years (from 15) for investments in FZs in these regions. Second, the law provides that companies that set up in the border region can obtain loans on preferential terms from the Central Bank. Finally, the law provides the CNZFE with flexibility to waive certain requirements for FZ companies investing in this region. But despite these benefits, only two zones are in operation in these provinces, and both are government owned. One (Pedernales) has only one operating company, and the other (Esperanza) has six. Together, they provide only 3,500 jobs.

- *Honduras:* The government of Honduras initially sought to promote geographic diversification by selectively expanding the zone policy to targeted regions. Government attempts to nurture an export-oriented manufacturing cluster around the capital, Tegucigalpa, failed to move investment from the San Pedro Sula region for several reasons. The cost of living is higher in Tegucigalpa, and there is a scarcity of suitable land. Transporting containers overland is always a challenge in Honduras, given the country's hilly landscape and security problems. Manufacturers based in San Pedro Sula benefit greatly from its proximity to Puerto Cortés, which is the entry and exit point for seaborne goods. The San Pedro Sula region also has a first mover advantage. It hosts a number of influential industrial families and has a small, preexisting garment sector; a wide range of key input suppliers; and a social infrastructure that is attractive to local and international managers.

Besides Lesotho, the African countries included in this study have not developed zones with an explicit regional development agenda. Yet, even in these countries, it is obvious that zones located in more peripheral regions are unlikely to be successful, particularly if they are not designed around specific sources of comparative advantage.

- *Nigeria:* While location decisions of zones in Nigeria generally came bottom-up from specific state initiatives rather than through a national spatial policy, the first two EPZs (Calabar and Kano) were established in locations far from the main commercial areas where foreign investors are likely to locate and far from operating ports. More than a decade after the launch of the program, these zones together house fewer than 20 active companies. Most of the new zone projects are located near Lagos or Port Harcourt.

• *Ghana:* The government's intention was to develop three zones, one at the Tema port outside Accra, another (a technology park) in Ashanti, and a third at the country's second port in Sekondi. However, after almost 15 years, only the project near Accra has been developed.

The experiences outlined here underscore the importance of having a clear and transparent set of criteria by which location decisions are made, and going through a proper process of feasibility assessment before moving forward with zone investments. This does not mean that governments cannot target their zone strategies to address inequalities and adjustment processes that result from the structural changes to which zones contribute. Rather, it simply means that investing in developing zones in peripheral areas may not be an effective way to address regional inequalities. Box 7.1 describes an example of an innovative use of economic zones in a regional development context.

Governments often take on large obligations, create expectations, and risk distorting markets by undertaking large-scale demarcations of land for eventual zone development.
Political economy is one of the main reasons many countries end up using their zone programs for regional development. Even when a government accepts the arguments against using zones to address spatial inequality, it may not want to appear to direct government resources to the core, rich regions at the short-term expense of poorer, peripheral regions. A common outcome of this political process is to identify and earmark land for zones across the country. For example, in Tanzania, the rollout of the new zone program created political demands for zones in every region. In response to the demands, the government asked each region to identify and set aside land for development of township-sized economic development zones. The result is that 14 sites across the country, each of at least 2,000 hectares, have now been earmarked for future development.

Even if these projects never go forward, governments can create problems for their zone programs by setting aside land in this manner. First,

Box 7.1

Leveraging Public Assets for Zone Development in Bangladesh

After the EPZs in Chittagong and Dhaka filled quickly in the 1990s, there was pressure to develop new industrial areas under the EPZ program in Bangladesh. However, access to industrial land is extremely constrained and the time it takes to secure and develop land can be prohibitive. In this environment, the Bangladesh Export Processing Zones Authority and the government have made effective use of obsolete assets; specifically, large state-operated enterprises that have closed. The Adamjee EPZ was developed on the grounds of an old jute-milling complex. This zone is now fully operational and has been attracting investment at a rapid rate. Currently, the Karnaphuli EPZ is being developed at the site of a former steel mill.

Not only has the use of these assets for SEZ development helped overcome severe land constraints in the country, but it offers the potential for employment opportunities in communities that previously relied on jobs in industries in which the country is no longer competitive.

Source: Author.

undertaking too many developments at once raises significant risks of creating an oversupply, with commercial implications for existing private developers. Second, government involvement in these developments risks crowding out the private sector. Merely by setting aside large tracts of land for these developments, the government can crowd out private sector opportunities elsewhere. Third, zone programs risk taking on significant expenses; for example, the payment of land compensation claims.

But perhaps most important, even in the absence of specific immediate expenses, there may be financial implications for governments in securing very large tracts of land and identifying them as locations for zones. Making zones successful requires substantial investment in connecting infrastructure to the zones: road access, utilities, even port or airport infrastructure. This will almost always be the responsibility of government, although in some cases there may be room for private sector participation (e.g., for utilities provision and toll roads). By acquiring large tracts of land for future development of SEZs, governments effectively incur an obligation—to potential private investors as well as local communities—to deliver on this infrastructure. This is a huge commitment. And unless these sites have already been defined as strategic nodes for investment, potential exists for conflicts in relation to the government's long-term economic and social infrastructure plans.

Land acquisition, compensation, and displacement issues are still receiving insufficient attention in many zone programs.
Finally, in several of the zone programs under study, there is evidence of continued problems related to land acquisition, resettlement, and compensation. For example, in Vietnam, more than 57,000 hectares—most of it formerly occupied by small farmers—is under construction or operation as industrial zones. Many rural villagers have been displaced, and it may be that resettlement and retraining have not been conducted equitably or efficiently, and resettlement areas have not been adequately planned or serviced. A 2005 report estimated that more than 100,000 households were displaced for the development of industrial zones and complexes, and that less than two-thirds of those households benefited through enhanced work opportunities, improved social and technical infrastructure, or adequate compensation for appropriated land (Action Aid Vietnam 2007).

In Nigeria's Lekki SEZ development—a joint venture between the Lagos state government and a consortium of private and state-owned enterprise (SOE) investors from China—communities around the project protested over land-taking, resettlement terms, the construction of utility lines through their communities, and the employment of Chinese workers in construction. These protests caused project delays and resulted eventually in the local community being granted an equity stage in the Nigerian partner's shareholding. Negotiations also resulted in more employment opportunities for workers from local communities.

Registration, Licensing, and Administrative Procedures

Having a one-stop shop is the objective of virtually all zone programs, but although many countries have made significant progress (for example, in shortening the time between application and license provision), truly effective administrative delivery remains hampered by weak institutional authority and coordination in most zones.
Most of the zone programs studied offer some type of one-stop service to their investors. This service is primarily focused on helping investors obtain business licenses, export and import licenses, work permits, health

and safety certificates, environmental clearances, and a wide range of other authorizations. But the services extend beyond the initial set-up stage and involve mitigating the day-to-day constraints of bureaucratic processes. Investors typically value these services—in most countries, they perceive the zone authority as being "on their side" and rely on it to resolve problems with government on their behalf. However, zone authorities in Africa are only partially effective in delivering these services. A contributing factor to the failure of the original zone program in Senegal was the fact that it often took up to a year to get a key license or permit. For the most part, African zones today are generally efficient in dealing with firm approvals and business licenses, but they may have problems facilitating environmental impact assessments, immigration permits, and local municipality approvals. Moreover, zone authorities often have to dedicate more resources than they had planned to provide responsive aftercare. As discussed in detail in Chapter 6, the main reasons for this situation are a lack of clear institutional authority for delivering on these services and the inherent challenges of coordinating across multiple government agencies.

In Vietnam, the government decided from the outset to establish formal, empowered one-stop shops in each zone, along with dedicated onsite customs clearance. These two services were considered to be fundamental to providing an internationally competitive operating environment for investors. Evidence from the case studies and firm surveys summarized in Chapter 5 suggests that the approach was effective. Zone-based firms in Vietnam reported the shortest waiting times for getting applications approved and obtaining business licenses, construction permits, and utility connections, and the shortest customs clearance times of almost any country in the survey.

But few zone authorities are likely to have enough specialists to deliver all the necessary services to investors while also meeting the wider needs of government (e.g., protecting workers, the environment, and the local private sector). Only very large zone programs would consider spending the resources needed to develop or acquire such expertise. The approach taken in Vietnam may not be transferable to smaller low- and middle-income countries; in these countries, the issues of coordination discussed in Chapter 6 will be critical. An approach taken by many zone authorities is to have staff seconded from the agencies to the authority sit together to form a physical one-stop shop; although some challenges related to authority are inherent to this model (see Box 7.2).

Box 7.2

Lesotho's One-Stop Business Facilitation Centre

LNDC has always supported investors as they establish themselves in Lesotho. The services provided by LNDC include—

- Business start-up (reserving a company name, registering a company, getting a manufacturing license, registering for tax, registration of a workplace, registering for municipal rates).
- Immigration (visitor visas, residence permits, six-month border concessions).
- Connecting to utilities (electricity, water, telecommunications).
- Labor issues (work permits).

However, the process has still been relatively burdensome for investors, particularly in relation to immigration and work permits. According to LNDC, the entire process takes approximately 90 days to complete for foreign investors. In addition, difficulties in business registration for domestic companies (who do not have access to LNDC assistance) was restricting the creation of better links between the export-oriented FDI and local producers. In response to these problems, the government introduced the One-Stop Business Facilitation Centre in Maseru in September 2007 to streamline investor services. The steering committee includes representatives from the Ministry of Labour, Ministry of Home Affairs, Ministry of Trade and Industry Cooperatives and Marketing (MTICM), and the Commissioner General (Customs & Excise). Staff from all these ministries and agencies work in the Centre, under the coordination of MTICM. The Centre offers services related to company registration, obtaining a manufacturing license, work permits, residence permits, the export license, and import licenses. It is open to all investors, although work and residence permits are available to investors in the manufacturing sector, which is prioritized by the government. Foreign investors still generally go to LNDC first; LNDC then helps them through the process of working with the Centre.

Unfortunately, the Centre was relatively ineffective at first, primarily owing to poor coordination across ministries and agencies, and ineffective use of IT. Regarding the former, although the Centre is managed by MTICM, staff report to their individual ministries, making it difficult for the manager of the Centre to coordinate activities and enforce discipline. As for IT, none of the services are available online. For example, manufacturers in Lesotho must obtain a license every time they import an item from outside SACU. As a result, many manufacturers

(continued next page)

Box 7.2 (*continued*)

must send a staff member or agent to the Centre every day. For manufacturers outside of Maseru, this is an even greater burden; a satellite center is being planned for Maputsoe.

To respond to these challenges, the Centre revived the steering committee, which had become moribund, in February 2009, and its members signed an MOU on operations and deployment of personnel. They also began the process of moving some registration activities online. Sources suggest that despite the difficulties, the Centre has had some effect on reducing the amount of time required to start a business and obtain export and import licenses.

Source: Author.

Another way to bring some authority to the one-stop service (in the absence of a true delegation of authority) is to operate under a principle of "automaticity"—ideally supported by a service agreement or MOU with the relevant agencies. This is the approach taken by APIX in Senegal. Automaticity is essentially the same as a "no objection" approach: If an applicant receives no response from APIX (neither a rejection or request to hold response) after 30 days, the authorization is granted by default.

Zone operators play an important bridging role between investors and the government; this can be a valuable source of differentiation for operators. While the one-stop services are normally the responsibility of zone authorities, zone operators (private or public) can assume at least some of the functions. Indeed, in countries in which the zone program is dominated by the private sector, the coordinating role of the one-stop service is often largely devolved to the private zone operators. For example, neither the Dominican Republic nor Honduras offers a formal one-stop service to free zone investors. Instead, the investors look to their landlords for the coordinating function (see Box 7.3). For private zone developers, this role is fundamental to the value they bring to investors; in fact, they often compete on services rather than on rent. For the typical one-stop activities such as business licensing and permitting, the big difference is that private zone operators have no authority at all over the decision-making process. So, in truth, they really are "one more stop." However, they understand how the process works, have been through it countless times, and have cultivated relationships with government counterparts in the relevant agencies, so

Box 7.3

The Value Added Role of Industrial Zone Operators in Honduras

Honduran zone operators have done a good job of providing an environment that allows manufacturers to focus on their operations without major distractions from the challenges that affect entrepreneurs outside the zones. The quality of infrastructure and the sophistication of service delivery are the two main selling points in the zone operator market. The zone operator offers a security buffer against a sometimes turbulent external business environment, as well as a range of support and facilitating services tailored to the specific needs of clients.

The cost of rent is an important consideration for investors in deciding where to locate production. However, it is seldom one of the key concerns. In addition to rent, which covers security services, companies often pay directly only for telecommunications and electricity. Even electricity may be payable to the zone operator, who negotiates special deals with the national energy provider. The company's only direct interface with the government is the customs officials who control what goes in and out of the zone. Or, as one zone operator said, "A customer [foreign investor] who gets exposed to government-related corruption and other problems gets scared and wants to leave. The *maquila* operator functions as the interface that sorts out all the issues behind the scene, leaving the companies to do what they do best, which is manufacturing."

The increasing sophistication of the services offered by zone operators is striking. They offer fully serviced real estate, including facilities, utilities, security, waste removal, recycling, and worker transport. Some parks offer "shelter plans" for particularly footloose companies. These plans include accounting, payroll, recruiting, and training services. Some zone operators provide their own temporary labor services to manufacturers, and zones such as ZIP Buena Vista and ZIP Choloma, which provide engineers and builders who can be hired for short-term jobs. Thus, some zone operators are becoming manpower agencies as well as real estate agents. And manufacturers are increasingly willing to pay well for these value-added services.

Source: Authors.

they tend to be in a much better position than the new investors to manage the process.

Overall, evidence from the zone surveys suggests that privately operated zones tend to offer a broader range of value added services than public zones, and that the African zones offer fewer services than the non-African zones. Across all countries, provision of child care services is limited (they are offered in only one zone in Bangladesh and about one-third of zones surveyed in Honduras and the Dominican Republic). Onsite housing for workers is extremely rare.

Infrastructure

Too many African zone programs fail to deliver on basic infrastructure (such as utilities) inside the zones. Upfront investment in the core infrastructure is not enough; zones need to ensure that the authorities that control service delivery (e.g., electric companies, municipal water authorities) meet their obligations and are in a position to maintain the equipment.
A fundamental promise of SEZs is to provide a quality operating environment by concentrating infrastructure investment in a defined area. The prospect of uninterrupted power and water are key criteria when investors consider location options. While some of the African zones (most notably Lesotho and, to some extent, Kenya) appear to offer fairly reliable infrastructure, infrastructure gaps have been a major cause of concern for investors in several of the zones.

For example, Nigeria's flagship Calabar zone has long had serious problems with electricity provision. According to its largest investor, the power crisis reached a peak in a week in May 2009, when production was run on generators for 115 hours out of 132 (i.e., 87%). The investor noted that even when power is delivered, its quality is so poor (low or high voltage) that it is of little use for the companies operating in the zone. A survey of companies in the zone indicated that all of them own or share generators and make extensive use of them.

Interviews with investors in Ghana's Tema zone indicated that several had been without water for more than a year and were forced to bring in water by tanker truck at a huge cost. In addition, although the zone invested in its own substation, power cuts were reported to be frequent, and investors said they rely on generators for 5–10 hours each day. Finally, two investors reported that in order to access a 2 megabyte (MB) broadband Internet connection, they pay a fee of US$5,000 a month. Such a fee is high enough to effectively shut out many prospective entrepreneurs in the IT or IT-enabled services field.

Looking at the factors that contribute to these infrastructure gaps yields useful insights into what must be done to address them. In the case of Calabar in Nigeria, the zone apparently purchased state-of-the-art equipment at the time of investment, but it was not properly maintained and quickly fell into disrepair. From the beginning, the zone ran on a generator at least three hours a day, and outages occurred every day during the switchover from the mains to the generator (this was a manual process). In Tema, water shortages are related not to the infrastructure per se but to the fact that the municipal water authority on which the zone relies has not increased its capacity in response to the demands of the zone, as well as decisions made by the water authority to ensure that water is available to nearby residential areas. Zone authorities must take proactive responsibility to address the factors that constrain their investors, whether these factors lie inside or outside the gates of the zones. These problems also underscore the need for interagency cooperation in the implementation of zone programs.

While zones have been surprisingly inept at resolving infrastructure challenges, some useful practices have been employed. Like many zone programs, Lesotho has dedicated substations in its large industrial parks; but unlike most other programs, it also works with the national electricity provider to ensure that power to industrial areas is prioritized to minimize downtime when national power shortages are known to be coming. Bangladesh and Vietnam also follow this approach. For example, the Dhaka EPZ has established a power plant through a PPP that provides 100 percent of the electricity needed in the zone. The company sells electricity at a wholesale rate to the zone operator, who then distributes and sells it to the firms in the zone.[5] In addition, all four of the non-African zone programs try to involve the private sector in electricity provision by allowing them to purchase electricity from the grid and service zones. There does not appear to be any such private participation in the African zones.

In most zones, infrastructure considerations stop at the gate. Effective programs tend to plan the zones as part of much larger, integrated regional development initiatives, with a specific focus on transport and social infrastructure.

In Chapters 4 and 5, we discussed some of the effects of poor transport infrastructure on outcomes in many African zones. Although governments may invest significant resources in zone infrastructure, they often fail to consider the wider system in which the zones operate. Road access to many of the zones is poor (e.g., Athi River[6] in Kenya and Calabar in Nigeria), increasing costs and time for moving goods in and out, and making public transport for workers problematic. In Vietnam, foreign investors operate with international-quality infrastructure inside the zones but face huge bottlenecks in accessing ports, highways, and airports. In Kenya and Tanzania, poor infrastructure and operational performance at the ports has had a negative effect on the competitiveness of the firms that operate in their zones.

Some zone programs, however, pay attention to integrating the zone into a wider trade infrastructure. For example, in Honduras, a toll road was developed on the motorway linking the *maquila* factories in the valley outside San Pedro de Sula and Puerto Cortes, in order to speed up delivery times. In Ghana, the development of the Tema zone was part of a wider gateway strategy that integrated the zone with the port and the airport, including both hard and soft infrastructure.

Another critical infrastructure issue that is seldom taken into account in zone planning is social infrastructure—schools and hospitals in particular but also recreational and other facilities that workers and managers rely on. For example, in El Salvador, most of the private zones provide facilities such as football pitches and children's playgrounds. Social infrastructure is particularly important in two situations. First, in the rapid growth stage of labor-intensive zone programs, the zones may attract large pools of migrant labor—often young females from rural areas. This can put tremendous pressure on the public infrastructure in the communities around the zones. Second, as zones upgrade to higher value added activities, the surrounding communities must offer the kinds of schools and public health facilities that will attract skilled workers. This was an important part of the upgrading strategy in Malaysia, for example.

Customs, Trade Facilitation, and Transport

In successful zones, customs operations are identified as critical sources of competitive advantage and are given the authority and capacity to deliver an efficient clearance service.

Most zone programs under study have been fairly effective in establishing an environment for efficient onsite customs clearance. Anecdotal evidence across countries indicates that, from a customs clearance standpoint, investors benefit substantially from operating in an SEZ environment over duty-drawback or bonded warehouse schemes, which are administered poorly in many countries.

As we have stressed throughout this report, the institutional arrangement through which the customs service is delivered in the zone appears to be critical to its success. This is true for two reasons: (1) customs regimes are a significant source of corruption in some countries, and

(2) because government tax revenues are at stake, customs processes are often a source of cross-institutional conflict. Some of the programs studied, including those in the Dominican Republic and Vietnam, address these risks by establishing a dedicated customs subdirectorate for the zone program. This tends to give the regulator greater authority over customs processes in the zones. In the Dominican Republic, the subdirectorate is governed by an interagency commission that includes the customs authority, the zone regulator, and the association representing companies operating in the free zone. In Honduras, substantial authority was given directly to private zone operators, who are responsible for paying a share of the costs of the customs officials (this is over and above the cost of the facilities to house these officials, which is the responsibility of zone developers/operators in almost all SEZs). This arrangement gives zone operators the power to pay overtime wages if officials are required to work at odd hours and to report any problems with service delivery or corruption to Customs. The zone operator also assumes responsibility for tenants' behavior with respect to customs, giving the operator an incentive to ensure that companies comply with rules and procedures. Where customs officials are not part of a dedicated zone subdirectorate, they are often rotated in and out of zones to limit the potential for corruption.

Some of the African zones do not have the scale to support dedicated customs personnel. This has been the case in Tanzania and Ghana, and both counties' programs have suffered from clearance delays and uncertainties. Customs can be a Catch-22 situation, particularly in the early stages of a zone.

Customs effectiveness goes well beyond the gates of the zones; it depends critically on the facilities and operations at ports and airports.
As discussed throughout this report, effective zone programs address issues that go well beyond the gates of the zones. Efficient onsite customs clearance is of limited value if there are long delays in getting the goods through the ports. This is a significant problem for many zone programs, and it undermines the good work that has been done with regard to onsite customs clearance in the zones.

Tanzania is a good example of the challenges posed by poorly operating ports and less-than-efficient customs. Tanzania has significant potential to expand its role as a logistics/storage hub into the EAC customs territory along the Central Corridor supply chain for products bound for Rwanda, Burundi, and the Democratic Republic of Congo. However,

Tanzanian producers and service providers struggle with the lack of capacity and poor performance at the Dar Es Salaam port. This struggle was compounded in the early days of the EPZ program by a lack of awareness of the program and the duty-free access arrangements on the part of many related government agencies, especially the customs authority. As awareness of the program has grown, the situation has slowly improved, although problems arise whenever new staff are assigned to handle EPZ-related shipments. And despite the efficiency and expediency arrangements of customs services for EPZ operators, the lack of a one-stop center at the zones in Tanzania meant that EPZ goods still had to line up for clearance.

Programs that have made significant efforts to improve their ports and integrate them with the zones have reaped the rewards. One example, discussed earlier in this chapter, is Honduras. Another is the Suzhou Industrial Park in China (see Box 7.4)

Promoting Linkages with the Local Economy

Achieving linkages between zone-based firms and the domestic economy has long been a major challenge in zone programs, particularly those in low-skill, labor-intensive, footloose sectors such as garments. Moving beyond these sectors may create additional opportunities for improved links.

Across most of the countries studied, zones are largely enclaves with limited links to the domestic economy. This has significant implications for the potential of these zone programs to contribute dynamic benefits to the economy, particularly in terms of facilitating industrial upgrading through knowledge and technology spillovers from zone-based FDI.

While traditional EPZ assembly activities present inherent challenges to integration between zones and local economies, challenges are less daunting in activities related to the agriculture and natural resource sectors, in which local supply relationships are fundamental. In the African context, this may help argue for a refocusing of zone strategies toward natural-resource-based comparative advantage. And, if comparative advantage exists in these areas, the countries should be in a better position to absorb the resulting spillovers from FDI. Thus, even with smaller scale zone programs, African countries could realize more dynamic benefits from zones by reorienting their strategic focus. Moreover, if the refocus strengthens links with supply chains, it might also result in greater overall job creation from the zone program, primarily through indirect employment.

Box 7.4

Overcoming a Landlocked Location: Integrated Customs and Trade Facilitation at Suzhou Industrial Park

The China-Singapore Suzhou Industrial Park (SIP), a joint venture between the governments of Singapore and China, is one of China's most successful industrial parks. Despite its generally advantageous location in China, the park is land-locked. Thus, one of the most important areas for government support in the development of the park has been transport, logistics, and trade facilitation. The continued streamlining of customs procedures and port handling, which have been adapted and upgraded over the years, has been one of the most important contributions of government to the success of the zone.

From the inception of the park in 1994, a customs subadministration was planned; it was formally launched in 1999. SIP now operates as a virtual port and is allowed to handle customs clearance of exports and imports directly. SIP firms enjoy an efficient "green lane" and independent customs supervision, which has run 24 hours a day, seven days a week since 2003. An integrated free trade zone (IFTZ) was established in SIP in 2008 by integrating two processing trade zones, one bonded logistic center, and one customs checkpoint.[7] The IFTZ serves as a platform to promote the development of a business process outsourcing (BPO) industry in SIP. Some multinational corporations—including Fairchild Semiconductor Inc., Samsung, and Chi Mei Optoelectronics—have established or are planning to establish their distribution centers in the IFTZ, so an international logistics and distribution base is gradually taking shape.

Source: Zhao and Farole (2010).

SEZ models have a significant advantage over traditional EPZ models in facilitating improved links.

Traditional zone programs, built around labor-intensive assembly designed to exploit trade preferences, face structural barriers to achieving integration between the zones and the domestic economy. This is because the structure of trade preferences often works against sourcing from the local market. For example, many of the trade agreements that allowed African and other low-income countries to gain duty-free access to the U.S. and EU markets for apparel were originally designed so that firms would source fabric from those end markets. In some cases (e.g., under

AGOA), most African countries are now free to source fabric from any third country. While this generally allows exporters from Africa to compete more effectively, it also means that they have strong incentives to access these materials from the lowest cost locations. And, because they are based in a zone, they can access these inputs without paying any duty. This situation provides little incentive (and in some cases a clear disincentive) to purchase locally.

The traditional EPZ model also biases against participation of local firms by (usually) placing tight restrictions on sales to the local market, forcing firms to be export-oriented. Moreover, many zones set a minimim level of investment to qualify for participation; for example, in Tanzania and in Senegal's original program, local firms have had to invest at least US$100,000 to qualify.[8] Thus, local firms are much less likely to be in the zones. This does not necessarily restrict them from supplying zone-based firms but, as discussed below, it raises another barrier and limits the kinds of interactions that could contribute to spillovers across firms. Critically, this situation also prevents local firms from accessing the benefits available to zone-based firms (e.g., fiscal and nonfiscal incentives, duty-free access to inputs). Equal footing policies are a start, but in many countries weaknesses in the business environment result in domestic firms that cannot compete with alternative international suppliers. This has been the finding of in-depth studies in the Dominican Republic and Lesotho that sought to identify the reasons for the failure of zone programs to create significant supply links in sectors such as garments. For example, it was found that in the Dominican Republic's apparel sector, local spending in the early 2000s was only 1.5 percent of the export value of free zone companies (Sanchez-Ancochea 2006).

Thus, co-location might play an even more important role than expected. SEZ regimes that do not place any restrictions on local ownership or require export-orientation are more effective models for contributing to integration of the zones. An alternative is the concept of hybrid zones that allow local firms to be co-located with export-oriented firms in the same EPZ. An innovative approach following this model is the multipurpose industrial park (MPIP) at Tema in Ghana (see Box 7.5).

One of the most important sources of spillovers from FDI is through forward and backward supply linkages. To facilitate spillovers, zones must remove policy and administrative barriers to local market integration.

Box 7.5

The MPIP at Ghana's Tema Free Zone: A New Approach for Integrating Local Firms with FDI

As part of the relaunch of the Tema zone following the departure of the initial private developer, Business Focus of Malaysia, the Ghana Free Zones Board (GFZB), with support from the World Bank, decided to open part of the enclave to non-export companies. The board set aside about 70 hectares as an MPIP. The MPIP is designed to support the development of smaller scale domestic industries and create links with major exporters. Although companies within the MPIP will not have access to a special fiscal and customs regime, the plan is to facilitate competitiveness by establishing critical common infrastructure and cluster-based business support services, such as common packaging and labeling facilities, kiln drying, and warehousing.

The creation of the MPIP represents an innovative shift in the enclave model in Ghana into that of a hybrid EPZ that combines free zone and non-free-zone investors in the same location. MPIP should offer a substantial opportunity for local firms to become better integrated into the supply networks of exporters in Tema.

Source: Author.

In small markets such as Lesotho, strong supply linkages would not be expected, given the limited scale and specialization of local supply and the limited size of the local market opportunity. But we found that even in Bangladesh, Vietnam, and Nigeria—where end markets are large and there are a large and dynamic local industrial bases that could supply SEZ-based companies—linkages are weak. It is clear that the very nature of EPZ enclaves contributes to this situation and that SEZ rules and procedures tend to make links difficult to achieve.

In terms of forward linkage, the main policy barriers in the zones are the restrictions on local sales. Only Nigeria and Lesotho (and the upcoming zone in Senegal) have eliminated all de jure barriers to zone-based firms selling to local markets. In Bangladesh, significant restrictions remain: only 10 percent of sales are permitted to the local market; zero in the garment sector, which is the mainstay of the EPZs. And difficult customs administration creates additional barriers to selling into local markets. This issue was mentioned specifically by investors in Ghana, Vietnam, and Bangladesh, but it is a barrier to forward links in most countries. Partly as a result of these barriers (and partly because of the strategies pursued by FDI in the traditional EPZs), local market sales in most countries are actually far below the limits set by zone legislation. Finally, restrictive regional trade agreements also diminish the potential for forward linkage through regional markets. For example, the Arab FTA, Mercado Común del Cono Sur (MERCOSUR), and ECOWAS all exclude products produced in free zones from their free trade arrangements.

Even bigger problems exist with backward integration; that is, domestic firms supplying FDI based in the zones. This is where the biggest opportunities exist for local economies to benefit from zones, both in the short term and by taking advantage of the dynamic effects of knowledge spillovers. These links also have the potential to help overcome financing constraints of local SMEs; for example, by obtaining financing directly from large firms or, more likely, by collateralizing receivables from large, credit-worthy companies in the supply chain (e.g., through factoring).

However, we found that both policy and administrative factors have played a role in limiting backward integration. On the policy side, a major issue has been the lack of a level playing field (mentioned previously) between local and foreign suppliers to the zones. For example, in Honduras, until recently, SEZ-based firms were required to pay a 12 percent VAT on all purchases from the local market but could access those same goods from international suppliers on a tax- and duty-free basis. Beyond this obvious misalignment, policies that fail to offer benefits to suppliers as indirect exporters also hamper their competitive position vis à vis international suppliers. In Ghana, the government has attempted to address these barriers through the following policies, designed to promote local supply into the free zones:

- Sales of goods and services by a domestic enterprise from the national customs territory to enterprises in a free zone or single factory zone are considered exports, which gives local suppliers benefits as indirect exporters.
- A domestic enterprise is eligible to benefit from the export incentives available to a national exporter and does not require an export license for the sale of any goods and services to enterprises in a free zone or single factory zone.
- An enterprise in a free zone or single factory zone may purchase goods and services sold by a domestic enterprise with local currency obtained through conversion of foreign currency through a bank or a licensed foreign exchange bureau.

In addition to policies, administrative issues raise barriers in most zone programs. The extremely restrictive extraterritoriality of many zone regimes results in regulations and procedures that restrict sales between firms inside and outside the zones. As a result, zone-based firms often find it easier to import goods from abroad than to source from the local market. The most common problem is the administration of the duty drawback regimes, which enable direct and indirect exporters based outside the zones to access production inputs on a duty-free basis. In most countries, delays and heavy paperwork requirements make it difficult for local firms to take advantage of the benefits. In Bangladesh, for example, backward links are not prohibited and are, in theory, encouraged. However, a number of regulatory, administrative, and general market factors place significant barriers in the way of such links:

- First, although local producers selling into the EPZs can obtain duty drawback on imported inputs (as indirect exporters), smaller suppliers rarely claim it because of the heavy bureaucracy of the drawback system and the hugely understaffed organization that administers it.[9]
- Second, concerns regarding security and leaks of EPZ products into the local market have resulted in restrictions on the movement into the EPZs of trucks from the domestic territory. For example, trucks may only travel into and out of the zone during certain hours. This has made the process of getting supplies from local companies more difficult.
- Finally, according to many garment manufacturers inside the EPZs, local supplies are often of insufficient quality to meet the standards of international buyers. As a result, the large majority of fabric is sourced from China. According to interviews with EPZ companies and BEPZA officials, no formal programs are in place to try to improve the links between EPZ companies and local suppliers.

Despite these problems, the large local supply base is making some inroads into the EPZ exporters. BEPZA points to the Swedish clothing retailer H&M, which sources inputs from 27 different local suppliers. This is certainly the exception to the rule, but it underscores the size and diversity of the local supply base, something that is not the case in many EPZ programs in Africa.

Some examples exist of programs being undertaken in the zones to improve local links—programs in Vietnam and Kenya are discussed in Box 7.6.

Box 7.6

Programs to Support Local Linkages: Vietnam and Kenya

Vietnam-Japan Joint Initiative

In Vietnam, Japanese organizations have been particularly prominent in promoting a support industry network within the electronics and automotive sectors. Specifically, the Vietnam-Japan Joint Initiative to Improve Business Environment with a View to Strengthening Vietnam's Competitiveness, signed in December 2003, calls for the "development, introduction, and utilization of supporting industry in Vietnam." The Japan External Trade Organization, in association with investment and trade promotion centers in northern and southern Vietnam, holds an annual exhibition in which Japanese buyers are matched with Vietnamese suppliers. In early 2009, Vietnam's first dedicated industrial zone for supporting industries was established in Bac Ninh province near Hanoi.

Kenya's incubator program at Athi River

Recognizing the opportunities for the local SMEs and the interest shown by local small enterprises to enter the export market, Kenya's Export Processing Zones Authority (EPZA), along with partners Kenya Industrial Estates Ltd. and the Kenya Export Promotion Council, established the EPZ Business Incubator Program at Athi River to help local SMEs grow into exporting enterprises. The program provides purpose-built infrastructure and support services at subsidized rates and offers standard EPZ tax benefits and a special dispensation for incubator firms to sell a higher percentage of their output to the local market than is normally allowed during the first four years of operation.[10] The program helps incubator firms establish direct exporting and subcontracting relationships with larger firms (not strictly limited to EPZ firms).

Source: Author.

Effective training programs and vibrant local labor markets are critical to facilitating knowledge spillover.

Besides supply relationships, the main channel for spillovers from FDI are likely to be through the movement of skilled labor across firms. Low worker skills, limited vocational training, and rigid labor markets are major barriers to integration, particularly in the countries studied. Countries such as Senegal and Ghana—in which high proportions of local management are employed in the zones—have some of the most rigid labor markets in the world, according the Doing Business ratings (World

Bank 2009). Thus, the likelihood of these managers moving across firms or setting up their own companies is limited.

Training and skills development play a critical role by upgrading the workforce and putting it in a position to take advantage of opportunities to absorb new knowledge and technology. There is a strong argument for the provision of training as a public good, as individual firms may be unwilling to invest in training if there is a possibility that workers will move to other (competitor) firms before the original firm gets its return on investment in the training. To overcome this problem, government and zone authorities often partner with the private sector to identify skills development needs, create programs to address them, and find sustainable funding sources. The best example of success in this area is the Penang Skills Development Centre in Malaysia, a public-private effort that is considered to be one of the key factors in the success of Malaysia's economic transformation over the past two decades. A smaller scale private initiative in Honduras provides another example of the role of training in zone upgrading. These programs are described in Box 7.7.

Box 7.7

Training and Skills Development to Support Upgrading in Zone Programs

Malaysia: Penang Skills Development Centre

The Penang Skills Development Centre (PSDC) was the first industry-led training center established in Malaysia. It was conceptualized in 1989 in response to an urgent sense that if Penang was going to continue to attract FDI, its human capital would have to be trained to keep pace with changes in technology. The initiative, the land, and some financial support came from the state and federal governments, but Malaysian and foreign private companies played the leading role in establishing the center. Not only did these companies provide the initial trainers and equipment, they also designed the training programs to meet their needs.

The PSDC now has 140 members and operates as a nonprofit society. Its mission is to pool resources among the free industrial zones and industrial estates in Penang to provide up-to-date training and educational programs in support of

(continued next page)

Box 7.7 *(continued)*

operational requirements, and to stay abreast of technology. The center operates on a full-cost basis—companies pay to send employees for training. To ensure that the training meets the needs of industry, the programs are continually upgraded and adapted to evolving skill needs.

Today the PSDC caters to the firms in the free industrial zones and industrial parks in Penang, which in late 2007 had 1,277 factories employing approximately 220,000 workers. The center has trained more than 150,000 workers through more than 7,000 courses; pioneered local industry development initiatives; provided input and helped formulate national policies for human capital development; and contributed directly to the Malaysian workforce transformation initiatives. Recently, the PSDC set up a new Shared Services Centre that houses Malaysia's largest electromagnetic compatibility (EMC) lab, which will provide training programs aimed at fast-tracking the work-readiness of university graduates. The program will be conducted in partnership with member companies to address the competency gap between what these graduates know and the needs of industry.

The PSDC was unique, but the model has since been adopted throughout the country—skills development centers operate in 11 of the 13 states in Malaysia.

Source: Penang Skills Development Centre/PenInvest (www.psdc.org.my, accessed May 16, 2010).

Honduras: Instituto Politécnico Centroamericano (IPC)

IPC is a nongovernment, not-for-profit vocational training institute that was founded in 2005. An assessment of the vocational training system in Honduras had concluded that the system was broken—instructors were incapable of teaching, and 95 percent of the equipment was broken, irrelevant, or missing. IPC was established to design courses for current and future workers in all sectors of the economy, including manufacturing and textiles and clothing. IPC's objective is to provide workers with the skills demanded by industry, so its curriculum is strongly influenced by input from employers. The institute strives to offer the best technical equipment, courses, and instructors; for example, a majority of the 12 instructors are from North America, Europe, and Latin America. In the spring of 2009, IPC had 270 full-time students and some 1,400 workers who were upgrading their skills in courses lasting 2–18 weeks. A majority of the graduates join SEZ companies; for example, Gildan (the Canadian company that sponsored the original assessment of the country's vocational training system) hires 60 students from IPC every year.

(continued next page)

Box 7.7 *(continued)*

Ninety percent of the students come from large families earning less than US$300/month; the fee for a year of full-time training is US$1,500. Expenses are partly covered by companies, charitable organizations, and governments; for example, a U.S. NGO covers transportation and a daily meal; a Swiss company that supplies chemicals to the local textiles industry donated a chemistry lab; a French company provided design equipment; and an Italian company donated sewing equipment. Roughly 95 percent of the students receive a corporate scholarship that covers 75 percent of their fees. In return, they commit to work for the sponsor for two to four years.

Source: Author.

Monitoring, Enforcement, and Learning

Monitoring and enforcement of labor and environmental standards in zones is improving but remains a source of weakness and risk.
As discussed previously in this report, most zone programs have made significant improvements over the past decade in their de jure standards for workers' rights. With some significant exceptions, most zone programs are now in compliance with ILO standards and operate labor regimes that do not differ from those that prevail in the national economy. But a gap remains between the de jure and de facto environments in many zones. Data are relatively limited, but anecdotal evidence suggests that labor standards, including monitoring and enforcement, tend to be better inside than outside the zone regimes in most low-income countries.

In traditional assembly-based EPZs—where competition for footloose, cost-conscious investment is fierce—there is a serious risk of a race to the bottom in terms of standards enforcement. In sectors such as garments, strict codes of conduct imposed by international buyers on zone-based suppliers are increasingly prevailing over those set by the regulatory authority. But given the demands of some international buyers for ever lower costs and flexibility, it remains to be seen whether the suppliers will be able to (or choose to) comply with the codes.

Despite the problems, some programs are beginning to establish structures to improve compliance and the quality of the work environment. For example, in Bangladesh, where the rights to organize labor unions and enter into collective bargaining were long banned in the zones, workers have gained increasing legal rights since 2004. The launch of the Labor

Counselor Program (see Box 7.8) has probably had an even greater positive impact on workers.

Lesotho has also made substantial efforts to improve its labor situation in recent years, through training, better relations with unions, and support

---

Box 7.8

Bangladesh's Labor Counselor Program

BEPZA is responsible for ensuring compliance with social and labor regulations in its zones. Acknowledging that its activities in these areas were limited, BEPZA initiated a unique and innovative program in 2005. The program, funded by the World Bank, recruited 67 counselors to work closely with employees and management to address proactively issues related to wages, working conditions, food, child care, benefits, and security. These counselors worked on behalf of BEPZA but were perceived more as facilitators than as regulators or enforcers. The young recruits paid almost daily visits to their designated factories to work with management on the correct application of labor and compensation regulations, and acted as informal arbitrators between management and workers to resolve grievances. They reported existing and potential issues to BEPZA. The International Finance Corporation (IFC) estimated that the improved implementation of existing rules facilitated by these counselors resulted in a 32 percent increase in wages for the workers in the EPZs.

The program appears to have been greatly appreciated by both management and workers. The initial funding expired in 2009; at BEPZA's request, the Bangladesh Investment Climate Fund (BICF) supplied additional funding to continue the counselor program. BEPZA has committed to integrating the program into its mainstream operational budget. In 2006, allegations of unpaid wages led to massive demonstrations and serious unrest in the country. A couple of factories were set on fire in the Dhaka EPZ. All stakeholders hope that the presence of the counselors will prevent such situations from arising in the future.

Despite significant unrest that shook Bangladesh's garment sector in 2010, no incidents were reported in any of the EPZs. There is no doubt that the labor counselors, since the BICF started working with them in 2007, have been instrumental in maintaining this stark contrast between inside and outside the zones. The counselors have acted as an effective and informal arbitration mechanism, and have begun to build a relationship of trust between worker and employer in all the EPZs. As evidence of this improved relationship, in the Dhaka EPZ, grievances declined from 2,000 in 2007 to only 400 in 2009.

Source: Author.

for programs such as the Apparel Lesotho Alliance to Fight AIDS (ALAFA), a nonprofit coalition of companies that provides education and treatment for Basotho garment workers, more than 40 percent of whom are estimated to be afflicted with HIV/AIDS. The industry-wide program provides education and prevention, voluntary testing and counseling, and management of AIDS through the roll-out of care and treatment for HIV-positive workers. Since 2009, the service has been extended to spouses of workers. The existence of programs such as ALAFA has helped to reposition Lesotho as a location for sourcing high-quality clothing manufactured under ethical conditions. The country's relative success to date with this enlightened approach suggests the benefits of developing an alternative to the old sweatshop model of EPZs. Kenya's zone program also recognized the growing importance of labor standards to attract investment in the garment sector. In Kenya, perceptions of poor labor conditions and ineffective enforcement were a barrier to investment, particularly by large companies serving global brands.

Monitoring and enforcement of environmental standards also tend to be relatively weak in many zones. This is problematic because the activities in most zone programs have significant environmental effects, most often in terms of wastewater, which has been a particular problem for the zone programs in Lesotho and Vietnam.

Lack of effective monitoring and evaluation (M&E) is a critical weakness in most African SEZ programs.

One of the most critical and underappreciated roles of zone authorities is monitoring and evaluating the performance of zones across a wide range of outcome indicators. The role of M&E links back to the overall strategy and objectives of the SEZ program and should be a fundamental part of the government's ongoing decision-making process regarding investment in the program. The SEZ strategic plan should make it clear how success will be defined, determine how it can be measured, and establish mechanisms to collect the necessary data to monitor progress against these measures on an ongoing basis.

Because of the closed and regulated nature of zone programs, authorities are in a good position to collect detailed and valuable data from the firms that operate within them. However, few of the African zone programs appear to take advantage of this opportunity. Kenya and Ghana track and analyze some valuable data on economic outcomes (e.g., exports, investment, employment, taxes, local purchases), but other African programs in the study appear to have no systematic process for data collection, despite the fact that many of them require (at least nominally) their licensed investors to fill out relatively detailed forms on a quarterly or annual basis. In contrast, the non-African zones in the study—particularly those in Latin America—provide valuable standardized annual data (see Box 7.9).

In the absence of an effective program to monitor the activities and results of companies operating under their zone regimes, African zone

---

Box 7.9

CZNFE's Annual Free Zone Statistics

Consejo Nacional de Zonas Francas de Exportacion (CNZFE) is responsible for overseeing the Dominican Republic's free zone program. Among CNZFE's many responsibilities are monitoring and evaluating free zone policy and making recommendations to the president for future development and strategy.

In addition to evaluation, investment promotion, and customer services, an important activity in CNZFE is the compilation and dissemination of statistics related to the free zone program. The Dominican Republic, like most countries with established free zone programs, requires companies to provide information on their activities on a regular basis. In the Dominican Republic, they must also file a specific set of data with the Central Bank every month. A detailed compilation of statistics—for the program overall and in each zone—is published annually; reports going back to at least 1992 are available (in Spanish) on CNZFE's Web site.

In terms of monitoring and the evaluation of performance statistics, the main differences between this program and many others around the world are as follows:

- The Dominican Republic enforces the data requirements, so compliance rates are high.
- CNZFE complements these statistics with a mandatory, detailed annual survey of zones and companies.
- CNZFE conducts a valuable analysis of the data and makes it available to the industry, the government, and the public.

Thus, CNZFE fulfills its monitoring and evaluation role in a highly effective way to assess the evolution, oportunities, and risks in the developing free zone program. This information is an important part of policy discussions related to the program.

Source: Author.

regulators are (1) unable to enforce regulations effectively, which results in abuse of the system and negative externalities (e.g., environmental); (2) unable to determine whether programs have been successful; and, therefore, (3) unable to make informed decisions about future investment, participate effectively in policy dialogue, or respond appropriately to the changing needs of the investors and the government.

Notes

1. Benjamin William Mkapa SEZ in Mabibo, an industrial suburb of Dar Es Salaam.
2. Both of these figures are as of November 2009, based on an interview with the general manager of NEPZA.
3. The exception is often in mining or oil and gas sectors, where returns can be extremely high.
4. Mongla is located next to the country's second main seaport, but the port is not of international standard and no international shipping lines call there. In December 2009, the government signed an MOU for a US$3b PPP to modernize the port (http://bangladesheconomy.wordpress.com/2009/12/03/govt-plans-3-billion-ppp-project-to-develop-mongla-port).
5. The PPP arrangement also allows the company to sell excess capacity into the national grid at an agreed-upon rate.
6. A major road upgrade is ongoing on the Nairobi-Mombasa highway. In the short term, this is making access even more difficult for Athi River, but eventually the upgrade should greatly improve the situation.
7. After its success in SIP, the scheme was extended to 20 other cities.
8. In Tanzania, however, local firms are privileged in comparison with foreign investors, who face a minimum investment level of US$500,000.
9. Small indirect exporters often complain that they cannot claim drawback because they are unable to attach the original bill of export with their claims (as this is held only by the final exporters). It has been estimated that less than 10 percent of eligible duty drawback is claimed through the system.
10. The program calls for incubator firms to be able to sell 80 percent of their output to the local market in the first year, decreasing to 40 percent by the fourth year.

References

Action Aid Vietnam. 2007. *Food Security for the Poor in Vietnam.* Hanoi: Action Aid International Vietnam.

Sanchez-Ancochea, D. 2006. Development trajectories and new comparative advantages: Costa Rica and the Dominican Republic under globalization, *World Development* 34 (6): 996–1015.

World Bank. 2009. *Doing Business 2010*. Washington, DC: World Bank.

Zhao, M., and T. Farole. 2010. "Partnership Arrangements in China-Singapore (Suzhou) Industrial Park." Mimeo (March). World Bank, Washington, DC.

CHAPTER 8

Policy Conclusions: SEZs in Africa—When, What, and How?

Introduction

In this report, we have documented the scale, scope, and nature of SEZ programs across a number of African countries. We have provided detailed quantitative and qualitative evidence on the main factors that contribute to SEZ performance in both the short and long term, and assessed the performance of African zone programs against these factors and benchmarked them against select global peers. Finally, we have outlined good practices and lessons learned on strategic and operational aspects of economic zone programs.

We find that while performance varies across countries, economic zone programs in Africa have, by and large, failed to deliver significant benefits to date. Investment, exports, and employment generated in the African zones are low, and many of these benefits have come from single factory schemes, which in most African countries are unlikely to have the catalytic effect that is the objective of economic zone programs. Most importantly, the African programs show little evidence of progress in capturing the dynamic benefits of FDI and, thus, of leveraging the zone program to

With a contribution from Claude Baissac.

support diversification, upgrading, or broad-based economic reform. Indeed, evidence suggests that several of the programs have already stagnated at levels of employment and exports that are far short of their objectives. However, although the success of the non-African zones studied as part of this project is qualified, these zones seem to have the potential to deliver static benefits such as employment and foreign exchange on a large scale, and to function as useful instruments (alongside other policies) to support structural economic transformation.

As outlined in Chapters 4, 5, and 6, a number of factors appear to contribute to the underperformance of African zones in meeting both static and dynamic objectives. These include issues that can be fairly readily targeted and addressed, such as poor infrastructure (inside and outside the zones), insufficient attention to trade facilitation issues (again, going beyond the gates of the zones), and weak program planning and management. However, success is also limited by more complex and entrenched challenges, including institutional coordination, the political economy, and wider national competitiveness, which negatively affect planning and performance in the short term, and undermine the dynamic potential of the zone programs to adjust to changing economic circumstances.

Most of the African programs studied in this report are in the early stages of their development, and several are experiencing some signs of growth. The challenge for the African zone programs—most of which were designed along traditional EPZ lines—is to remake themselves, building on sustainable sources of comparative advantage rather than relying on factors such as low wages, incentives, and trade preferences, which have not provided a sufficient base on which to carve out a competitive position in global markets.

In the remainder of this chapter, we will draw policy conclusions—specifically for the African and low-income countries—from our findings. A number of challenges are inherent in this undertaking. First, the lack of high-quality data on economic zones has limited the scope and depth of quantitative analysis we could present in this report, which makes it difficult to draw firm policy conclusions on some issues. Second, the outcomes of zone programs result from complex interplays of policy, implementation, and context—a context that includes factors such as timing (e.g., the state of global and local economies, trends in global production networks, trade agreements), sector structures, and the specific nature and quality of local and national institutions. What works well in one place today may fail somewhere else tomorrow. This problem is not unique to economic zone policy, but it requires a focus on context and a cautionary approach to making broad generalizations about the appropriateness of economic zones and of specific policies related to them. Therefore, we focus our policy conclusions on the African country context; specifically on low-income and lower middle-income countries, bearing in mind that here, too, we encounter significant heterogeneity. The policy conclusions do not go too deeply into day-to-day operational aspects in the zones but address policy and institutional factors that bear directly on operational performance.

When Are Economic Zones an Appropriate and Effective Policy Choice?

There is no economic context or set of objectives in which economic zones are likely to be more or less successful. They have worked (and not worked) in many different situations.

SEZs have clearly shown their potential to generate meaningful static economic benefits to their host countries, such as employment, investment, foreign exchange, and exports. The results in our four non-African zones (Bangladesh, Vietnam, Honduras, and the Dominican Republic) and in zones around the world—including African zones such as Lesotho, Madagascar, and Mauritius—bear testament to this. These benefits may in themselves be significant net contributors to the economy, notably in the case of least-developed countries. However, they may have a high opportunity cost if the SEZ is used solely to avoid or displace reforms. In a more limited range of cases, SEZs have also played an important role in creating the conditions for long-term (dynamic) changes in the structure of the economy and, critically, minimizing opposition to reform through progressive demonstration effects and by encouraging domestic investment in SEZs. However, while almost all countries in the world have implemented some form of economic zone program, only a small handful are recognized as major success stories. The failures tend to go undocumented, and the majority of programs deliver net benefits that are moderate at best.

The success of some zones, however, suggests that they have the potential to benefit economies at various stages of their development and to meet various objectives. Table 8.1 provides a basic structure for organizing some of the examples of economic zone success. In small markets, successful zone programs have tended in the first stage to take advantage of location, trade preferences, and labor arbitrage to create large-scale employment and support a transition away from reliance on natural

Table 8.1   Framework for Organizing Examples of Successful Zones

	Transition from inward focus to global integration	Transition from natural-resource-based economy	Upgrading from factor-cost-based economy
Small markets	• Malaysia (stage 1)	• Dominican Republic • Honduras • Mauritius (stage 1) • Costa Rica (stage 1) • Lesotho • United Arab Emirates	• Mauritius (stage 2) • Costa Rica (stage 2) • Malaysia (stage 2) • Colombia
Large markets	• Korea (stage 1) • China (stage 1)	• China (stage 1) • Philippines • Bangladesh • Mexico	• Korea (stage 2) • China (stage 2)

Source: Author.
Note that "stage 1" and "stage 2" refer to situations in which zone programs have developed over relatively long time periods and have transitioned through several stages of development.

resource sectors (normally agriculture) toward the development of a light manufacturing sector. Countries in this group have been successful in terms of employment creation and foreign exchange contribution by attracting investments within global value chains. The challenges for many of these zones, with small product and labor markets, have been to move the zone beyond enclave status and to maintain a sustainable competitive position as inevitable wage increases erode the traditional basis of comparative advantage. Some of the small countries have used the zones as a tool to support further upgrading away from a reliance on labor-intensive manufacturing to higher technology and more knowledge-based activities. As we discuss later in this chapter, the experiences in these countries have certain commonalities: namely, state capacity, proactive government support, integration of the zone program within a broader framework of growth policies, and ongoing exchange between the zones and the domestic economy.

Many of the large countries with successful zones (most of them in Asia) used the zones to leverage an existing capacity and comparative advantage in factor-cost-based manufacturing to facilitate a transition away from inward-looking development policies to export-led growth. These zones have offered foreign investors the potential to operate in a protected environment while the government uses the zone to test reforms. In many of these markets, the emphasis on upgrading to medium technology activities became an important priority shortly after integration, and the zones have played an important role in attracting the foreign technology needed to support the transformation of domestic industrial capacity. Also, by concentrating economic infrastructure and public goods in one geographic area, the zones have helped unlock natural agglomeration processes and supported the exploitation of scale economies in emerging sectors.

By facilitating these structural transitions, economic zones in both large and small markets have played an important catalytic role in the policy reform processes that are part of the transition. They did this by allowing governments to protect the rents of powerful elites (traditionally dominant industry sectors and their connected political interests) in the broader economy while using zone enclaves to test reforms, provide a safety valve for political compromise with alternative interests (e.g., powerful minority interests, secondary regions), and provide a demonstration effect to facilitate broader reforms over time.

Thus, despite the limited success rates of economic zones on a global basis, they have had an impact in a wide variety of situations. Economic zones may be less effective as a policy tool on the opposite end of the investment climate spectrum (see Figure 8.1), where the national investment climate is so poor that implementing a successful zone is virtually

Figure 8.1   Schematic of the Potential Effect of SEZ Policy across the Investment Climate Spectrum

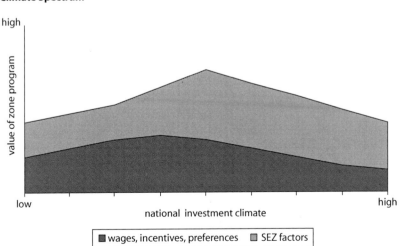

Source: Author.

impossible, and where the investment climate has so few constraints that the cost to government of maintaining a special trade and investment regime for the program is likely to outweigh any incremental benefits. Using economic zones as an enclave may be most tempting when the domestic investment climate is a complete disaster, but the findings from this report raise some doubts about this use: A zone is unlikely to be sufficient to protect investors from the investment climate around them, particularly if it is unable to fully free itself from the influence of the state. However, further research is needed to understand the role of SEZs in postconflict environments—it is likely that the specific context of a postconflict environment will have a bearing on the potential of zones to catalyze investment and private sector activity. If a dynamic private sector existed before the conflict and the most pressing investment climate concerns relate to infrastructure, zones may have a strong catalytic effect. But in the absence of a strong domestic private sector and where the state is weak (or powerful but predatory), SEZs may struggle unless they can almost fully circumvent the state.

In contrast, if an economy operates well on most aspects of its investment climate and land is not an issue, natural, efficient, and broad patterns of investment and agglomeration should occur, making economic zones largely unnecessary. There are three exceptions to this in high-income countries: (1) the government uses economic zones as a tool of regional policy to encourage investment into lagging regions; (2) the government uses economic zones as a tool of sector-specific industrial policy to attract FDI that would otherwise invest offshore (e.g., trade zones that provide substantial incentives to host mainly foreign automotive assembly operations in the United States); and (3) the government uses economic zones to provide collective goods and promote clustering in new and advanced industries (e.g., the promotion of technology parks). In the first two cases, zones are unlikely to deliver a positive net benefit to the national economy. In the third, the argument is less clear, as market uncertainties and coordination challenges may make economic zones a valuable tool.

Between the two extremes, the evidence from many years of economic zone research suggests that zones can play an important role in helping catalyze processes of economic transition. Where national investment climates are poor, investors are attracted primarily by low wages and fiscal incentives, although administrative efficiencies and quality infrastructure also play an important role. However, as the national investment climate improves, the likelihood of zone success and the potential impact of a zone program should also improve, and the main contribution of the zones progressively moves away from low wages and incentives toward factors such as quality infrastructure, administrative superiority, customs facilitation, and the benefits of local clusters in the zones.

Finally, timing and the confluence of external factors can contribute to success in SEZs. For example, much of the early investment in Bangladesh's EPZs came from investors escaping the civil war in Sri Lanka; Lesotho's garment sector was born as a result of apartheid-era sanctions against South Africa; and Honduras opened its zone program to private investment just as a preferential trade agreement with the United States helped stimulate a major trend in offshoring and while conflict enveloped most of its Central American neighbors (its competitors for investment). But while an element of serendipity exists in the experience of many of the successful zone programs, the case of Honduras underscores an important finding of this study: Timing aside, the success of an economic zone program requires attention to infrastructure, SEZ policy, trade policy, and committed domestic investors.

What factors exogenous to the zones determine whether a zone will be successful?

While economic zones have shown that they can play a role in a wide range of economic policy contexts across various levels of a country's development, certain factors remain outside the control of the policymakers who plan and implement these programs. These factors are likely to determine the success of a program and should dictate, to a certain extent, which zone policies are put in place. In Chapter 4, we focused on two of these factors: national competitiveness and the size of the domestic (and possibly regional) markets accessible from the zones.

Empirical evidence (see Chapter 4 and, for example, Schrank 2001) suggests strongly that SEZs are more effective in countries with large domestic markets. This effectiveness is apparent in both supply and demand channels. First, the greater the scale of domestic market opportunities, the more attractive the location is for foreign investors (market-seeking FDI),[1] which leads to greater investment and employment in the short term. Second, the supply side of the domestic market tends to be more developed in larger markets, with more highly skilled and specialized workers and greater depth and specialization among suppliers.[2] Thus, FDI in the SEZs is more likely to develop extensive and deep links with the domestic economy in a larger market, leading to transmission of knowledge and technology and contributing to strong dynamic effects from the zones. For smaller economies, reaping the benefits of zone policies is likely to require a more proactive planning and implementation effort, including the following:

- Developing a clear competitive position based on sustainable sources of comparative advantage.
- Ensuring that the package on offer to investors is attractive; it may include some fiscal incentives, but these incentives should be carefully considered and strictly limited (see discussion later in this chapter).
- Making a comprehensive and proactive effort to maximize the integration of SEZ firms into the local economy and to absorb the resulting spillovers. Such an effort will require policies that go well beyond the zone program to integrate economic zone policy with wider industrial and trade policies, a critical issue.

The relationship between zone success and national competitiveness discussed earlier in this report seems to be unambiguous. An investor is unlikely to locate in a zone if the national investment environment is not competitive in the chosen sector or task. As shown in Figure 8.1, the likelihood of a zone program being successful in a very poor national investment climate is small. Zones appear to be able to tip the competitiveness balance at the margin, but they will not generally shift the paradigm. This may have important implications for many low-income countries, including these:

- In poor investment climates—especially where the government is weak or predatory—zones may not provide sufficient protection from catastrophic investment climates unless they can almost fully circumvent the state.
- If a country goes forward with an economic zone program despite a poor domestic investment climate, it is important to identify specific niche areas of competitiveness or activities with particularly high rents for investors to make the program attractive despite the risk.
- Weak investment climates tend to force the use of ever-greater incentives to offset competitiveness gaps and investor risk. This is an expensive strategy and runs the risk of undermining the reform agenda over the long term.
- Ongoing, progressive reform of the national investment climate is a must to avoid creating a permanent enclave and, with it, path dependence and stagnation in the zone. Again, the need to integrate zone policy into wider national policies and programs is clear.

In addition to national competitiveness and the size of local markets, a third success factor lies outside the control of zone program policymakers and tends to change only over the long term. This is state capacity—the effectiveness with which the government plans and implements its policies. The empirical evidence suggests that SEZs are more effective in countries with strong state capacity and less effective in countries with weak capacity. As with national investment climate, this issue affects the short-term success of zones in attracting investment, but its main effect is in the potential of the zones to contribute to meeting long-term policy objectives. A common thread in many of the zone success stories, from East Asia to Mauritius, is the commitment of senior policymakers to comprehensive export-driven growth policies and the technical competency of the wider public bureaucracy responsible for implementing them. It is telling that in much of Latin America, the zone programs that succeeded despite relatively weak state capacity were those that allowed a dynamic private sector in the region to take the lead. This factor has implications for many low-income countries contemplating or managing economic zone programs:

- In the absence of state capacity, countries are highly unlikely to be able to manage the complex set of policies, institutions, and practices required to make a zone program successful over the long term. Such countries should consider carefully before embarking on an economic zone program.
- Where state capacity is weak, countries should consider turning as much of the program as possible over to the private sector. This suggestion comes with two major caveats, however. First, even with strong private sector leadership in the zone program, government will play a critical role in many important policy decisions affecting the zones, so the state capacity problem will not go away. Second, in many low-income countries—including some of the African countries in this study—the domestic private sector is also weak and unlikely to be willing or able to play a leadership role in a zone program. Donors might be able to play a delivery support role in the short term, while capacity is developed.
- Zone program integration with wider economic policy will always be an issue. The challenge of weak state capacity is accentuated when successful implementation of a zone program requires delivery of policies, infrastructure, and services beyond the confines of the program.

The successful economic zone is usually only one piece of a larger success story. One of the clearest messages in this report is that the success of a zone is closely intertwined with the success of the national economy in which it is based. This is apparent in the East Asian cases of China and Vietnam and is also true in smaller markets, such as Mauritius and the Dominican Republic, where the success of the zones was closely linked to wider policies of economic liberalization implemented at the same time. Although it is difficult to assess the counterfactual scenario and disentangle the specific impact of the zones, the evidence presented in this report suggests that they can play an important role. The key is planning the right type of zone for the context, and then implementing it effectively. Which leads us to the next question: What is the context in which African economic zones are operating and what are the implications for the role and nature of SEZs?

What Type of Economic Zone Approach Is Most Likely to Be Effective in the African Context?

African countries are operating in an increasingly challenging global trade and investment context.
The rapid growth of economic zone programs around the world and their success in contributing to export-led growth in regions such as East Asia are one aspect of an unprecedented era of globalization of trade and investment that has taken place since the 1970s and that accelerated during the 1990s and 2000s. This period of globalization (trade grew 85 percent faster than GDP between 1983 and 2008) was particularly beneficial for developing countries and contributed to their rapid economic diversification: The share of manufactured products in total exports from low- and middle-income countries rose dramatically from 15 percent in 1970 to 57 percent by 2008. This increase was enabled by the vertical and spatial fragmentation of manufacturing into highly integrated "global production networks," which in turn was made possible by (1) major technological revolutions in transport (containerized shipping) and communications technologies that dramatically lowered the cost of shipping intermediate goods and managing complex production networks, and (2) trade liberalization that significantly reduced the applied tariffs on manufactured goods.

These trends are behind the rapid globalization of light manufacturing sectors such as electronics, automotive components, and especially apparel that have accounted for the large majority of investment in traditional export processing zones over the past three decades. Especially for countries with low labor costs, scale economies, and preferential access to major consumer markets such as the United States, Europe, and Japan, economic zones (with their access to duty-free inputs; high-quality, flexible infrastructure; and often generous fiscal incentives) proved to be the perfect instrument through which to capture increasingly mobile foreign investment. But African countries, most of which are in the relatively early stages of economic zone development, are facing changes in the global environment that are likely to have important implications on their approach to economic zones. These changes are summarized as follows:

- *Dampening growth of trade and investment in the postcrisis environment*: While trade has recovered significantly from the depths of 2008 and early 2009, it is clear that the U.S. and European economies can no longer function as the twin engines of global demand. In the short to medium term at least, levels of trade and investment—particularly those linked to the consumer goods that drive the light manufacturing sector—are not expected to return to the levels of growth experienced in the 1990s and 2000s. For African countries, this means much greater competition for traditional sources of investment in economic zones.

- *Consolidation of global production networks*: As a result of evolving business strategies, the fallout from the economic crisis, and a changing regulatory environment, lead firms are increasingly consolidating their production networks in terms of both suppliers and production locations. Thus, apparel buyers are concentrating sourcing through Tier 1 suppliers and concentrating production in a limited set of supply markets. In sectors such as garments and electronics, the initial evidence suggests that African countries are likely to be among the losers from these changes compared with markets that can offer low production costs and substantial scale (e.g., Vietnam, China, and Bangladesh).

- *The entrenched position of "factory Asia"*: A particular challenge for African countries is that most of them launched their zone programs after the trends outlined above were well entrenched and, critically, after China and other Asian investors had built massive scale and competitiveness in light manufacturing. Thus, the competition African countries encounter as they seek to attract investment into their economic zones is on a completely different level than what the Asian and Latin American zones faced when they launched between the 1970s and early 1990s.

- *End of the Multi Fibre Arrangement (MFA) in the apparel sector:* The expiration of the MFA at the end of 2004 (discussed in Chapter 3) effectively eliminated the likelihood that African zones could become large-scale global export platforms in the apparel sector. For programs such as those in Lesotho and Kenya, which have large existing positions in the sector, the focus since 2005 has been on rescuing the sector and retaining whatever firms and employment are possible. But major growth in this sector (which still accounts for the largest share of all employment in economic zones worldwide) may be off the agenda.

- *WTO Agreement on Subsidies and Countervailing Measures:* Although most African countries are exempt from the prohibition on export subsidies, Kenya will have to make substantial changes to its program by 2015 to remain compliant, as may Ghana, Nigeria, and Senegal soon thereafter.

- *Expanding network of regional trade agreements:* While the multilateral trade agenda has failed in recent years, bilateral and regional trade agreements are increasing rapidly around the world. Africa is no exception; indeed, its regional blocs are making substantial progress in their integration efforts. This will open up regional markets and create opportunities for manufacturing and trade-and-logistics-oriented economic zones, but it will also create a number of challenges (of administration and policy, as well as competitive positioning) for existing programs.

- *Growth of South-South trade:* While not yet offsetting the decline in demand from developed markets such as the United States, Europe, and Japan, the emergence of trade networks anchored in the global South (particularly in markets such as China, India, and Brazil) may open up significant new opportunities for trade and investment in African countries, for which economic zones have the potential to play an important supporting role.

- *Growth of services offshoring:* The most dynamic segment of global trade is services, from ICT-enabled activities such as call centers, back-office outsourcing, and business services to tourism, logistics, and financial services. Some African countries have begun to explore these opportunities, but none have yet made effective use of the potential power of economic zones to facilitate these activities.

In this context, African zones are not likely to be competitive using the traditional zone model that many of them employ.
African countries—indeed, all countries in this study—have followed similar approaches in the development of their economic zone programs, which have the following characteristics:

- A focus on attracting investment in light manufacturing sectors, with a particular emphasis on garments and textiles.
- Related to this, a focus on unskilled, labor-intensive activities.
- An emphasis on attracting investment that wishes to access markets through trade preferences, primarily aimed at the United States (through AGOA) and, in some cases, Europe.
- Use of a traditional EPZ model, designed for simple assembly and transformation activities using imported inputs, with few links to local markets.
- Government planning, investment, and operation.
- Substantial fiscal incentives, particularly exemptions on corporate taxes, VAT, and local taxes.

In the changing international context, this approach is unlikely to serve the interests of African countries. Already, a clear mismatch exists between this approach and the competitive strengths and weaknesses of most African countries. Most African countries have failed (with or without zones) to become deeply integrated into global production networks, leaving them increasingly on the periphery of global manufacturing trade. On the other hand, until the global economic crisis, African countries were enjoying a boom in growth, trade, and investment, driven not by the Asian model of export-led manufacturing but rather by natural resources; specifically, the demand for commodities (which, in turn, is driven strongly by expanding South-South trade links).

So, is there a disconnect between the traditional EPZ model of trade and the comparative advantage of most African countries? The evidence presented in this report shows that African countries struggle to compete as global export platforms for labor-intensive manufacturing. High labor costs (linked in part to high transaction costs and risk) combined with lack of scale make most African manufacturers uncompetitive with most Asian producers at the factory gate (see Table 8.2). This rough quantitative assessment is supported by the foreign producers in Africa's SEZs, who say that in a global comparison, African salaries are high and productivity is low for low-skilled workers, and there is a serious shortage of skilled workers, particularly those with vocational training. Add to this the challenges of geography and distance, aggravated by poor infrastructure (hard and soft) to support trade-related transport and a weak national business climate, and there are few situations in which establishing a base in an African zone rather than one in Asia or elsewhere would be part of a firm's competitive global manufacturing strategy.

If most African zones are unlikely to be competitive as manufacturing export platforms, they may need to rethink their strategies and move away from the traditional EPZ model and toward, for example, natural-resource-based activities, including agricultural and minerals processing. This does not mean that there will not be manufacturing or services opportunities worth pursuing (as well as the potential for zones to play a role as regional logistics and trading hubs), just that traditional assembly of imported components is unlikely to be the main driver of success. African SEZs will also require a much greater focus on building regional value chains and promoting industry clusters. This will require much more integration with local and regional economies than is possible under the existing enclave models, as well as a refocusing on generating efficiencies through external scale and coordination rather than simply through internal efficiency.

If this argument is accepted, the agenda for African zones will expand. African countries will have to look beyond traditional labor-based assembly operations to activities in which they have specific sources of

Table 8.2   Comparison of Estimated Labor Productivity in Select SEZs[3]

	Output per worker (US$ 2008)	Average monthly cost of unskilled workers[4] (US$)
Bangladesh	11,715	46
Dominican Republic	45,063	225
Honduras	37,921	313
Vietnam	15,167	102
Ghana[5]	37,294	118
Kenya	13,646	117
Lesotho	9,913	150
Senegal	12,433 (2007)	225

Source: Author's calculations derived from data collected through the SEZ investor surveys.

comparative advantage, integrate more effectively with local and regional markets, and adopt a much more flexible zone model that will support both of these efforts. These issues are discussed below.

Look toward the flexibility of an integrated SEZ model: Zones as growth catalysts.

The global trend in economic zones has been shifting away from traditional EPZs and toward larger scale, more flexible SEZs. In Africa, several countries, including Kenya and Tanzania, are moving in this direction. The SEZ model is typically designed over a wide geographic area that includes residential development and may encompass entire towns. More important, bearing in mind the issues discussed above, the SEZ model allows for (1) a broader range of activities, moving beyond simply processing and including such activities as logistics, services, and even agriculture, and (2) greater flexibility regarding sources of investment and the markets to which outputs are sold. Specifically, this means greater openness to domestic investment and sales into local markets, which could contribute significantly to the integration of zones with local economies and to their dynamic potential.

The integrative potential of the wide-area SEZ could be particularly valuable in the African context, as one of the main problems in African zones has been that all the positive aspects of the zones (e.g., infrastructure, services, reduced corruption) tend to stop at the gates. This wide-area SEZ model addresses development on a broader scale and allows for better links between hard and soft infrastructure investments and the core industrial park. Again, however, success requires that governments in the host countries view the projects as catalytic components of wider development opportunities integrated with key infrastructure investments (e.g., growth pole initiatives).

Look toward sources of comparative advantage; this may mean greater attention to agriculture and natural-resource-based sectors in the short term.

Most African countries are at a competitive disadvantage in the light manufacturing activities that have traditionally been the basis for economic zone investment, and global trends in trade and investment are likely to make this situation worse, at least in the near term. But this does not mean that no opportunities exist to attract manufacturing investment to African zones (for example, see "regional opportunities" below). However, African zones are much more likely to be successful by focusing on sources of sustainable comparative advantage. In terms of attracting investment in global export platforms, in most countries these comparative advantages are to be found in sectors that are natural-resource-intensive—linked to agriculture, mining, or oil and gas. Using the wide-area SEZ approach, some of these land-intensive activities can be encompassed within a zone. But the bigger potential is in processing activities that are one stage or more downstream from production. Here, economic zones have the potential to tip the balance regarding whether to process near the source or near the end market. Focusing zones around these sectors also adds potential for integrating local value chains (providing raw material inputs, services, and support) with foreign investors, improving the likelihood of capturing the spillovers from FDI.

So, many of the activities would still be in manufacturing or processing, but they would be focused on sectors in which Africa has a comparative advantage in inputs. (Or, expressed a different way, where the region's poor competitiveness in manufacturing is partly mitigated.) This approach would also open up more opportunities in the services sector, as inputs to the natural-resource-based sectors and as export opportunities in their own right. Although most African countries still face significant hurdles to competitiveness in business services and ICT-enabled outsourcing, opportunities might be available in some markets. Finally, tourism (in effect, a natural-resource-based service sector) is another source of comparative advantage in many African countries that could be exploited through zone programs.

The evidence from the African zones covered in this study indicates that investment is already edging toward natural-resource-based sectors, whether or not the zone programs are targeting these sectors strategically. For example, around one-quarter of all firms surveyed in the six African countries were involved in agriprocessing-related activities, compared with less than 2 percent of firms in the four non-African zones. In Ghana, the rapid growth in investment and exports under the free zone licensing program is heavily concentrated in cocoa, timber, and other agriprocessing activities. In Kenya, much of the diversification away from traditional garment manufacturing has taken place in agriculture and agriprocessing. And in Nigeria, the failure of the free zones to attract manufacturing investment contrasts with the huge boom in investment in services related to the oil and gas sector.

Take advantage of regional opportunities.

While most African zones have not established themselves as attractive locations for export platform investment, some evidence suggests that investors see their potential as platforms for selling into regional markets. For example, in many of the African zones—particularly those in West

Africa—there appears to be substantial production of end products destined both for consumers and business, such as metals, building products, chemicals, and food to neighboring countries. With the challenges of scale in most African countries and the significant transaction costs in production and cross-border trade, tapping into the potential of zones to serve as platforms for regional markets (including those that specialize in trade and logistics) represents a significant opportunity in some countries.

Promote agglomeration and scale—zones as a tool for spatial industrial policy.
Regional trade through the zones might model efficient patterns of regional specialization and trade. In the African context, zones can benefit from regional integration not only on the demand side but also on the supply side. In other words, economic zones may be attractive to investors not simply as platforms from which to sell to regional markets but also as locations from which specialized regional inputs can be tapped and production scaled up. The latter points to the need for a strategic focus on economic zones as a component of spatial industrial policy. While the regional opportunities may be particularly exciting, using zones to promote agglomeration at the subnational and national levels also offers significant potential. By concentrating core infrastructure and sector-specific public goods around zones, a country can use its zones to catalyze processes of agglomeration and help industries reach scale thresholds that allow them to compete more effectively in regional and global markets. Once again, this approach underscores the importance of (1) integration of economic zone policy within the wider industry and trade policy framework, and (2) integration of economic zones with the domestic economy to reap the benefits of scale. The approach also raises questions about the value of single factory free zone schemes in most countries, which may not have the same potential for promoting agglomeration and developing regional industry clusters.

A note of caution is in order regarding the use of zones as a spatial policy tool—it should not be confused with using zones as tools to encourage investment in peripheral and lagging regions. As we have discussed in this report, the evidence from many experiments of this nature is clear: Economic zones are almost inevitably expensive failures when they are located in regions far from the economic core.

Opportunities for South-South investment.
The recent growth in South-South trade, particularly trade linked to Africa's natural resource sectors, has contributed to rapidly growing

interest in South-South investment in the region. This interest goes beyond mining and infrastructure to include manufacturing and services activities. Foreign partners have expressed interest in investing in the development of economic zones in Africa. The most high-profile activity is the announcement by the Chinese government that it will support the development of at least five economic and trade cooperation zones in Sub-Saharan Africa—two in Nigeria, and one each in Zambia, Ethiopia, and Mauritius. Investors from India, Turkey, and Egypt have also been active in zone development in the region. And Dubai World, a company linked to the Dubai government, is investing up to US$800 million in developing the new SEZ in Dakar (along a model already deployed successfully in Djibouti and Morocco). These trends may offer significant opportunities for African countries to attract large-scale investment in their zone programs. They also offer the potential for African governments and private developers to learn—as China did—from other countries and private companies that have substantial experience in planning, developing, and managing zones.

Economic zones as catalysts for reform.
Finally, in light of the serious competitiveness weaknesses in the region, the challenges of state capacity, and the political economy factors that slow reform, the economic zone programs in the region should be reexamined to see how they can serve as reform catalysts. Again, this means using the zone programs as more than simply an instrument of trade and investment policy. So far, none of the African zone programs appears to have taken this approach; indeed, few programs globally have done so. But the programs that are held up as success stories—most notably China but also Mauritius—used their economic zones *expressly* as a vehicle for broader economic reform. In many African countries, this is the role in which economic zones can potentially have the greatest long-term effect on the economy.

How Can African Governments Plan and Implement Effective Economic Zone Programs?

The issues discussed in this section are covered in substantial detail in Chapters 6 and 7. Here we offer a brief summary of the most important policy-related issues that follow from the conclusions drawn in this chapter.

The economic zone program must be integrated as part of the country's long-term trade, industrial development, and wider economic growth strategy.

A critical finding of this report is that the success of a zone is closely inter-twined with the long-term success of the national economy in which it is based. One of the main differences between zone programs that have been successful and sustainable and those that have failed to take off or have become stagnant enclaves is how well the program was integrated into the broader economic policy framework of the country. Zones have generally failed to have a catalytic effect in most countries in part because they have been disconnected from wider economic strategies; they are often put in place and then left to operate on their own, with little effort to support domestic investment in the zones or to promote links, train-ing, or upgrading. Unlocking the potential of zones appears to require clear strategic integration of the program as well as active government leadership to facilitate the positive impact of the zone.

Successful programs use zones as more than static instruments of trade and investment policy; they use them to support dynamic processes of agglomeration and spillover; as tools for spatial industrial policy. Virtu-ally all the African countries in this study nominally promote a wide range of objectives with their programs (e.g., employment, foreign exchange, exports, FDI, technology access), but few, if any, appear to treat the pro-gram as an important pillar of wider economic growth, industrialization, and trade strategy. In contrast, successful programs such as those in Mauritius, Malaysia, and China use their zones as part of a group of instruments designed to promote wider economic policy reform, diversi-fication, and upgrading.

Policies to promote links between SEZs and the domestic economy are critical to achieving long-term dynamic benefits.
Countries that have been successful in deriving long-term benefits from their economic zone programs have established the conditions for ongo-ing exchange between the domestic economy and firms (mainly FDI) based in the SEZs. This includes investment by domestic firms in the zones (and by zone-based firms in the domestic market), supply links (forward and backward), business support and other value added services, and, critically, the seamless movement of skilled labor and entrepreneurs between the zones and the domestic economy. From a policy perspective, this model suggests a number of priorities for free zone programs, includ-ing the following:

- Shift from the EPZ to SEZ model to eliminate legal restrictions on for-ward and backward links and domestic participation, and to promote physical integration with the local economy.

- Eliminate policy biases against local companies supplying zone-based firms, and establish incentives for indirect exporters (e.g., accessing imports duty-free).
- Encourage domestic investors to locate in the zones by eliminating policy restrictions and investment-level requirements (or, if necessary, developing alternatives for smaller local firms).
- Address challenges to the local private sector, including access to finance and the culture of entrepreneurship.
- Promote training and knowledge-sharing across companies inside and outside the zones.
- Promote the development of industry clusters as a source of scale economies and competitiveness for local firms.
- Support the integration of regional value chains, and address constraints to competitiveness across value chains.
- Support public-private institutions, both industry-specific and transversal.
- Ensure that labor markets are free to facilitate the movement of skilled labor across firms throughout the economy, and eliminate barriers that restrict movement between zone-based firms and the domestic economy.

This broad agenda underscores, yet again, the fact that the zone program cannot be treated as a stand-alone policy instrument.

More active, high-level political commitment is needed to support most African zone programs.

High-level, active government commitment to zone programs is a significant contributor to their success. This support must be consistent over the long term: The evidence from even the most successful zone programs suggests that it normally takes 5–10 years after launch (thus, possibly 15 years or more from when a project was first conceived) before a zone begins to show signs of success. In analyzing the East Asian successes with economic zones, the role of political leadership—in terms of both vision and active support along the path of planning, implementation, and operation—is clear. African zone programs have largely failed to secure this kind of consistent and active commitment from senior political leaders. Indeed, many African countries have shown only a half-hearted commitment to their zones; for example, passing zone laws but failing to implement regulations; failing to provide adequate resources for program management, infrastructure, and promotion; and failing to ensure consistency in policy and approach.

Priorities at the outset are to secure a very senior political champion for the zone program and to build broad commitment through, for example, an interministerial committee.

African zone programs must focus on improving strategic planning and implementation. This requires improving the capacity, budget, and accountability of the zone regulatory authority, and reforming the institutions that support zone programs.
A sound legal and regulatory framework is a necessary first step for a successful zone program, particularly one designed around private sector development and operations. Implementation of the framework is equally important. Some of the African zone programs under study have problematic legal frameworks, but most were broadly sufficient to meet investor needs. However, good laws often were applied poorly, particularly with respect to the authority of the regulator, administrative clearances for registration and operation, and monitoring and enforcement. In addition, few of the legal frameworks under study appear to derive effectively from the strategic aims of the zones, owing, in part, to a lack of appropriate focus on those strategic objectives. Because the legal framework acts as a guide to the overall program, this failure may explain the strategic drift in many zone programs. A stronger focus on proper strategic planning—including rigorous needs assessment and feasibility analysis—is necessary in most African zones. But the implementation challenge remains—many zones that look great on paper fall apart quickly when the project moves into the development phase.

These problems in planning and implementation raise serious concerns about whether state capacity is sufficient to deliver effectively on the zone programs, particularly given their integrated nature. In many of the programs studied for this report, the authority responsible for developing, promoting, and regulating the program lacked the resources and capacity to fulfill its mandate, or the institutional authority to do so. Countries should consider putting their economic zone authority under the president, the prime minister, or a central ministry, such as the ministry of finance; delegating clear authority to the agency; and, equally important, ensuring that it is appropriately staffed and given a sufficient, predictable budget. In addition to resources, zone authorities need proper incentives to ensure that they take a long-term, strategic view of the programs they oversee. This means, for example, creating a program that aligns with national development objectives; prioritizing quality over quantity of investors (too often, zone authorities are encouraged to "sell licenses" rather than attract quality investors); and promoting exchange between the zones and the domestic economy. Reforming the institutions that oversee zone programs means ensuring that their boards are independent and include representatives of the relevant stakeholders (e.g., the private sector, unions, affected communities).

Finally, improving the functioning of the economic zone regulatory authorities also means addressing institutional issues beyond the zone authority; specifically, improving coordination across the many ministries and agencies whose authority and expertise are required to deliver on the zone program.

Greater private sector participation and public-private coordination should reduce risk and improve the quality of outcomes in African zone programs, but the scale and nature of private participation may vary depending on the country context.

Some of the recognized success stories (e.g., China and Mauritius) have been led mostly by the public sector. In other parts of East Asia, both private (e.g., the Philippines) and public (e.g., South Korea and Taiwan-China) models have been successful. In Latin America, the turnaround of many zone programs during the 1990s can be partly attributed to the dynamic role of the private sector. In Africa, both models have been tried and neither has been a success. What seems to matter is not so much who runs the program but how—their objectives, incentives, and capacity. In Asia, individual zones have been government run but with a profit motive; moreover, the government management units overseeing these programs were, by and large, competent and effective bureaucracies. As discussed earlier, government-run zone programs in Africa have suffered from problems of both governance and capacity. But where public sector governance functions poorly, there is no guarantee that the private sector will offer a viable alternative. Indeed, several African programs that engaged with private sector developers experienced problems with rent-seeking, capacity, and public-private relations. Moreover, the private sector in some African countries may be too weak to take on a leadership role in large-scale economic zone development. That said, given the large investments required to support zones and the uncertain returns, private sector participation can play an important role in reducing government's risk in zone programs. Moreover, as a major stakeholder in the outcomes of zone programs, the private sector needs to be involved in a significant way. For these reasons alone, private participation should be encouraged. However, ideological prescriptions for private investment and management should be avoided in favor of what is practical in the context.

Regardless of the role the private sector plays in zone development and management, more private sector participation is needed in strategic planning and policy decisions affecting zone programs, and this includes a greater voice on zone authority boards. Finally, public-private institutions (such as the Penang Skills Development Centre in Malaysia) can play an invaluable role in supporting the exchange between zones and the domestic economy, and supporting the ongoing process of upgrading the quality of the firms in the zones.

Incentives may continue to play a role in economic zone programs, but they must be limited and strictly controlled.
Most zone programs rely heavily on fiscal incentives to attract investors. In large countries (e.g., China, India, Bangladesh, and Vietnam) with significant pools of unskilled labor, low wages may be a sustainable source of comparative advantage into the medium term and may outweigh the need for incentives. But, as discussed previously, this is not the case in Africa. The reaction to the competitiveness gap in many of Africa's economic zone programs is to treat the symptom rather than the disease, so they use the levers of fiscal incentives (and, in some cases, aspects of labor policy) rather than addressing more fundamental aspects of competitiveness, such as productivity or labor market rigidities. This is not surprising; in fact, it is a logical use of the instruments available to the zone policymakers, at least when the policymaking and implementation of zones is viewed in a narrow way. However, when wages and incentives are the bases of competitiveness, they create pressure for distortions and race-to-the-bottom policies, including extending and increasing incentives and granting exemptions on minimum wage and labor rights. In addition, traditional fiscal incentives are becoming increasingly problematic in the WTO context, and many African countries will be required to eliminate them within the next five years. Finally, the evidence presented in Chapter 4 suggests that although incentives may attract some investment in the short term, there is no evidence that they lead to positive outcomes in zone programs; in fact, the more successful zone programs generally make less use of incentives than the less successful ones.

African zone programs should begin to reduce their reliance on fiscal incentives. This will be easier to do with a strategic focus that shifts away from activities in which they are uncompetitive and toward those in which they have comparative advantage. Shifting to more focused incentive regimes (for example, targeting specific sectors or activities) is a first step in the process; emphasizing nonfiscal incentives (particularly services) is a bigger step.

Of course, getting rid of fiscal incentives is a challenge that requires collective action. Regional trade bodies may be able to play a valuable role in establishing frameworks that control the use of incentives in economic zones.

Infrastructure quality is a critical gap in many African zones; delivering more effectively on hard and soft infrastructure inside the zones and integrating it more effectively with the domestic market must be a priority for African zone programs.
Most of the African zones offer an infrastructure inside the zone that, while not world-class, is of significantly higher quality than that typically available in the country. However, in some cases, zone infrastructure mirrors the worst experiences in the country, including water shortages; electricity failures; and health, safety, and environmental shortfalls. If basic internal infrastructure needs cannot be met, even generous fiscal incentives will not be enough to attract and retain investment in the zones. In contrast, the zones studied in Asia and Latin America offer a higher quality infrastructure overall and an infrastructure environment inside the zones that is dramatically superior to what is available outside.

Although most of the problems in Africa's zones relate to hard infrastructure, soft infrastructure—specifically, customs and trade facilitation—is also an important determinant of success or failure. Zones worldwide have made significant progress over the past decade in establishing efficient onsite customs processes, but several of the African zones have ongoing problems with customs clearance. Various models exist for efficient delivery of this service—a dedicated customs subdirectorate and clear service agreements between zone authorities and customs authorities seem to be the most important improvements a zone can make.

A more widespread problem—common to virtually all the African zones and, to a lesser extent, the non-African zones—is that quality infrastructure stops at the zone gates. If zones are to be successful, countries need to address the wider trade-related infrastructure: Poor road connectivity and serious port-related delays undermine the competitiveness of many zones. One of the most effective and cost-efficient ways to ensure integration between zones and trade gateways is to co-locate them. Thus, the development of new zones should focus, wherever possible, on locations that are inside or adjacent to major ports, airports, or other key trade infrastructure.

Finally, the sustainability of zone programs depends on the availability of social infrastructure (education and health) to attract skilled workers.

Addressing the infrastructure gap should be a primary role of government in zone programs, and it will require significant financial resources. The SEZ model, which covers much wider geographic areas and can encompass key trade-related infrastructure, offers much greater potential to address this challenge than the traditional fenced-in EPZ.

African economic zones need to improve their approach to social and environmental compliance issues. At the national level, economic zones should be seen as an opportunity to experiment with policy innovations. While most zone programs have made significant improvements over the past decade with regard to workers' rights, a gap remains between the de jure and de facto environments in many zones. In most of the countries we studied, the labor conditions inside the zones were better than those in similar firms outside the zones, but monitoring for compliance with labor standards is limited in many zones, and enforcement is often weak. Despite the large proportion of female workers in most zone programs, there has been a serious lack of effort to address gender-specific issues in the zones under study. Enforcement of environmental standards in zones is also generally weak. Increasingly, however, social and environmental standards are being set by international buyers rather than national governments, and zones that allow investors to flout environmental and labor standards create a reputational risk for investors who are supplying these global buyers. In the long term, it is in the interest of zone authorities to ensure that investors comply with acceptable standards of operation.

SEZs offer an ideal environment for policy experimentation, not only because of their enclave nature but because they have built-in compliance mechanisms that do not normally exist outside the zones, such as the ability to issue licenses, to monitor firms within a short time frame, and to revoke a license, terminate a lease, or impound containers. This context could offer interesting opportunities to test innovations in social and environmental policy.

Implications for Future Support to SEZ Programs

Are economic zones appropriate in the African context?

Economic zones can be expensive and risky projects; the margin for error is small, and successful zones take time to develop. They rely on effective state capacity, and their success is tightly intertwined with that of the wider national economy in which they are based. Clearly, they are not for the faint-hearted. But economic zones have proved to be a powerful instrument to attract investment and promote exports in some countries and, more important, to catalyze processes of structural transformation, including diversification and upgrading. So, the flip side of high risk is, unsurprisingly, high reward (although, in the case of economic zones, it may be difficult to disentangle their specific effects on the observed outcomes).

Most African countries have the potential to derive valuable benefits from special economic zones. These countries are in need of diversification and are in the early stages of industrialization. To diversify, they need to attract private investment, particularly FDI. By overcoming infrastructure and land constraints and facilitating economies of scale, SEZs offer the potential to leverage trade preferences to attract investment and support diversification, if they are implemented effectively.

Thus, there is sufficient reason for continued support of SEZs as a policy instrument—but not blanket support. The environments in which zone programs are developed are complex and heterogeneous, so overly deterministic approaches should be avoided.

What are the preconditions for successful implementation of a zone program?

This report sheds light on the factors that determine success in economic zone programs, and follows in a line of analytical work by academics, multilateral organizations, and others stretching back some 30 years. Thanks to this body of work, we understand much about what it takes to make zones successful. Combining this knowledge with some new information that has emerged in this report, we can outline a framework for situations in which SEZs are appropriate, as well as preconditions for their success. This framework includes the following:

1. Ensure that the SEZ program is focused where it can best complement and support comparative advantage, as validated through a detailed strategic planning, feasibility, and master planning process.
2. Integrate the SEZ as part of a broader package of industrial, trade, and economic development policies.
3. Integrate the SEZ with support to existing industry clusters rather than as an alternative or greenfield approach to cluster development.
4. Ensure high-level political support and broad commitment before launching any program, including the establishment of an interministerial committee to oversee program development.

5. Promote exchange between the zone and the domestic environment through both policy and administrative reforms.
6. Support the provision of high-quality hard and soft infrastructure encompassing zones, key urban centers, and trade gateways.[6] The focus should be on leveraging SEZs to support existing and planned infrastructure to facilitate the potential for growth catalysts/poles.
7. Put SEZs on the regional integration agenda, with an emphasis on their role in facilitating regional production scale and integrating regional value chains.
8. Ensure the development of sound legal and regulatory frameworks, and cement them by addressing the challenges of institutional design and coordination.
9. Promote private sector participation and public-private partnerships, along with technical assistance with structuring and negotiating PPPs.
10. Consider the capacity of the government to deliver on an SEZ program, particularly in light of the integrated and long-term nature of SEZs. This will require a focus on institutional development and political economy factors that influence zone policy and implementation.
11. Establish clear standards with regard to environmental, labor, and social compliance, and identify regulatory responsibilities for monitoring and enforcement.
12. Develop and implement a comprehensive monitoring and evaluation program from the outset, with safeguards in place to ensure that SEZ program developments remain aligned with strategic and master plans.
13. Recognize the long-term nature of SEZ program development. This means planning beyond short-term project cycles and monitoring progress on an ongoing basis.

Obviously, given the breadth of the activities recommended in this chapter, no single donor or government will be able to support all the financial and technical needs of a country's economic zone program. Coordination of all actors, including the private sector, will help ensure effective delivery, particularly in light of the limited absorption capacity in many zone authorities. Table 8.3 provides a very rough sketch of where different actors might be positioned to support the agenda outlined here.

One of the most important areas for coordinated support from donors, governments, and other actors is in the provision of high-quality data, research, and analysis on SEZs, as well as practical advice for SEZ practitioners.[7] The final section of this report makes suggestions for a research agenda.

Table 8.3   Potential Areas of Support across Different Stakeholder Groups

	International financial institutions: lending, technical assistance (TA)	Other donors: grants, TA	Private sector: (TA, investment)	Country governments
Strategy; legal and regulatory framework	✓	✓		✓
Institutional reform	✓	✓		✓
Capacity building	✓	✓		
Support for public-private bodies	✓	✓	✓	✓
Supporting private sector participation	✓	✓	✓	✓
Feasibility studies	✓	✓	✓	✓
Monitoring and evaluation	✓	✓		✓
External (integrative) infrastructure	✓		✓	✓
Zone infrastructure			✓	
Clusters, value chains, and small and medium enterprise support	✓	✓	✓	✓
Regional integration	✓	✓		✓
Research and knowledge	✓	✓		✓

Source: Author.

Research Agenda

The number, variety, and economic importance of special economic zones have increased at an accelerated pace over the past 20 years or so, as documented in this report. However, research on economic zones has not grown commensurately. While academic and policy interest in zones is increasing, as illustrated by the expanding body of academic papers, it remains narrow. Few academic research programs are focused on economic zones[8]; few research centers and think tanks show more than occasional interest in the subject[9]; and few international organizations dedicate resources to SEZ research.[10] In Chapter 2, we offered an in-depth summary of the state of policy research on economic zones and concluded that, as a result of the ongoing research, it is becoming possible to determine whether specific countries should develop SEZs and, if they do, to better structure the required zone policies and components. However, a number of important questions remain to be addressed.

An agenda for SEZ research should have two primary objectives:

1. To contribute to essential research and analysis on SEZs in the fields of economics, political economy, spatial analysis, industrial research, social studies, environmental studies, and so on. This contribution should seek to consolidate existing research, identify critical gaps, provide essential data in normalized formats, and offer empirical analysis and theoretical foundations.
2. To contribute to policy analysis and formulation with a view to improving strategic and operational practices to ensure that zones are properly employed, effectively developed, and consistently monitored and adapted to changing conditions.

Although the distinction between academic and policy research capabilities is important, in practice there would be significant overlap in research agendas, notably in data gathering and analysis, in economic modeling, and in policy analysis. Researchers should cooperate to maximize resource allocation and applicability of the findings.

Priorities for empirical and policy research

- Researchers should inventory, acquire, and organize data on SEZs, building on existing databases such as those of the ILO, the discontinued WEPZA International Directory of Free Zones, and the World Bank's International Trade Department database. Consideration should be given to maintaining a live database that can be updated on an ongoing basis.

- A dedicated research effort should focus on empirical and formal analysis of the economic impact of SEZs, updating theories, models, and cost-benefit approaches. Some valuable directions for research are (1) consolidating the models of dynamic impact assessment and deriving policy lessons from them; (2) updating cost-benefit analysis models to incorporate dynamic impacts; and (3) creating a practitioner's manual for project economic impact forecasting and a reference database of model economic impact studies.

- We need to improve our understanding of the political economy of SEZ policy formation. Purely economic analyses (with the exception of game theoretic and public choice models) tend to avoid questions of decision making—they are too abstract to be sufficiently descriptive. We need to apply political economic models—models that account for historical processes, class relations, and the relationship between state and dominant social groups—to the SEZ decision dynamic. A global comparative analysis across regions and time would provide critical insights, especially if it included a typology of policies correlated with economic conditions and apparent political motivations.

- We also need to better evaluate the impact and implications of the end of the MFA in particular and the effects of the WTO in general. While some work has been done on these topics, no cross-national or cross-regional research exists. Yet, as illustrated by some of the case studies in this report, these changes in the international trading order have had profound effects on investment, production, and trade patterns, with very significant consequences for developing and emerging countries.

- With the observed shift toward SEZ models and the recommendations in this report for African countries to move away from traditional manufacturing-oriented zones, services is likely to be a primary area of demand for future zone programs, particularly the development of zones to support call centers, ICT and ICT-enabled services, and other business offshoring activities. Research on the role and value added of SEZs (above and beyond providing industrial infrastructure) is limited. A deeper understanding of these issues and the performance of service-related zones is needed to support policy decision making.

- We need to increase our comprehension of the spatial dimension of SEZs, especially in terms of their complex international economic geography and international, regional, and national locational factors. We do not understand enough about concentration versus dispersion, centralization versus diffusion, and the issue of SEZs and economic decentralization. One line of research that would yield valuable insights would be the mapping of regional trade and investment patterns, showing the origins and destinations of production inputs (imports) and outputs (exports). Historical analysis of zones in a select number of countries would help demonstrate the impact of the MFA and WTO, as well as regionalization patterns. This information could have valuable implications for SEZ feasibility analysis.

- The relationship between SEZs and clustering is another subject that requires research, especially in light of recent SEZ projects that have attempted to foster the emergence of clusters. There is a dearth of case and comparative knowledge about this relationship.

- With regard to the question of dynamic impact, we need to investigate the role of SEZs in the diffusion of innovation, technology, and entrepreneurship. Available evidence is ambivalent, suggesting a marginal role in some cases and a critical role in others. We need comparative research to determine the factors (international economic factors, commodity and production systems, domestic private sector characteristics, and regulations) that influence these processes. Evidence suggests a positive correlation between the intensity of the impact of SEZs on the one hand and innovation, technology transfers, and entrepreneurship on the other. Domestic entrepreneurs appear to play an essential role in ensuring that SEZs become rooted in the national economy.

- Similarly, we need research in the area of the SEZ life cycle to update existing work and connect the life cycle with broader international and domestic issues. In particular, we need a better understanding of the correlation between diffusion of the SEZ into the domestic economy and changes in regulation. For some, this diffusion or absorption is a manifestation of failure and limited relevance; for others, it is a manifestation of success and relevance.

- Additional work should be conducted to empirically assess the respective economic and financial performances of public and private zones, including the cost of direct and indirect subsidization. It is widely believed that private zones outperform public ones but, as this report shows, evidence to suggest this is lacking. Understanding the optimum conditions and factors for success of public and private zones is crucial. A related research requirement is to determine the conditions under which private, public, or public-private partnerships apply best and to understand the conditions under which public sector investment is warranted. It is usually assumed that public subsidization of zones (whether the zones are public, private, or PPP) is a requirement of most "developmental" zones. In marginal cases, subsidization is often the principal condition for later commercial success. Improved economic modeling and empirical research should address this issue.

- In related research, it may be interesting to study the role of private free zone associations (e.g., ADOZONA in the Dominican Republic, AHM in Honduras) to understand their role, functions, and effect on SEZ program outcomes.

- The concept of jump-starting economic growth in postconflict environments by establishing a physically and administratively secure environment through the SEZ instrument is appealing. But issues related to the wider investment climate and public sector capacity in fragile states may constitute significant obstacles. Conceptual and empirical research is needed to better understand the applicability of the SEZ instrument and the conditions for effectiveness.

- We need to develop a coherent position on SEZ tax regimes, taking into consideration current practices, the effects of changing the tax regimes of existing SEZs (especially when these zones are only marginally successful but are essential providers of investment and employment), and country-wide issues. The consensus is that fiscal incentives do not contribute to the outcomes of SEZ programs in the long term, but some evidence suggests that they do attract investment in the short term. Moreover, all successful zone programs had fiscal incentives in place for some period. We need to understand how these incentives contribute to initial investor behavior and how they affect early-stage and longer term zone development. On the flip side, the policy advice for developing SEZs as "administratively superior" environments that do not benefit from special fiscal or customs regimes requires some empirical attention to test its validity.

- Turnkey zones present both opportunities and challenges to their host countries. These zones are different from the public-private partnership zones that have become the preferred funding, development, ownership, and management model over the past 15 years or so. These zones are funded, developed, owned, and managed by foreign concerns that select a location from a group of potential "candidate hosts."

Most often, these zones are closely affiliated with foreign governments. The Chinese trade and economic cooperation zones are the most high-profile form of turnkey zones. Anecdotal evidence raises questions about their economic benefits to the host economy and the political-economic implications.

- Key methodologies employed in strategic and operational decision making, as well as in monitoring and evaluation and ex post evaluations, remain loosely defined and lack broadly accepted standards and norms. This is true, for example, with regard to methodologies for evaluating whether an SEZ should be considered as a policy option in a specific case. It is also true with regard to methodologies for conducting feasibility analysis. As noted above, there is a critical lack of integration between academic research and policy analysis on the one hand and the methods practitioners develop and use on the other.

Improving technical assistance

In terms of technical assistance, there has been ample discussion, and numerous attempts have been made to establish best practices in both the architecture of zones and their development cycle, but a major effort is still required to improve methodologies in the following areas:

- Opportunity analysis (often called competitiveness analysis or comparative benchmarking) is the first step in determining whether an economic rationale exists for a specific SEZ. Methods to evaluate competitiveness lack clear standards and tend to involve simple compilation and comparison of fairly broad sets of country-level and industry-level indicators.

- Demand/market analysis or forecasting usually follows. This is a crucial step to confirm the extent of the opportunity, its economic configuration (activities and sectors), its life cycle (phases), its physical footprint, its locational attributes, and so on. This is where an SEZ is right-sized or wrong-sized, right-placed or wrong-placed. Various approaches can be taken to this very essential step, but there is no defined best practice, little informed debate on how to conduct it or improve on it, and no known attempts to revisit past forecasts to learn from them.

- Economic and financial analysis is conducted using the data from the previous steps; this step also includes key master planning and engineering design concepts. The twin analyses are meant to test the internal and external return of the proposed SEZ under a set of assumptions and scenarios. In practice, the lack of a set methodologies for the exercise results in a tendency to overstate benefits and understate costs. Budgets are rarely sufficient to allow proper data gathering, analysis, and integration. As with demand forecasting, this step is crucial, and the results should be a critical factor in the ultimate decision to go forward with a project, redesign it, or terminate it. In practice, economic and financial analysis tends to be a mechanistic exercise that rarely contradicts the initial policy intent.

The following four steps could be taken to address these issues:

1. The development of methodologies and guidelines for the feasibility and implementation cycles, including comprehensive methodologies for key feasibility analysis components. These guidelines should be developed through formal exchanges between theoretical experts and policy practitioners to ensure that a solid theoretical foundation is combined with essential practical experience and knowledge. This undertaking should include a revision of competitiveness analysis to include in-depth analysis of comparative advantage, encompassing investment, trade, and economic data. An improved methodology or methodologies would provide guidance on the relevance of the SEZ option for specific situations; it would be based on a comprehensive economic diagnosis of needs and would determine whether an SEZ might provide an opportunity and which type of SEZ would be best. Researchers should apply advanced techniques in project economics (such as reference class forecasting) to demand forecasting and economic and financial modeling. These methods will provide more accurate results with greater transparency.

2. The creation of accessible resource databases for practitioners, including methodologies and guidelines, reference projects, and accessible experts who can be consulted on questions and problems of methodology, in general or in relation to specific projects.

3. The introduction of systematic peer review mechanisms for all major components of feasibility analyses, to be incorporated in the feasibility cycle. This review would ensure the use of best practice methods.

4. The inclusion in the feasibility cycle of a medium- and long-term ex post evaluation designed to compare forecasts with actual outcomes.

This evaluation would encourage more realistic forecasting and provide opportunities for learning and improvement.

The *SEZ Practitioners Guide* (IFC, forthcoming) should go a long way toward standardizing and enriching the technical assistance provided for SEZ programs.

Developing research and development capabilities.

In terms of both general and policy research objectives, there is a critical need for the establishment of permanent multidisciplinary research capabilities on SEZs. Two capabilities should be developed: one in theoretical research and one in applied and policy research. This could take the form of a permanent effort engaging academic institutions, think tanks, donors, and clients. While some capability exists within donor institutions (e.g., ILO on labor issues and the World Bank/IFC on technical assistance to governments), the focus is relatively narrow and tends to be dispersed across the organization. Among the initial tasks of an SEZ research group or groups would be to inventory and critically assess existing research, index it, and make it accessible through a database. Another task would be to develop a more detailed research agenda to address the most critical research requirements. This could also be initiated as a first step under the aegis of a donor.

Notes

1. Restrictions on local market sales in many SEZs places significant limitations on this opportunity in many zone programs.
2. Depending on the domestic business environment and competition policy, larger markets tend to result in more competitive firms.
3. Data for Nigeria and Tanzania are excluded owing to a very small sample size.
4. Includes average reported monthly wage plus benefits.
5. Data for Ghana are skewed by a high level of reexport activity; data from the Ghana Free Zones Board show exports higher than production for many years.
6. The Ghana Gateway and its MPIP offers a model in this regard.
7. The forthcoming IFC publication *SEZ Practitioners Guide* is an example of the kind of knowledge products that will play a valuable role in supporting more effective planning and implementation of SEZ programs.
8. One such institution is the China Center for Special Economic Zones at Shenzhen University.

9. The Flagstaff Institute—manager of the World Economic Zones Processing Association—once paramount in the domain, has been dormant for several years.

10. The International Labour Organisation has been the most consistent in its efforts.

References

IFC. (Forthcoming.) *SEZ Practitioners Guide.* Washington, DC: World Bank.

Schrank, A. 2001. "Export Processing Zones: Free Market Islands or Bridges to Structural Transformation?" *Development Policy Review* 19(2): 223–242.

Country Case Selection

Table A.1   Benchmark Selection Criteria

	Country	Specific zones in each country
Comparability and generalizability	• International Development Association (IDA) country[1] • Ongoing SEZ program • Broad geographic coverage • Comparability with African countries in terms of size of economies, geography, market access, institutions	• Operating for at least 3 years (where possible) • Light manufacturing focus

Potential for learning	• Size and growth of SEZs: investment, employment, exports
	• Examples of good practices as well as pitfalls to avoid in relation to:
	  ○ Efficient business processes: procedures, customs, etc.
	  ○ Mainstreaming reforms
	  ○ Domestic market links
		• Focus on zones located in relatively prime locations in the country
		• Include at least one private sector owned/operated SEZ (where possible)
		• Specific examples of good practices or pitfalls to avoid

(continued next page)

Table A.1   Benchmark Selection Criteria *(continued)*

	Country	Specific zones in each country
	° Export diversification and upgrading ° Creating sustainable employment and entrepreneurial opportunities for women • Experiences with private sector owned/operated SEZs	

Source: Author.

1. With potential to include one or two lower middle-income non-IDA countries if necessary to ensure case examples that may offer valuable lessons for African IDA countries.

Table A.2 Summary Assessment of Potential Sample Countries against Benchmarking Criteria—African Countries

Criteria	AFR (6)									
	Ghana	Nigeria	Senegal	Kenya	Tanzania	Uganda	Lesotho	Madagascar	Mauritius	Mozambique
IDA country?	Yes	Yes	Yes	Yes	Yes	Yes	Yes	Yes	No	Yes
Program ongoing since 2005 or earlier with at least 2 operational zones?	Yes (1995)	Yes (1991)	1 zone only*** (1974)	Yes (1993)	Yes (2002)	No	Yes** (N/A)	Yes (1991)	Yes/No* (1970)	Yes 1 zone only (1999)
Comparability with other African countries (scale, geography, market access, institutions)	✓✓	✓	✓✓	✓✓	✓✓	✓✓	✓	✓	–	✓✓
First cut: meeting basic requirements	✓	✓	✓	✓	✓	X	✓	✓	X	X
Learning potential	✓	✓	✓✓	✓✓	✓	N/A	✓✓	✓✓	✓✓	N/A
Significant constraints to carrying out research?	No	Some	No	No	No	No	No	Yes (current instability)	No	No
Final assessment: ranking within region	2	4	6	1	3	9	5	7	10	8

Source: Authors.

* Zones being phased out, with policies mainstreamed across the island.

** Single factory EPZs, most of which are housed in government-operated industrial parks/factory shells.

*** Second currently in development.

N/A—not applicable or unknown at time of country selection for study.

✓ – meets criteria.

✓✓ – meets criteria and is highly relevant.

X – does not meet criteria.

Table A.3   Summary Assessment of Potential Sample Countries against Benchmarking Criteria—Non-African Countries

CRITERIA	LAC (1–2)			EAC (1–2)			SAR (0–1)	
	Dominican Republic	El Salvador	Honduras	China	Philippines	Vietnam	Bangladesh	India
IDA country?	No	No	Yes	No	No	Yes	Yes	Yes*
Program ongoing since 2005 or earlier?	Yes (1969)	Yes (1976)	Yes (1977)	Yes (1979)	Yes (1972)	Yes (1991)	Yes (1980)	Yes (1965)
Comparability with African countries (scale, geography, market access, institutions)	✓	✓	✓✓	–	✓	✓	✓✓	–
First cut: meeting basic requirements	✓	✓	✓	x	✓	✓	✓	✓
Learning potential	✓✓	✓	✓	✓✓	✓	✓✓	✓	✓
Significant constraints to carrying out research?	No	No	No	Some (size/nature of zones)	No	No	No	Some (large # of zones)
Final assessment: ranking within region	2	3	1	3	2	1	1	2

Source: Author.

* Blend country.

✓ – meets criteria.

✓✓ – meets criteria and is highly relevant.

x – does not meet criteria.

Table A.4 Basic Economic and Trade Indicators of Selected Sample

Country	GDP[1] in 2007 (constant 2005 US$, billion)**	GNI[2] per capita, purchasing power parity in 2007 (constant 2005 US$)**	FDI, average net inflows in 2004–06 (% of GDP)**	Merchandise exports in 2007 (current US$, bn)**	Merchandise imports in 2007 (current US$, bn)**	AGOA eligible (incl. apparel) (US)	Everything But Arms eligible (EU)
Ghana	29.6	1,260	2.1	4.3	8.0	2 Oct 2000 (20 Mar 2002)	No
Kenya	54.4	1,449	0.2	4.1	9.2	2 Oct 2000 (18 Jan 2001)	No
Lesotho	2.9	1,455	7.0	0.81	1.7	2 Oct 2000 (23 April 2001)	Yes
Nigeria	276.2	1,867	2.5	66.5	27.5	2 Oct 2000 (14 Jul 2004)	No
Senegal	19.5	1,573	0.7	1.7	4.3	2 Oct 2000 (23 Apr 2002)	Yes
Tanzania	46.1	1,141	3.1	2.0	5.3	2 Oct 2000 (4 Feb 2002)	Yes
Bangladesh	185.9	1,173	1.1	12.4	18.5	N/A	Yes
Dominican Republic	61.6	6,316	4.1	6.7	13.1	N/A	No
Honduras	25.5	3,597	3.7	2.2	6.8	N/A	No
Vietnam	209.0	2,454	3.7	48.4	60.8	N/A	No

** Source: World Development Indicators.
1. Gross domestic product.
2. Gross national income.

APPENDIX B

Large-Sample Dataset

Table B.1   Countries in Large-Sample Dataset

ARGENTINA	GRENADA	PAKISTAN
BANGLADESH	GUATEMALA	PANAMA
BELARUS	HAITI	PERU
BELIZE	HONDURAS	PHILIPPINES
BOLIVIA	HUNGARY	POLAND
BOSNIA-HERZEGOVINA	INDIA	ROMANIA
BRAZIL	INDONESIA	SAUDI ARABIA
BULGARIA	IRAN	SENEGAL
CAMBODIA	JAMAICA	SEYCHELLES
CAMEROON	JORDAN	SOUTH AFRICA
CAPE VERDE	KENYA	SRI LANKA
CHILE	KYRGYZSTAN	SUDAN
CHINA	LEBANON	SYRIA
COLOMBIA	LESOTHO	TANZANIA
COSTA RICA	LITHUANIA	THAILAND
CROATIA	MACEDONIA	TOGO
CUBA	MADAGASCAR	TRINIDAD AND TOBAGO

(continued next page)

Table B.1   Countries in Large-Sample Dataset *(continued)*

CZECH REPUBLIC	MALAWI	TUNISIA
DOMINICAN REPUBLIC	MALAYSIA	TURKEY
ECUADOR	MALDIVES	UNITED ARAB EMIRATES
EGYPT	MALI	URUGUAY
EL SALVADOR	MALTA	VENEZUELA
FIJI	MAURITIUS	VIETNAM
GABON	MEXICO	YEMEN
GAMBIA	MOLDOVA	ZIMBABWE
GHANA	NICARAGUA	

Table B.2   Summary of Large-Sample Dataset Population by Region[1] and Income Level[2]

	Low income	Lower middle income	Upper middle income	High income	TOTAL
East and Central Europe	1	1	8	4	14
East Asia and Pacific	2	4	2	0	8
Latin America and Caribbean	1	7	13	1	23[3]
Middle East and North Africa	1	5	1	2	9
South Asia	2	3	0	0	5
Sub-Saharan Africa	10	4	4	0	18
TOTAL	17	24	28	7	77

1. Regions defined according to World Bank classification.
2. Income level categories defined according to World Bank classification based on 2008 GNI per capita, Atlas Method (Source: World Development Indicators). Low income: <US$995; lower middle income: US$996–$3945; upper middle income: US$3946–$12,195; high income: >US$12,196.
3. Includes Cuba, which is unclassified.

Survey Methodology

The approach selected for capturing quantitative data on the SEZs in the 10 countries is based largely on the methodology of the World Bank's Enterprise Surveys.

Enterprise Surveys: Overview

The Enterprise Surveys capture business perceptions on the biggest obstacles to enterprise growth, the relative importance of various constraints to increasing employment and productivity, and the effects of a country's business environment on its international competitiveness. The surveys cover more than 100 indicators from 110 countries.[1] They were developed by the Enterprise Analysis Unit of the World Bank Group and have been running since 2002. The Enterprise Surveys cover 49 indicators in 11 main subject areas. The Enterprise Surveys follow a well-established methodology, using a survey instrument that is standardized across countries. Most importantly, this survey instrument can be readily tailored to the SEZ environment, and it offers the ability to compare SEZs with existing data on the national environment.

The Enterprise Survey methodology does have some limitations. First, there are some concerns about the comparability of perceptions-based surveys across countries, which may limit the extent to which the results can be compared across the benchmark sample. However, most of the firms operating in these zones are foreign direct investors, so there should be less culturally induced response bias in the surveys. On a longer term basis, these surveys are relatively expensive to replicate because of the necessity of surveying individual firms. Thus, tracking ongoing performance of SEZs may not be realistic using this methodology. Finally, there may be practical challenges in undertaking surveys of enterprises within SEZs, making them more difficult to survey than firms outside zones. The main challenge is that zones tend to be secure environments that restrict access. This security-consciousness is compounded by sensitivity to bad press (regarding, for example, labor and environmental practices) that may keep zone managers and firms from accommodating researchers. It is often necessary to work with national authorities and zone management to get their support for the survey process.

Description of Survey Methodology

The surveys were conducted through face-to-face interviews with firm managers and owners in the countries and zones listed in Table C.1. Surveys were carried out by trained local consultants using a standard questionnaire. The differences in size and composition among SEZ programs resulted in two different approaches to select firms to participate in the study. In Africa, all firms established in enclaves were contacted and asked to participate in the survey, and efforts were made to include a substantial number of SEZ firms with single unit status.[2] In Ghana and Senegal, the prevalence of single unit zones resulted in a relatively low share of firms asked to participate.

In the non-African countries—where most SEZ firms are located inside enclaves—the three or four most important enclaves were selected and all firms inside them were approached for the survey. While the selected zones included a significant percentage of SEZ firms and were representative of the overall programs, generalization to national SEZ program results should be done with some caution.

Although all firms in selected enclaves were asked to participate in the survey, some declined. Nonresponse could affect our estimates, especially if some element of self-selection is involved. The firm nonresponse rate inside enclaves varies by country and is relatively higher in non-African countries. However, because the universe of firms inside selected enclaves was exhausted, not much could be done to improve the estimates for those enclaves. Not all single unit firms were approached for the survey, and their selection was not random,[3] mainly owing to costs and difficulties of surveying geographically dispersed

Table C.1   Summary Data from Survey Samples

Country	Dates of survey	Zones	Completed surveys	Operational firms	Percentage surveyed
Ghana	Jul–Aug 2009;	*All Country*	*33*	*131**	*25%*
	Oct–Nov 2009[4]	Tema	11	11	100%
		Single units	22	120*	18%
Kenya	Jul–Aug 2009	*All Country*	*40*	*56*	*72%*
		Athi River	17	23	74%
		Sameer	6	6	100%
		Kipevu	2	2	100%
		Single units	15	25	60%
Lesotho	Jul–Aug 2009	*All Country*	*35*	*66*	*53%*
		Maseru West	16	23	70%
		Thetsane	9	15	60%
		Nyenye	6	18	33%
		Maputsoe	4	7	57%
		Single units	0	3	0
Nigeria	Nov–Dec 2009	*All Country*	*65*	*98*	*66%*
		Calabar	12	13	92%
		Onne	53	85	62%
Senegal	Jul–Aug 2009	*All Country*	*30*	*304**	*10%*
		Zone Franche			
		Industrielle	4	4	100%
		Single units	26	300*	9%
Tanzania	Jul–Aug 2009	*All Country*	*16*	*17*	*94%*
		Hifadhi	7	7	100%
		Benjamin			
		William			
		Mkapa SEZ	2	2	100%
		Millennium			
		Business			
		Park	1	1	100%
		Kisongo	1	1	100%
		Single units	5	6	83%
Bangladesh	Oct–Nov 2009	*All Zones*	*148*	*254*	*58%*
		Chittagong	71	140	51%
		Dhaka	64	96	66%
		Comilla	13	18	72%
Dominican	Sep–Oct 2009	*All Zones*	*107*	*138*	*78%*
Republic		Santiago	51	65	79%
		San Pedro	35	42	83%
		Itabo	21	31	68%
Honduras	May–Jun 2009	*All Zones*	*40*	*60*	*67%*
		Green Valley	5	9	55%
		Indhelva	17	20	85%

(continued next page)

Table C.1   Summary Data from Survey Samples (continued)

Country	Dates of survey	Zones	Completed surveys	Operational firms	Percentage surveyed
		Bufalo	13	25	52%
		Choloma	5	6	83%
Vietnam	Aug–Sep 2009	*All Zones*	*117*	*217*	*54%*
		Tan Thuan	85	138	62%
		Linh Trung 1	16	38	42%
		Linh Trung 2	16	41	39%

*Estimate, no exact data available.

units. The results for single unit zones in Ghana and Senegal, in particular, should be treated with caution.

Although the response rate for the majority of the questions was very high, some firms declined to respond to more sensitive questions (e.g., those related to sales and wages). When item nonresponse is high and could present a problem for our estimates, we highlight this in a footnote; if too few observations were available for a country, we did not include the information.

Notes

1. The data are collected using a standard survey instrument tailored to specific industry sectors (manufacturing, services, global). The surveys are administered by private contractors on behalf of the World Bank. The survey is completed by managing directors, accountants, human resource managers, and other company management. It uses a stratified random sampling methodology; sample sizes range from 250 to 1,500 businesses. For detailed methodological information, go to www.enterprisesurveys.org/methodology.

2. In Kenya, Lesotho, and Tanzania, the concentration of SEZ firms in enclaves meant that a significant number were asked to participate in the survey.

3. In Ghana and Senegal, selection of the firms to approach for the survey was determined by (1) location—only firms located in or near the capital (Accra and Dakar, respectively) were included in the population, and (2) industry—only firms in manufacturing and processing activities were included. Taking these two factors into account, the sample was constructed randomly.

4. Surveys were conducted in the Tema Export Processing Zone during July and August 2009; additional surveys of single factory free zones in the Accra region were conducted during October and November 2009.

Index

Figures, notes, and tables are indicated by *f*, *n*, and *t*, respectively.

ECO-AUDIT
Environmental Benefits Statement

The World Bank is committed to preserving endangered forests and natural resources. The Office of the Publisher has chosen to print *Special Economic Zones in Africa* on recycled paper with 50 percent postconsumer fiber in accordance with the recommended standards for paper usage set by the Green Press Initiative, a nonprofit program supporting publishers in using fiber that is not sourced from endangered forests. For more information, visit www.greenpressinitiative.org.

Saved:
- 4 trees
- 1 million BTU's of total energy
- 369 lbs of CO_2 equivalent of greenhouse gases
- 1,777 gallons of waste water
- 108 pounds of solid waste